BERNINI AND THE IDEALIZATION OF DEATH

BERNINI AND THE IDEALIZATION OF DEATH

The *Blessed Ludovica Albertoni* and the Altieri Chapel

Shelley Karen Perlove

THE PENNSYLVANIA STATE UNIVERSITY PRESS
University Park and London

Library of Congress Cataloging-in-Publication Data

Perlove, Shelley Karen.
Bernini and the idealization of death : the Blessed Ludovica Albertoni and the Altieri Chapel / Shelley Karen Perlove.

p. cm.

Includes bibliographical references.
ISBN 0-271-00684-6
1. Bernini, Gian Lorenzo, 1598–1680. Blessed Ludovica Albertoni. 2. Albertoni, Ludovica—Portraits. 3. Bernini, Gian Lorenzo, 1598–1680—Criticism and interpretation. 4. Counter-Reformation in art. 5. Altieri Chapel. I. Title.
NB623.B5A65 1990
730′.92—dc20

89–16336

Printed in the United States of America

It is the policy of The Pennsylvania State University Press to use acid-free paper for the first printing of all clothbound books. Publications on uncoated stock satisfy the minimum requirements of American National Standard for Information Sciences—Permanence of Paper for Printed Library Materials, ANSI Z39.48–1984.

For R. Ward Bissell

Inspired Professor,
Supportive Colleague,
Dear Friend

Contents

List of Illustrations

Unless otherwise specified, works of art and architecture are in Rome.

Photographic Credits

Alinari/Art Resource, N.Y.: 18, 20, 36, 40, 46. Ashmolean Museum, Oxford: 48. Biblioteca Vaticana, Rome: 60. Bibliothèque Interuniversitaire, Montpellier: 35. Barbara Bini, Rome: 6–8, 10–15, 17, 21–25, 58. Luigi Cipriani, Rome: 2. Biblioteca Hertziana, Rome: 3, 33, 41, 44, 50, 54, 57. Istituto Centrale per il Catalogo e la Documentazione, Rome: 37–39, 42, 47, 51, 54, 55, 59. Museum der bildenden Künste, Leipzig: 27–28, 32. National Gallery, London: 56. New York Public Library: 49. Shelley Perlove, Ann Arbor: 1, 4, 5, 9, 16, 19, 30, 34, 53. Réunion des Musées Nationaux, Paris: 52. Galleria degli Uffizi, Florence: 26. Victoria and Albert Museum, London: 29, 31.

Acknowledgments

This study of Bernini's *Blessed Ludovica Albertoni* and the Altieri Chapel began in 1979, when many thoughtful, unanswered questions were raised in discussions with R. Ward Bissell regarding Bernini's late masterpiece. It seemed curious to me that a sculpture of such complexity and beauty should be, by comparison with other works by the artist, relatively unknown.

I am deeply indebted to two distinguished scholars of Bernini studies, Irving Lavin of the Institute for Advanced Study in Princeton and the late Howard Hibbard of Columbia University, who were both extremely helpful in encouraging my investigation. I would like to think of this work, if I may, as a modest memorial to Professor Hibbard, whose book on Bernini stimulated my interest in the sculptor when I was an undergraduate at New York University.

Professor Lavin's magisterial study of the Cornaro Chapel (*Bernini and the Unity of the Visual Arts,* New York, 1980) was essential to this inquiry. Especially influential was his insightful discussion of the "bel composto," the concept that Bernini's art was a carefully orchestrated ensemble of painting, sculpture, and architecture, the parts of which contribute to the meaning of the whole. Professor Lavin was the first scholar to deal in any depth with this significant aspect of Bernini's art. His investigation of the artist served as a model for my study of the complex network of meaning in the Altieri Chapel. Other noted scholars to whom I am indebted for their expertise are Christoph Frommel of the Biblioteca Hertziana, Laurie Nussdorfer of Wesleyan University, Thomas Tentler of the University of Michigan, Jack Wasserman of Temple University, John Pinto of Smith College, Nathan Whitman of the University of Michigan, John Varriano of Mount Holyoke College, and Philipp Fehl of the University of Illinois. P. Celso Luigi Cipriani, O.F.M., of San Francesco a Ripa was most patient in allowing me to spend countless hours consulting the church archives. Permission to investigate the cloisters and the exterior of San

Francesco (the property is not open to the public) was kindly granted by Dr. Giovanni Di Geso, Superintendent, and Dr. Paola Degni, Architect, of the Soprintendenza per i Beni Ambientali e Architettonici del Lazio. My studies of the clay statuettes of the *Ludovica* in the Hermitage in Leningrad and the Victoria and Albert Museum in London were facilitated by the kind assistance of Dr. Nina Kosareva and Dr. Anthony Radcliffe, respectively. The late John D'Amico of George Mason University helped me tackle challenging problems of paleography regarding the papal briefs.

Many of the fine photographs of the Altieri Chapel that appear in this monograph are attributable to the talents of Barbara Bini, photographer of the American Academy in Rome.

I am also appreciative of the efforts of my colleague and friend, Gerald Gardner, who patiently helped me deal with the technical intricacies of word processing.

Most of all, I am eternally grateful to R. Ward Bissell, Joy Kenseth, and Irving Lavin, who generously devoted time and diligence to the careful reading of the manuscript, and whose support and astute advice were invaluable to this publication. Philip Winsor, Senior Editor of Penn State Press, was a model of wisdom and good judgment throughout the duration of this project.

A personal and immeasurable debt of gratitude is owed my husband, Warren, and daughters, Jennifer and Nina, whose love, devotion, and moral support were essential to the completion of my work.

Funds to support the research for this book were provided by the Kress Foundation and a Horace H. Rackham Faculty Grant from the University of Michigan. A Horace H. Rackham Publication Subvention Grant of the University of Michigan and an award from the Campus Grants Committee of the University of Michigan at Dearborn lent financial support to the publication.

Introduction

In 1671, the year in which Ludovica Albertoni was beatified in an elaborate ceremony in Saint Peter's, Gianlorenzo Bernini (1598–1680) was nearly seventy-three years old. Always devoted to his religion, the artist in his late years had become even more fervently concerned with spiritual matters. The accounts of his biographers and the works of art produced or designed by Bernini during the last decade and a half of his life clearly establish that his mind was as keen as ever and his knowledge and understanding of the intricacies of religious thought most impressive. Padre Giovanni Paolo Oliva, General of the Jesuits and a personal friend of the artist, once remarked that discussing theology with Bernini was like attending a doctoral defense at a seminary.[1]

Although his mental abilities were not impaired in his old age, his physical strength had waned after many years of hard work. Burdened by the demands of such patrons as Pope Clement X (1670–76) and Louis XIV of France (1643–1715), Bernini was forced to rely upon his assistants in carrying out many artistic projects, notably the tomb of Pope Alexander VII.[2] It is astonishing, therefore, to be confronted with Bernini's *Blessed Ludovica Albertoni*, executed when the artist was in his seventies (Fig. 17). The outstanding quality of this exquisite marble sculpture, installed in the Altieri Chapel in the church of San Francesco a Ripa in Rome, strongly suggests that it was worked by the master himself, with only minor participation by assistants. The esteemed critic John Pope-Hennessy bestowed lavish praise upon this work of art: "It is on this sublime figure rather than on the *Saint Theresa* that his [Bernini's] claim to be accepted as the peer of the very greatest Italian artists must ultimately rest."[3]

Scholarly interpretations of this piece have been various and, at times, contradictory.[4] My study proposes an interpretation of the precise nature of the experience that Ludovica is undergoing, and explores the significance of the event in light of contemporary theological thought. For the first time, the work is analyzed in the full context of the painting, sculpture, and architecture of the chapel. A reconstruction of the history of the Altieri Chapel and the cult of Ludovica Albertoni clarifies the situation at the time of the commission to Bernini and illuminates the sculptor's contribution, both artistically and iconographically, to the chapel.

This study, tracing the history of the Albertoni/Altieri family, the Altieri Chapel, and the cult of Ludovica over a period of 141 years, offers a telling glimpse of the politics of canonization and its impact upon the patronage of members of the *Popolo Romano,* the lay patrician class to which the Albertoni/Altieri family belonged. The Altieri Chapel itself demonstrates how art and architecture reflect the importance of preserving and emphasizing the physical evidence of Ludovica's cult, as proof of her sanctity.

Viewed in conjunction with its chapel setting, other works of art, biographical material on Ludovica, and contemporary religious literature, the sculpture is revealed as a masterpiece of deep spiritual meaning, the study of which tells us a great deal about Bernini's genius in his old age and about dying and salvation in the Baroque age. This investigation dramatizes the imaginative way in which he drew upon literary and visual sources, as well as his own personal concerns, to evolve an inventive and unique work of art.

1

The Altieri Chapel and the Cult of Ludovica

Not long after the sixteenth-century Roman matron Ludovica Albertoni was beatified (1671) by Pope Clement X Altieri, the pontiff's adopted nephew, Cardinal Albertoni/Altieri, commissioned Bernini to memorialize the *beata* and dignify her place of burial in the family chapel in San Francesco a Ripa in Trastevere. There he created a sculpture of Ludovica and placed it within a setting that dramatized the theological significance of her pious life and sublime death. Bernini's contribution to this project, both iconographically and artistically, is illuminated by tracing the history of San Francesco a Ripa, the Altieri Chapel, and the cult of Ludovica.

Prior to the thirteenth century, San Francesco a Ripa in Trastevere (Figs. 1 and 2) was the site of the Benedictine church of San Biagio, a monastic complex consisting of a hospice and hospital for pilgrims entering the city through the nearby Porta Portuensis.[1] The strategic location of this site, close to a gate of entry to the city, would govern its use up to 1870 as a charitable center for the aid of pilgrims visiting the churches of Rome.[2] In fact, one such visitor—Saint Francis of Assisi (1182?–1226)—was to have a decisive impact on the future of the church. The sainted friar stayed at the church on one of his sojourns in Rome, and since that moment the room in which he slept has been venerated as a shrine by the brothers of the convent.

In 1229, upon the decree of Pope Gregory IX (1227–41), San Biagio and the adjacent complex became the first nucleus of the Friars Minor in Rome. With the financial support of the local nobility, the church, rededicated to Saint Francis, was reconstructed, and Pietro Cavallini (1229–c. 1321) was commissioned to fresco the vault of the nave and transept with scenes from the life of the saint.[3]

The number of brothers living at San Francesco steadily declined from 1249 to 1549, a period in which Santa Maria in Aracoeli was the center for the Friars Minor. The fate of the Trasteveran church changed in the sixteenth century, however, when its convent became a base for the *riformati.* Upon the separation of the Franciscan order into the Conventuals and the Observants, the brothers of San Francesco a Ripa adhered to the latter. While the Conventuals believed that the order could own corporate property, the Observants advocated strict obedience to Saint Francis's rule of poverty. In general, the Conventuals tended to be the scholars of the order and the Observants were preachers more directly involved with the indigent. In 1517 Pope Leo X (1513–21) made the Conventuals nominally subject to the Observants, a reversal of the previous situation. With the issuance of this decree, the reform movement at San Francesco a Ripa became strengthened, the friars at the convent calling for a more rigid adherence to the vow of poverty. The number of brothers at the church grew, and the local aristocracy, whose patronage of the convent was essential for its growth, took a renewed interest in the friary.

Since the fifteenth century, the nobility of the region, who had become wealthy merchants over the years, had demonstrated a commitment to the Franciscans, both for religious and political reasons. These Trasteverans, members of the *Popolo Romano,* the lay patrician class involved in the government of Rome,[4] relied upon the friars to help them gain support among the local citizenry. The conflict between the desires of the nobility to make the church more splendid and the wishes of the more austere brothers (the Zealots), who wanted to adhere rigidly to the Rule of Saint Francis, colored the future development of the church and the conventual complex.

It is in this climate of reform and resurgence that one encounters the holy and ascetic figure of Ludovica Albertoni. Born in 1473 of a Roman noble family, Ludovica became famed for her virtue and sanctity. The events of her life are related in the hearings of her beatification of 1671 and in her biography of the same year, written by Giovanni Pauolo, a friar of San Francesco a Ripa and a descendant of Ludovica.[5] These accounts inform us that the *beata* was intensely religious throughout her life. When she was a young woman, she wished never to marry, but to cling only to Christ. Yet in spite of her desire to remain a virgin, she humbly obeyed her parents and married a wealthy Roman nobleman, Giacomo Della Cetera. Shortly thereafter the couple moved to Trastevere, where they raised three daughters, two of whom married members of local noble families—the Muti and Mattei.

Widowed at the early age of thirty-three, Ludovica donned the black sackcloth and white veil of the tertiary order of the Franciscans at the church of San Francesco a Ripa and devoted the remainder of her life to acts of penance and piety, modeling herself after Saint Elizabeth of Hungary, the founder of the order. As a member of this lay order of *Penitenti,* Ludovica was able to live the ascetic life of a Franciscan without being confined to a convent.[6] The period in which Ludovica served was one of great hardship and tragedy: Rome was sacked by the troops of Charles V in 1527, and the bubonic plague of 1528 ravaged the city, killing many who had escaped the attacks of the invaders. Hardest hit by these events was the area of Trastevere. Known as the "mother of the poor,"[7] the Franciscan tertiary cared for the injured, sick, and indigent of this region, giving all of her riches to the needy by concealing pieces of gold and silver inside the bread she distributed in the streets. She believed that God would see to it that the most deserving would receive the coins.

The accounts relate that she was most assiduous in her devotions, often submitting to repeated acts of penitence and mortification.[8] At times, during her prayers, she would miraculously levitate, her face inflamed by a religious rapture. At the age of sixty Ludovica was stricken with a fever, the pain and suffering of which she bore with great courage and patience.[9] Caring little for her physical needs, she longed only for the moment when her soul would be released from her body and united with her spouse, Jesus. She took communion more often, finding comfort in the "sacrosanct body of Christ."[10]

Her illness worsened and, having predicted the day of her death, she called for her confessor, begging him not to abandon her "in this step so perilous for the soul."[11] Kneeling on her bed, she received the viaticum and sent everyone from the room and shut the door. She was alone all day, and when her servant finally entered the room, Ludovica's face was flushed. As described by the servant, "she seemed full of joy," as if she had "returned from paradise."[12] Ludovica immediately called her lawyer and witnesses to draw her will, with instructions that her body be interred in the family chapel in the left transept of San Francesco a Ripa, in the sepulcher of her husband.[13] It was clear to everyone that she was quite "anxious to achieve the blessed vision of Jesus Christ."[14]

The hour of Ludovica's death is described in some detail by her biographer. The Franciscan tertiary held the crucifix in her hands, fixed her eyes upon it, and begged for the mercy of Jesus. She also called upon the Virgin to liberate her soul from the snares of Satan. Tenderly and compassionately kissing the wounds of the effigy of Christ, she uttered, "In manus tuas Domine commendo spiritum meum." In fervent prayer, her soul at peace, she "fell asleep in God" on 31 January 1533.[15]

In accordance with her will and testament, Ludovica was buried in the chapel that is now known as the Altieri Chapel. Her funeral, a most glorious event, was attended by cardinals, conservators, and the poor. The burial expenses were paid by members of her family—the Albertoni, Altieri, Muti, and Mattei.[16]

Immediately after her death, Ludovica was called a *beata* and a saint. Her body was said to work miracles, and her sepulcher, installed in the Altieri Chapel, became the focus of a cult. Guidebooks dating from as early as 1554 report that her grave was a place where "miracles are wrought" and pilgrims were encouraged to visit this holy site.[17] Witnesses who testified at the proceedings of her beatification related that people of every class and condition came to beg for her intercession, leaving numerous votives on her sepulcher.[18] It is not surprising, therefore, that the cult of Ludovica was to be a major determining factor in the evolution of this chapel.

At the time of Ludovica's death, the chapel, presumably dating from the end of the fifteenth century, was smaller than it is today. Ludovica's father-in-law had been interred there before the death of her husband and, in a will of 1506, her husband referred to the chapel as new.[19] Information on its history is provided by a chronicle of San Francesco a Ripa of 1696, written by a friar at the church, Ludovico da Modena.[20] According to his account, the chapel, the oldest in the church, was originally dedicated to the Holy Crucifix. The oldest crucifix in the church, which at the time Ludovico was writing was hung over the sacristy door, may have been previously installed in this chapel. Painted on canvas, it was a copy of the crucifix used by Saint Francis of Assisi at the beginning of his conversion.[21]

Although our knowledge of what the chapel looked like in the sixteenth century is incomplete, its appearance in the early years of the seventeenth century may be reconstructed by consulting the testimony of Ludovica's beatification hearings. Virtually ignored by scholars, the proceedings, or *processi,* are a rich source of information on the chapel as well as on Ludovica's cult. The aged witnesses at the trial tell us that prior to 1622 Ludovica's coffin was stored in a crypt under the floor of the chapel, her place of interment marked by a brick sepulcher, slightly raised from the pavement, in the middle of the chapel.[22] A white epitaph, now embedded in the chapel pavement, was initially placed on her sepulcher.[23] The slab records the date of her death and identifies the deceased as the Blessed Ludovica, daughter of Stefano Piermattei Albertoni, wife of Giacomo, and mother-in-law of D. Niccolò Muti:[24]

> Iacet Hic Beata Ludovica, Filia
> Stephani. Petri Matthaei De Albertonibus,

Uxor Iacobi Et Socrus D. Nicolai Muti.
Vixit Annos LX. Anima [m] Altissimo Creatori Suo.
Reddidit Die ultima ianuarii,
MDXXX.III
Coelituu[m] Consors Frueris Quibus Ocia, Posce,
Ludovica, Tuis; Nosq[ue] Tuere Malis.
Da Modo Te Facilem,
Sanctissima, Numine Dextro,
Quo Miracla Facis Tot
Pia, Et Affer Opem.

The epigram on this stone thus implores the *beata,* who enjoys heavenly bliss, to intercede for the worshipper, to work miracles, and to grant protection from evil. Testimony at the proceedings of her beatification, hereafter referred to as the *processi,* also informs us that a lamp was always kept lit over her grave.[25]

The frescoes of Saint Clare and the Blessed Ludovica, now flanking the altar (Figs. 13 and 14), were commissioned by the conservators of Rome.[26] The painter Giovanni Battista Gaulli ("Baciccio") and the famous art critic Giovanni Pietro Bellori, each of whom testified at the *processi,* affirm that the painting of Ludovica had been done at least one hundred years earlier.[27]

The next campaign on behalf of the chapel never progressed beyond the planning stage. A project drawing that may be dated to about 1600 shows an ambitious plan for the Altieri Chapel.[28] This plan for Ludovica's burial chapel, considered much too extravagant for a church of the reform movement, was apparently scrapped by the friars.[29]

A better fate awaited the chapel in 1622, when a major restoration was initiated by the grandson of Ludovica, the Marchese Baldassare Paluzzi degl' Albertoni. Ludovica's biographer, Fra Pauolo, informs us that Baldassare made the chapel as magnificent as the poverty of an institution of Saint Francis would tolerate.[30] The chapel, designed under the direction of the Lombard architect Giacomo Mola, was enlarged and revetted with marble. The Altieri Chapel as seen today closely reflects the intervention of 1622.

Set off from the nave of the church by the arched entrance and raised floor, the starkly plain chapel, roughly octagonal in plan, is surmounted by a dome whose summit is pierced by a fenestrated lantern (Figs. 4–6). The two angled walls flanking the recess on the end wall, the perspective arch surmounting them, and the moldings decorated with cherub heads all relate to Giacomo's designs (Figs. 4 and 29).[31] The end wall, which today is open above the altar to accommodate a statue chamber, was in the Lombard architect's plan entirely closed, pierced only by a lunette window. (The altar now in the chapel, like the rectangular niche, belongs to a later campaign.) Previously in another location in the chapel, the sixteenth-century frescoes of Ludovica and Saint Clare (Figs. 13 and 14) were reinstalled by Giacomo to their present position on the splayed walls flanking the altar (Fig. 15).[32]

The frescoed decoration of the dome, entrusted by Baldassare to the Jesuit painter Gaspare Celio, reveals a heavenly vision of cloud-borne angels who sing and play musical instruments, while above them a host of cherubim revolve around the fenestrated lantern in a ring of golden light (Fig. 6). Surveying the universe from the summit of the lantern, a sharply foreshortened figure of God the Father raises his arm in blessing. The four pendentives of the dome are decorated with images of the Roman Virgin-martyrs Saint Agnes and Saint Cecilia and the Roman holy women Santa Francesca Romana and Ludovica Albertoni. Santa Francesca appears with an open book and a guardian angel (Fig. 7), and Ludovica is depicted giving bread to a beggar (Fig. 8). Ludovica and Francesca, both wearing white veils of the tertiary orders, closely resemble each other.

Celio was probably responsible for the fresco of Charles Borromeo on the left lateral wall of the chapel (Fig. 15).[33] The half-length portrait of Borromeo represents the cardinal in fervent prayer, his head turned to the upper right toward a shaft of light. A date of around 1622 would reasonably situate the fresco soon after Borromeo's canonization of 1610. The portrait of the saint constitutes an appropriate choice of subject matter for this church and chapel, since Borromeo, like the brothers of the convent, was strongly in favor of the reform and was, as well, an enthusiastic supporter of the tertiary orders to which Ludovica belonged.[34] As the embodiment of faith and charity, Borromeo serves as a saintly analogue to the *beata.*

Precursor to the altarpiece now installed in the chapel niche, Celio's painting of the Madonna and Child with Saint Anne was hung on the end wall, above the altar.[35] In honor of the restoration of 1622, the chapel dedication was changed from the Holy Crucifix to Saint Anne, thus necessitating a new altarpiece devoted to the titular saint. The altar of the chapel was officially rededicated in 1631, and it may be safely assumed that Celio's altarpiece was finished and in place by this date.[36]

The church of San Francesco a Ripa was devoted to the cult of Saint Anne, the Franciscans having always been advocates of the veneration of Mary's mother.[37] The Franciscan pope, Sixtus IV, added the feast of Anne to the Roman calendar in 1481, and when in 1584 Pope Gregory XIII issued a bull extending her feast to the universal church, the Franciscan friars were jubilant. Fra Innocenzo da Chiuso, who lived in the convent of San Francesco a Ripa in the first half of the seventeenth century, was so devoted to the cult of the saint that he was called "Innocenzo of Saint Anne."[38] Two relics of Mary's mother were preserved at San Francesco a Ripa.[39] In 1622, the year in which the Altieri Chapel was dedicated to Saint Anne, Pope Gregory XV issued a bull calling for the observance of her feast day. Other documents at San Francesco a Ripa affirm that the festival of this saint was celebrated by the brothers with great solemnity and splendor.[40]

The present whereabouts of Celio's altarpiece are unknown,[41] but one may reconstruct its appearance by examining contemporary descriptions, as well as three studies by the artist preserved in the Uffizi (Fig. 26).[42] Witnesses at the *processi* report that the painting showed the Madonna, Child, and Saint Anne with Joseph and Joachim, the summit of the picture occupied by a glory of angels.[43] The drawings depict the Holy Family in a shallow interior, with rays of light shining down upon them from a glory of angels floating on clouds. Arranged as part of a formal, symmetrical composition, the Virgin, seated at the left with Joseph behind her, urges Jesus toward the figure of Saint Anne, who bends over to offer him flowers or, in one case, a wreath. Behind the aged grandmother is Joachim, who occupies a position analogous to that of Joseph.

The glory of angels at the top of Celio's painting, its strong lighting suggested by the illumination in the sketches, implies the presence of a lunette window (Figs. 4 and 26). The light streaming into the chapel from the window would correspond to the lighting in the painting hung beneath it. The subject of the altarpiece, the Madonna and Child with Saint Anne, traditionally refers to the Immaculate Conception: the idea that Mary, free of original sin,was sanctified in the womb of her mother.[44] The doctrine of the Immaculate Conception was strongly advocated by the Franciscans, and their adherence to it is expressed in the chapel dedication and the print of the Madonna and Child with Saint Anne that hangs on the right lateral wall of the chapel (Fig. 10). The print depicts the Christ Child as he is about to be received into the arms of his sainted grandmother, who is seated beside the Virgin. Around the border are small reproductions of holy images of the Madonna and Child housed in seven churches of Rome.[45] Church documents relate that this print was placed in the chapel upon the death (in 1631) of Fra Innocenzo da Chiusi, who, as an advocate of Saint Anne's cult, had kept this devotional work in his cell.[46] The inscription beneath the engraving clearly refers to the doctrine of sanctification:

> Ave Maria, gratia plena. Dominis tecu[m]. /
> Tua gratia sit / mecum. Benedicta tu in Mulierbus. /
> Et benedicta sit Sancta / Anna Mater tua, ex qua sine /
> macula et peccato / processisti Virgo Maria. /
> Ex te a / utem natus est Iesus Christus Filius dei vivi. /
> Amen.[47]

Set into the wall of the chapel beneath the print of the Madonna and Child with Saint Anne is a white tablet, dated 1625, commemorating Baldassare's restoration. This marble slab framed in dark gray molding informs us that the marchese rebuilt the chapel, which was in a state of ruin, and restored the very old fresco of Ludovica:

> SACELLUM HOC IN QUO OSSA
> BEATAE LUDOVICAE PETRI
> MATTHAEI DE ALBERTONIBUS ROMANA
> PIE ASSERVANTUR TEMPORUM INIVRIA COLLABASCENS
> BALTHASAR PALUTIUS DE ALBERTONIBUS
> PIO IN GENTILEM SUAM OBSEQUIO
> SACRIS OSSIBUS SUB VETERI MONUMENTO REPOSITIS
> ANTIQUISSIMI EIUS IMMAGINE PROPRIO IN LOCO RESTITUTA
> A FUNDAMENTIS EREXIT ORNAVITQ
> ANNO JUBILEI MDCXXV[48]

The crest above this plaque includes the crown of the marchese with the cross of the cavaliers of San Giacomo and the coat of arms of the Albertoni family, a lion with chevrons.

This inscription referring to Ludovica as a *beata* relates that her sacred remains were redeposited beneath the old monument. The ennoblement of Ludovica's place of burial was apparently the chief motivating force behind the intervention. Her sepulcher was covered with a veneer of white finished marble.[49] Its height was raised to about one palm, and witnesses at the *processi* tell us that the tomb was rectangular (*in forma quadrata*), with a length measuring about eight-and-one-half palms and a width of about four and one-half. The original epitaph was repositioned on the sepulcher, and an iron from which a lamp was hung was attached to the monument. The light on the tomb was kept perpetually lit, and Ludovica's biographer reports that the oil from this lamp worked miracles.[50] Another lamp, also burning constantly, was hung from the base of a cross that formed part of an iron railing closing the chapel.[51]

During the course of the restoration, Ludovica's casket was found and removed to the sacristy, where it was opened ceremoniously on 4 March 1625 in the presence of officials of the church and the Roman city government.[52] Witnesses, affirming her saintliness, remarked that her body seemed sweet, like the flowers of paradise, a conventional proof of saintliness.[53] At this time, the epitaph on her sepulcher, which called her a *beata* and referred to her powers of intercession, was read aloud, and her body, carried in a procession, was redeposited in the chapel.[54]

The evidence discussed above establishes that Ludovica was venerated as a *beata* immediately after her death. Yet, despite the honors accorded her, this pious woman and her cult were not to be recognized by the papal authorities until 138 years had passed from the date of her death on 31 January 1533.

2

The Beatification and the Commission

The "Senate and the People of Rome" constituted the greatest source of support for the papal sanctioning of Ludovica's cult.[1] The Capitoline, which initiated the proceedings of Ludovica's beatification in 1671, had been consistently devoted to her cult from the moment of her death.[2] Conservators and magistrates attended her funeral and commissioned the frescoes of Ludovica and Saint Claire that now flank the altar of the Altieri chapel. On 13 October 1606, the conservators declared that on Ludovica's feast day a chalice and four wax torches be presented to San Francesco a Ripa at an official ceremony held at the *Beata*'s grave.[3] Installed on the left wall of the Altieri Chapel in 1625, an inscription plaque surmounted by a crest of the Roman government records the conservators' decree to honor Ludovica's feast day on the Capitoline Hill:

QUOD SENATUS POPULUSQ ROMANUS
BEATAM LUDOVICAM PETRI MATTHAEI DE ALBERTONIBUS ROMANÃ
SINGULARI PIETATE PROSEQUUTURUS
ULTIMUM IANUARII DIEM QUO FELICISSIME CONVOLAVIT INCOELUM
PER CURIAM CAPITOLINAM ANNUA A IUDICIIS
CESSATIONE CELEBRARI
ATQUE HOC SACELLUM SOLEMNI POMPA UT MOS EST
A ROMANO MAGISTRATU CONSUETA LIBERALITATE ADIRI
SENATUS CONSULTO MULTIS AB HINC ANNIS IUSSERIT
BALTHASAR PALUTIUS DE ALBERTONIBUS

GRATI ANIMI MONUMENTUM POS
ANNO IUBILEI MDCXXV[4]

Twenty years later, Ludovica was commemorated by a painting showing her giving bread to a poor beggar, which was placed in the Cappella Vecchia of the Palazzo dei Conservatori. Underneath this canvas painting by Giovanni Francesco Romanelli, a memorial tablet tells us of the conservators' gifts on Ludovica's feast day.[5]

The honors paid to Ludovica's cult by the Capitoline may be traced to the political power exerted by the *Popolo Romano,* the Roman nobility who controlled the secular government of the city. Born near the Campidoglio, Ludovica, a member of the *Popolo Romano,* had many ancestors, relatives, and descendants who held important positions in the civic life of Rome.[6] One of her most illustrious relations was her cousin, the writer and activist Marcantonio Altieri (elected conservator in 1525), who fiercely advocated the cause of the Roman nobles against the interests of the foreigners in the Eternal City.[7]

The veneration of the *beata* by the Capitoline paralleled that accorded to Santa Francesca Romana (canonized in 1608), to whom Ludovica was often likened. The *beata* was depicted on a devotional print alongside Santa Francesca,[8] and Ludovica was said to have carried in her pocket a holy relic of the saint, a piece of Francesca's veil.[9] According to Ludovico da Modena, the conservators originally wanted the fresco of Ludovica in the Altieri Chapel to have as a pendant a painting of Santa Francesca rather than Saint Clare.[10] Ludovica is depicted on the pendentives of the chapel with Santa Francesca, whom she closely resembles in dress and appearance. The tradition of representing Ludovica with Santa Francesca probably derives from the Albertoni family chapel at Santa Maria in Aracoeli, where the two holy women, like the figures in the Altieri chapel, are shown with the Roman saints Cecilia and Agnes on the pendentives of the vault.[11] These frescoes in the Aracoeli were painted by Niccolò Trometta in the second half of the sixteenth century. The *beata* was depicted with Francesca, Cecilia, and Agnes in the Albertoni family chapels most likely because these devout women were viewed as Ludovica's saintly prototypes; they were, like the *beata,* Roman noble ladies who renounced earthly pleasures and wealth to pursue a life of piety, asceticism, and religious devotion.

Thus Ludovica was viewed as an important figure by the *Popolo Romano,* and presumably the political ties of her family and her popular appeal with the people played some part in inspiring this veneration. Moreover, she would have been revered by the advocates of the Franciscan reform movement, her self-imposed life of poverty serving as an exemplar for the friars. In a bull of 1532 favoring austerity for the Franciscans, Pope Clement VII (1523–34) praised the Strict Observants of San Francesco a Ripa.[12]

The history of papal interest in Ludovica's cult may be traced by focusing upon pertinent facts and events in the period between her death in 1533 and her beatification in 1671. Ludovica was not canonized officially in the years immediately following her death because no canonizations were enacted between 1522 and 1587 (a policy undoubtedly instituted in reaction to Protestant criticism of the cult of the saints).[13] In the years following this period of inactivity, however, the *Popolo Romano* and the church of San Francesco a Ripa, both of which were unquestionably in favor of Ludovica's canonization, received important concessions from two popes, Paul V Borghese (1605–21) and Urban VIII Barberini (1623–44). In 1608 Paul V canonized Santa Francesca Romana, the daughter of Roman nobility who was famed for her piety, miracles, and good works; in gratitude for this honor, the *Popolo Romano* incurred the costs of the celebration of this event.[14]

The Borghese pope extended favors to the Roman nobility in yet another way. He aided the baronial families of Trastevere, many of which were engaged in farming and husbandry, by building streets in this region to facilitate the transport of agricultural goods. A plaque set up by the conservators on a house facade near San Francesco a Ripa commemorates the completion in 1611 of the street connecting San Francesco a Ripa with San Callisto.[15] Among the conservators listed on the inscription tablet is "Alexandro Muto Laurentio Alterio," a probable descendant of Ludovica.[16] Paul V also demonstrated an interest in San Francesco a Ripa, the Trasteveran church of the Roman noble families of this region; in 1614 he constructed a viaduct to supply water to the monastery.[17]

Urban VIII offered special recognition to San Francesco a Ripa on 1 February 1639 by granting indulgences for all of its seven altars.[18] Ludovica's grandson Baldassare Albertoni, who restored the Altieri Chapel in 1622, was also granted favors by the Barberini pope; Baldassare, who held the prestigious office of *maestro delle strade* on the Capitoline, was awarded the title of Marchese of Rasina.[19] In view of the respect accorded Baldassare by the pontiff, one could reasonably assume that Ludovica's grandson played a role in influencing Urban to honor Ludovica's cult. The pope ordered the exhumation of Ludovica's body, a procedure that usually preceded hearings of canonization. Soon after the reburial, a lamp, whose flame was kept continuously lit, was installed on the sepulcher. Since the use of lights for unsanctioned cults was outlawed by Urban, the installation of the lamp was considered by Ludovica's biographer to be tantamount to official recognition.[20] Moreover, it may not be coincidental that Ludovica's cult, which began in 1533, just made it under Urban's rule that cults established before 1534 were of sufficient longevity to be deemed legal under papal law.[21]

The most successful bid to open proceedings for Ludovica's beatification presumably originated with Cardinal Paluzzo Paluzzi-Albertoni (1623–98), whose meteoric rise to power was achieved in the papacy of Clement X Altieri.[22] When the Altieri name was threatened with extinction, owing to the lack of a male heir, the Albertoni family, including Paluzzo, his brother Angelo, and his nephew Gaspare, all agreed to assume this family's name upon the marriage of Gaspare in 1669 to Laura Caterina Altieri, the niece of Cardinal Emilio Altieri.[23] About one year later, Cardinal Paluzzo Paluzzi-Albertoni, now Altieri, apparently played a role in getting Cardinal Emilio Altieri elected to the papacy after a long and arduous conclave.[24] The election had been swung by the powerful Chigi faction, which looked with favor upon Cardinal Paluzzo; he was immediately chosen cardinal-padrone under the new pontiff, Clement X Altieri. The pope was aged and frail, and therefore delegated many responsibilities to his adopted nephew, Paluzzo. The cardinal, who held such prestigious offices as Treasurer of the Holy See, Prefect of Propaganda, and Secretary of Briefs, was virtually the most powerful man in the Curia. A document in the Archivio di Stato reports that Paluzzo's nephew and brother were richly rewarded for having assumed the Altieri name;[25] Gaspare was appointed general of the militia of the Church and governor of the Castel Sant'Angelo and the Borgo; Angelo was designated general of the papal galleys, with an elevation in title from marchese to principe.[26]

In 1670, upon the request of the Capitoline, the hearings for Ludovica's beatification were officially opened before the Congregation of Rites.[27] The procurator of her cause was Fra Giovanni Pauolo of San Francesco a Ripa, a descendant of Ludovica's, who in 1672 authored a biography of the blessed one.[28] According to standard procedure established by Pope Urban VIII's decree of 1634, beatifications and canonizations could be granted only by the Holy See, and cults venerated without papal consent were deemed illegal.[29] During the course of the proceedings it was necessary to determine if the prohibition of public worship of the Servant of God (the individual under review) had been observed. Cults proved to have existed continuously for more than one hundred years before the decree of 1634, however, were not considered to be in violation of the papal interdiction. In the case of Ludovica, her cult, which began immediately after her death in

1533, just satisfied the one-hundred-year longevity requirement, and a declaration of *super cultu immemorabili* was entered.

As was customary in such cases, witnesses who were of sufficient age to testify to the antiquity and continuity of the cult were questioned. Among them were friars at the convent of San Francesco a Ripa and holy women at the Tor de'Specchi (the monastery founded by Santa Francesca Romana). Their testimony, virtually identical in every detail, suggests that Fra Pauolo "prepared" the aged witnesses for trial. The elderly religious recounted the miracles wrought at Ludovica's grave, where many votives were placed in gratitude for her aid. Some brothers described the celebrations at the church on Ludovica's feast day. They reported that a piece of linen spun by the *beata* was displayed as a relic on her sepulcher.[30] Images of Ludovica giving bread to the poor were printed on paper and taffeta and distributed by the *beata*'s descendants to "cardinals and great princes" and to the citizenry as well.[31] Witnesses also described the chapel and cited as evidence of her cult the following: the epitaph, the inscription plaques, the sixteenth-century fresco depicting Ludovica with rays signifying blessedness, and the sepulcher itself with the light burning constantly above it.[32]

On the basis of the testimony of the hearings, Pope Clement X sanctioned Ludovica's cult on 28 January 1671.[33] Her beatification, attended by the nobles of Roman society, was celebrated at Saint Peter's. As a blessed one recognized by the Church, Ludovica could be honored with masses and offices by the Franciscans, but she was not to be revered universally as a saint. In the event that it could be proved that she continued to work miracles some years after her beatification, the Franciscan tertiary would be eligible for canonization.

In honor of Ludovica's beatification and feast day, a special mass of the Virgin Mary was celebrated in the *beata*'s name in the Altieri Chapel on 31 January 1671.[34] The church was lavishly decorated for the ceremonial mass and a multitude of candles were lit over the *beata*'s sepulchre. This special event was attended by Christina of Sweden, prominent members of Roman society, and, of course, the entire Altieri family, who, in memory of Ludovica's charity, distributed bread and money to the poor. It was said that, through the intercession of the *beata,* miracles were wrought on this day. On 2 February of the following year, Clement issued a brief extending plenary indulgence to all the faithful who celebrated the feast day of the blessed Ludovica.[35]

Linked historically with the power and prestige of the Albertoni/Altieri family, the cult of the *beata* was accorded further recognition. Now that Ludovica was officially declared a *beata,* Cardinal Paluzzi-Albertoni/Altieri turned his thoughts to the glorification of his pious great-great-grandmother, whose elevated status enhanced the family name. His desires to honor the blessed Ludovica must have been stimulated by the prestigious marriage of Ludovica Altieri, the cardinal's relative, with the duke of Gravina on 9 April 1671, the celebration of which was attended by the pope.[36] Paluzzo commissioned Fra Pauolo to write a biography of Ludovica, which was published with a dedication to the cardinal in 1672. The printed book alone, however, could not suffice as a memorial to the *beata.* As the grandson of Baldassare and a direct descendant of Ludovica's, Cardinal Paluzzo wished to commemorate his illustrious great-great-grandmother by commissioning a work of art for the Altieri Chapel in San Francesco a Ripa. The funds for such a project were available through Baldassare's will of 1651, which stipulated that at least 10,000 *scudi* be spent on the chapel upon the canonization of Ludovica.[37]

The project, which called for a statue of Ludovica placed in the Altieri Chapel, was entrusted by Paluzzo to the greatest sculptor in Rome, Gianlorenzo Bernini.[38] The history of this commission, however, is colored by a scandal brought to light by Valentino Martinelli in 1959.[39] The unfortunate incident and the events that ensued were reconstructed from *avvisi* in the Vatican Archives. These documents, which are daily bulletins of events of the papal court, offer a vivid picture of Bernini's tribulations in the four-year period from 1670 to 1674. The scandal occurred in 1670, when Gianlorenzo's brother and assistant, Luigi, was discovered in Saint Peter's sodomizing a young boy in the vicinity of the equestrian sculpture of Constantine. A typically sarcastic *avviso* reported that Luigi was caught mounting the "stable boy of the horse of Constantine."[40] Rather than face arrest, Luigi fled to Naples, but soon all of Rome knew of his disgrace. His financial holdings were confiscated and he was virtually exiled from Rome. Gianlorenzo elicited the aid of his good friend Christina of Sweden, who spoke to the pope on Luigi's behalf. Bernini himself went to the pontiff on many occasions between 1670 and 1674 to beg for his brother's pardon. A generous monetary offer was made to the father of the young boy who had been violated, and apparently Gianlorenzo endeavored to gain favor by producing garden statues and reliefs to embellish the pope's family palace at the Gesù. Clement, however, was unmoved by Gianlorenzo's repeated requests. Every time Bernini broached the subject, the pontiff would interrogate him about the sculptures for the Palazzo Altieri.

Even less sympathetic to Gianlorenzo during this period were the people of Rome. The sculptor was bitterly criticized for his influence in the papal court and for the sums of money he made on large projects.[41] They were violently opposed to the release of Luigi and were presumably watching the affair very closely. The popular attitude seems best summed up by this *avviso* of 20 December 1670:

> Anche contro il gia scritto Luigi Bernino, si crede che la giustizia non sia per adempire, quanto si e divolgato contro di Lui, perche il Cav.re suo fratello, abbondante di dinari, favori et cervello, sapra navigare secondo i venti, e riparare ogni mina contro la riputatione della sua Casa.[42]

The weight of public opinion undoubtedly played a part in shaping the events of these years.

Cardinal Paluzzo had taken a hard position against Bernini's brother; in an *avviso* of 27 December 1670, the cardinal is characterized as one who "essaggerasse contro il Delinquente."[43] Paluzzo was the power behind the papal throne, and it was undoubtedly crucial to Bernini's cause to convince the cardinal to desist opposing Luigi's pardon. According to an acerbic *avviso* of 17 February 1674, Bernini had offered to do the sculpture of Ludovica free of charge in order to please Paluzzo:

> Desiderando il Card. Altieri alzar una statua di basso rilievo in honore della B. Albertoni, concorsi varij virtuosi, solo il Cav. r Bernino e stato preferito, perche si e esibito di lavorarla dall' esilio quel gran Luigi per servirsene poi di stalliere del Cavallo di Costantino.[44]

Although no documents record the specific date at which Bernini began the *Ludovica,* there is reason to believe that he initiated the project at least two years before the *avviso* of February 1674. An early study for the statue may be dated around 1672 (Fig. 27); the drawing on the verso of the sheet is a study for the vault of the Gesù, whose domical decoration was commissioned and initiated in that year (Fig. 28).[45] On 23 January 1672 a license was issued granting permission for Ludovica's remains to be exhumed from her marble tomb and reburied under the altar.[46] The removal of the *beata* from the chapel no doubt signals the commencement of the project, since it would be inconceivable that work could be done with her sacred remains in the chapel.

The sculpture of Ludovica must have been completed in 1674; a letter of 19 October of that year written by Carlo Cartari, archivist and librarian of the Altieri family, refers to the statue as finished.[47] This correspondence also mentions other works "*condote ad esquisito fine*" by Bernini: the

Tabernacle (1673–74), the *King of France* (that is, either the bust of Louis XIV begun in 1665 or the equestrian of 1671–73), and the "sepulcher of Alexander VII" (1671–78). Cartari's letter, however, is not entirely reliable, since Alexander's tomb, although well under way, was not completed by 1674. Another source significant to the chronology of the statue is Filippo Titi's guidebook of 1674, which reports: "Hora nella Cappella della B. Ludovica Albertoni li Signori Principi Altieri fanno metter là di lei statua in marmo scolpta perfettamente dal Cavalier Bernino." Printed in lettering discernibly darker than the rest of the text, this statement may have been added at a later point, after an initial printing.[48] Signaling the completion of the Altieri Chapel, the "second translation" of the body occurred on 12 January 1675.[49]

The pace of work on the *Ludovica* between 1672 and 1674 probably proceeded slowly. Bernini, no longer a young man, was weakened by illness and was burdened with other important projects, such as the decoration of the altar of the Cappella del Sacramento in Saint Peter's (1673–74). Moreover, the extremely high quality of the *Ludovica* suggests that much of the carving was done by the sculptor himself. When the denigrating *avviso* of 17 February 1674 was dispatched, the statue was most likely well under way, since the *avviso* refers to the circumstances of the commission as an event of the past.

Shortly after the sculpture was finished, Bernini's son, Pier Filippo, was awarded the position of Secretary of the Congregation of Water, an appointment that gave rise to the contemporary quip "the sculptor's chisel has struck water like the rod of Moses."[50] In the holy year of 1675, Luigi was presumably released from exile and his property restored.

The scandal of Bernini's brother and the chain of events leading to his release are not recalled by Bernini's biographers; in fact, Domenico Bernini seems to have dismissed the affair altogether by insisting that Gianlorenzo was well compensated for the sculpture.[51] Perhaps this is a case of one who "protests too much." Surely Bernini, who would have welcomed the opportunity to please the cardinal, may have done the sculpture for little or no compensation. Whatever his motivations, the humiliation and frustration he suffered during this period offer a highly humanized picture of Gianlorenzo as a man who cared deeply for his family.[52] If Bernini did the statue of Ludovica to help his brother, then one may think of it as an act of love. Moreover, the work of art itself, a masterpiece of the sculptor's old age, leaves no doubt that Bernini's commitment to the project was absolute.

3

Bernini's Contribution

Bernini's statue of Ludovica, set within a niche that opens the space above and beyond the altar, is the focal point of the Altieri Chapel. The worshipper is drawn to the sculpture by the splayed walls and the perspective arch that telescope the view of the aedicule designed by Gianlorenzo (Fig. 3). Lighting as well establishes the statue in its niche as the visual center of the chapel. While the chapel proper is only dimly lit by the lantern of the dome, which is its sole light source, the recess is intensely illuminated by a window at the left, hidden from view. The effect of the light was even more dramatic before the window at the right, visible today behind a curtain, was walled up by a small structure built outside the aedicule (Figs. 15 and 16).[1] With windows on both sides, the niche would have been illuminated by the east window during the morning mass and by the west window during vespers.

Infused with light, the white marble sculpture of Ludovica is the climactic element in the chapel. The statue depicts the *beata* in a semirecumbent pose, her head thrown back on a lace-bordered pillow, her eyes rolled back, and her mouth open (Figs. 17 and 18). Lying in bed with her knees bent and slightly apart, the agitated garments flowing over her body as if animated by an unseen force, Ludovica grasps her bosom and waist. The quietly enraptured figure seems to belong to another world. Her private, intimate communion is undisturbed by the intrusion of the observer, who feels compelled to tiptoe before her.

The consummate beauty of the figure is enhanced by the drapery, which serves as well to heighten the emotional tenor of the work. The veil, rising from behind Ludovica's right shoulder, gently caresses her cheek as it undulates about her head and falls in a long uninterrupted sweep over her left hand, where it gracefully rises in a curving loop. In the area in which she grips her body, the cloth becomes more turbulent, moving about her abdomen in whirlpools and meandering toward her loins to arch upward in tightly bunched folds. A thin strip of cloth, flowing through the center of these whorls of fabric, rushes between her legs like a rivulet. Parallel to the piece of drapery just described is a fold of cloth that falls over the edge of the pallet to create a subtle visual link between the statue and the masses of colored drapery beneath it.

Ludovica's garments, whose movements and disposition may not be explained by the laws of nature, impart a visionary quality to the sculpture. The colored drapery beneath the statue is most irrational in its arrangement, the masses of folds rather mysteriously repeating the configuration of the *beata*'s body. This visual connection between the statue and the cloth is not obvious, but, once perceived, may not be doubted. While the large fold beginning near the bolster of the pallet and falling in a long diagonal to the right repeats the shape of Ludovica's head and upper torso enclosed by her veil, the fringed piece of fabric that rises near the center of the bed to connect with a massing of drapery at the upper right recalls the configuration of the *beata*'s upraised knee. The colored cloth, made of jasper like the altar, links the statue effectively with the liturgical center of the chapel where the Eucharist is celebrated (Fig. 19). Placed on a raised, stepped platform, the altar, which recalls the shape of a sarcophagus, is pierced in the middle by a heart-shaped opening surrounded by flames (Fig. 12).[2]

Set within a gilded arched enframement above the marble sculpture, the altarpiece, rendered in warm glowing colors by Giovanni Battista Gaulli ("Baciccio"), depicts the Madonna and Child with Saint Anne in a lush landscape (Fig. 20).[3] The ebullient young mother, seated at the left, gently delivers her robust, eager son into the waiting arms of his loving grandmother.

The chapel recess is richly ornamented with stucco, the arch above the painting coffered with rose bosses, the pilasters enframing the altarpiece embellished with tall, flaming torches comprising such elements as a cherubic head with bound wings, an entwining snake, and Janus heads (Figs. 19 and 21–23). Beneath the painting and behind the *Ludovica*, a panel is decorated with pomegranates, some of which have burst open, revealing the ripened seeds within them (Figs. 17 and 23). Other stucco elements in the niche include a radiant dove and baskets of roses and lilies decorating the vault, and flaming hearts, similar to the one on the altar front, embellishing the panels beneath the windows (Figs. 19, 24).

White stucco cherubic heads, attached to the frame so that the doweling is hidden from view, seem to float on the shafts of light entering the niche from the left window (and originally from the right window also) (Figs. 29, 31, and 32).[4] The angels, arranged in a descending formation, appear to converge upon the figure of Ludovica, effectively drawing attention to her. The cherubs, serving as a compositional force, also engage the emotions of the observer. Their facial expressions are wonderfully individualized, each conveying sympathy and love. Clearly then, the elements just described establish Bernini's statue of Ludovica as part of a whole, a coordinated ensemble of painting, sculpture, and architecture (Fig. 19).[5]

The artist, no doubt, spent some time planning this project, which was completed over a period of two years. Yet it is difficult to trace the evolution of Bernini's ideas for the Altieri Chapel, since only a few known preparatory drawings have survived and, among them, only the Leipzig sketch of 1672 (Fig. 27) offers a revealing glimpse of the genesis of the statue.[6] Executed with quick, jerky strokes of the pen, this study shows two reclining female figures drawn diagonally across the sheet, their heads cut off by a later trimming.[7] The heavily inked lines suggesting deep shadows demonstrate that Bernini, at an early stage of the project, already contemplated a dramatic lighting.

The drapery folds, which play such an expressive role in Gianlorenzo's sculpture, are revealed in this study as an early preoccupation of the artist. Of major concern in the sketch is the large, deeply creviced fold that rises near the *beata*'s left hip and loops over to fall upon her right knee.

This fold is replaced in the sculpture by a complex arrangement of drapery that more effectively accentuates and energizes the lower abdominal region. The general appearance of Ludovica's veil is first established in the Leipzig drawing. Unlike the veil in the sketch, however, the marble drapery covering Ludovica's head rises near her left hand in a curving loop that punctuates the flowing rhythms of the cloth. Extending from Ludovica's right side, the large triangular fold of the drawing is utilized in the marble sculpture to link the figure of the *beata* with the jasper cloth and altar beneath it.

Bernini was also concerned in this sketch with the disposition of Ludovica's hands. The drawing informs us that Gianlorenzo initially conceived of the figure as simply pressing her hands against her chest—a gesture that was employed earlier by Bernini in the *Maria Raggi* (1643) in Santa Maria sopra Minerva.[8] In the sculpture, Ludovica's right hand is higher than the left, a reversal of the situation in the drawing. This change was probably occasioned by the artist's desire in the statue to emphasize Ludovica's gesture of clutching her breast; by raising the height of the hand closest to the viewer, Bernini was able to give greater focus to the gesture.

Investigation of another preparatory work, a *bozzetto* in the Victoria and Albert Museum (Figs. 29–31), further illuminates the process by which Gianlorenzo created the marble sculpture.[9] With the exception of the pillow, which is more rounded in shape and lacks an ornamental border, this clay statuette is extremely close to the *Ludovica.*[10] Executed by Bernini's own hand, the *bozzetto* probably served as both a presentation piece for the patron and a working model.

Despite unfortunate losses in the areas of the face and pillow, the high quality of this terracotta may be easily discerned. The statuette, with its animated draperies and rich coloristic effects, possesses the freshness and vibrancy of an autograph work. Tool marks applied to the clay in different directions enliven the surface of the piece. On the back of the sculpture and on the mattress and right knee, for example, shallow hatchmarks created with the aid of a toothed instrument suggest folds of cloth and soft shadows. In contrast to these subtle tool marks, deeply gouged hatchmarks beneath the pillow (Fig. 30) record the vigorous slashing movements of the artist's hand. Also testifying to the variety of surfaces in this work are the shadowed depressions in the drapery between Ludovica's right knee and foot and the mellifluous spiral fluting of her veil.

The back of the *bozzetto* (Fig. 31) tells us a great deal about Bernini's thinking regarding the *Ludovica*. Clearly, the artist conceived of the sculpture as consisting of two basic masses: one encompassing the head and upper body, and the other the triangular shape of the bent leg. The coil of clay that zigzags in the vicinity of Ludovica's elbow and then rises and descends, echoing the contours of her leg, underscores the basic rhythmic movements of the piece.

The posterior of the *bozzetto* (Figs. 19 and 31) may have stimulated Bernini to repeat the contours of Ludovica's body in his design for the jasper cloth. Summarizing the basic masses of the *Ludovica,* the back of the clay model seems to anticipate the arrangement of drapery folds in the colored cloth. The jasper fold that arches upward and descends toward the center reflects the shape of Ludovica's head and upper torso. Rising toward the right, fringed folds of colored cloth echo the configuration of her bent leg. The point at which the clay coil of the *bozzetto* zigzags, articulating the transition from the torso to the bent leg, corresponds to a similar point near the center of the jasper cloth where two parallel folds edged with fringe begin their ascent toward the right.

Few people realize that the jasper cloth now in the Altieri Chapel was not created until well after Bernini's death. A painted wooden cloth, or *legno dipinto,* preceded the jasper cloth placed beneath the *Ludovica* in 1702 at Don Angelo Paluzzo Altieri's expense.[11] Although the two versions of the colored cloth were not executed by Gianlorenzo, the stone drapery presumably replicated the painted wooden cloth of the artist's design. He was probably compelled to use a wooden colored drapery in order to economize on this project, for which he received little or no compensation.

In addition to the colored cloth, the sculptor was also responsible for the design of the recess in which the statue of the *beata* was installed (Fig. 19).[12] The artist opened the wall on which Celio's altarpiece had been hung and added a rectangular extension to create an appropriate setting for the *Ludovica.* A black chalk sketch by Bernini in Leipzig (Fig. 32) studies the upper left wall of the aedicule.[13] The drawing demonstrates that early on the sculptor planned an arched frame for the painted altarpiece, the enframement represented by curved lines. Bernini also experimented with an idea for the vaulting, a scheme he later abandoned.[14]

The sculptor initially envisioned a flat-roofed, boxlike enclosure for the *Ludovica,* perhaps much like the arrangement shown in a reconstruction drawing (cf. Figs. 32 and 34). The vertical and horizontal lines on the left and top edges of the Leipzig sheet represent moldings that articulate the corners where the back wall connects with the adjacent wall and ceiling. In his final design, however, Gianlorenzo did not use a flat ceiling. He spanned the space with a cross vault that harmonized more effectively with the arch shape of the opening to both the recess and the painted altarpiece (Fig. 3).

The drawing also studies the frame of the altarpiece, the cherubic heads, and the lighting. The inner curved line on the sheet marks the innermost edge of the frame, while the other curved lines indicate its outermost moldings. Bernini envisioned the placement of cherubs both on the frame of the altarpiece and on the spandrel of the back wall. Flooded with light, the celestial creatures on the spandrels appear to be lit by a concealed window at the upper left. The shadows that fall on the angelic heads of the frame, however, imply that the painted altarpiece and the innermost molding around it were intended to be slightly recessed, a conjecture supported by the definitive design. In the final version, the altarpiece is framed by pilasters and coffering and by moldings decorated with egg, dart, and acanthus motifs. Although the painting and its inner frame are not recessed appreciably, the cornice of the pilasters overlapping the inner molding of the altarpiece offers the illusion that the picture is set into the wall, an arrangement recalling Bernini's original intention. He also made other revisions in his definitive design: The cherubic heads were moved to a lower position on the frame, and the unfocused, poorly illuminated angels in the drawing were replaced by ten individuated cherubic heads, five on each side of the painting, which direct attention to the figure of Ludovica beneath them (Figs. 18, 19, and 32).

The statue recess is decorated with motifs that are not studied in the Leipzig sheet but certainly were designed by Bernini since they closely resemble those he employed on other occasions. The flaming hearts on the side walls of the recess and on the front of the altar, for example, also appear on the gate of the Cornaro Chapel of Santa Maria della Vittoria and in the emblematic frieze in the Raimondi Chapel of San Pietro in Montorio.[15] In a design of around 1656 for a staircase in the Vatican palace, the sculptor employed an ornamentation consisting of roses intertwined with lilies, which anticipates the floral decoration of the vault of the recess in the Altieri Chapel (Fig. 24).[16] The flaming torches on the pilasters flanking the altarpiece in the Altieri Chapel may be related to the tall burning lamps of the interior vault of the entrance doorway of Sant' Andrea al Quirinale.[17]

The decoration of the architectural space designed to house the *Ludovica* was completed around 1674, and the altarpiece depicting the Madonna and Child with Saint Anne by Baciccio (Fig. 20) was finished the same year.[18] The statue, nearly completed by 19 October 1674, was installed in the recess sometime late that year.[19] By 17 January 1675, when Ludovica's remains were exhumed from her sepulcher and reburied in the altar, the sculpture and altarpiece were in place and the decoration of the aedicule completed.[20] Ludovico da Modena described this celebration, which he claimed was attended by many important people.[21] The "holy relics" of Ludovica, he related, were deposited in a coffin that was placed within a stone box bearing the inscription "Corpus Beatae Ludovice Albertonie." The caskets were then deposited within a new altar commissioned by Cardinal Altieri (Fig. 12). Ludovico provided a description of the sepulcher: "Placed at the back of the chapel was a new altar of finished Sicilian jasper rendered in the shape of a most noble tomb with a heart in the center, where a lamp kept continuously lit was placed, and over this tomb was celebrated the offering of the Mass."[22] The *frate* also informs us that in conjunction with the exhumation and burial the cardinal (Paluzzi-Albertoni/Altieri) commissioned a beautiful statue of the *beata* by Bernini, which was placed above and behind the altar. Positioned within the same space, Ludovico related, is the "new painting of Saint Anne" by the Genoese artist "Baciccio Gauelli, a man who showed great spirit in his works."[23]

Baciccio undoubtedly painted the altarpiece after the design for the statue and niche had already been established. A sketch by Baciccio in Montpellier (Fig. 35) depicts the sculpture of Ludovica, the billowing cloth linking the figure to the altar, and the sculptural decoration of the recess, all details virtually identical to the finished work.[24] The Genoese painter clearly wished to study the *Ludovica* and its architectural setting before working out his ideas for the painted altarpiece.

The painting by Baciccio, like the work that preceded it in the Altieri Chapel, shows the Madonna at the left with the young Christ, the latter reaching with outstretched arms toward Saint Anne (Fig. 20). While recalling the composition of the previous altarpiece in the chapel, Baciccio's painting of the Madonna and Child with Saint Anne represents a significant departure from Celio's uninspired treatment of the same theme (Fig. 26).[25] The studies for Celio's altarpiece that have come down to us suggest a symmetrical composition consisting of the Virgin and Saint Joseph on one side, Joachim and Saint Anne on the other, and the Christ Child occupying the space at the center. In contrast to Celio's figures, the Virgin and Child with Saint Anne in Baciccio's painting are bound together by warm, human feeling; gently conveying the child into the arms of his grandmother, Mary looks with tenderness at her mother, who focuses her attention upon the precious burden she is about to receive. Joachim and Joseph, who stand behind their wives in Celio's composition, are relegated to the far distance in Baciccio's altarpiece. A probable source for the airborne *putti* and the gestures of the figures in Baciccio's picture is a painting of the Madonna and Child with Saint Anne in San Isidoro by a disciple of Bernini, Paolo Naldini.[26]

Rather than depicting the figures in a shallow, stark interior as Celio had done, the Genoese artist placed the Virgin and Child with Saint Anne in the foreground of a fertile landscape offering a distant view of a hilltop town. The idyllic setting of Baciccio's painting situates this work within the Venetian tradition of the *Sacra Conversazione* in a landscape, a type of subject typified by Palma Vecchio's *Sacra Conversazione* (c. 1517) and Titian's *Virgin with the Rabbit* (c. 1530).[27]

Surely Baciccio was directed in this project by the older and more experienced maestro. He and Bernini had only recently collaborated at the Gesù, where they were involved in the decoration of the vault. The close connection between the painting and its chapel setting suggests, along with the drawing in Montpellier, that Baciccio, under Bernini's guidance, conceived of the altarpiece as part of an ensemble. A number of elements in the painting may be related to the statue of Ludovica beneath it (Fig. 19). Saint Anne, who wears the white veil of the Third Order and who is much younger than her counterpart in Celio's altarpiece, resembles Ludovica in facial features and dress.[28]

Previously unnoticed by scholars, visual connections may be drawn between the Virgin and the *beata* and the lighting of the painted altarpiece and the statue recess. Mary's gesture of handing the Christ Child to Saint Anne echoes Ludovica's act of pressing her breast. The sleeves of the Madonna and the *beata* are nearly identical in line, shape, and distribution of light, while the

Virgin's veil, rising up near the nape of her neck, recalls the energetic movement of the fold of cloth that arches upward near Ludovica's cheek. The fictive light in the painting, depicted as entering from the sides, coincides with the actual illumination of the *Ludovica* in its aedicule. The light in the altarpiece, suggesting dawn or twilight, is consistent with the lighting of the marble sculpture, which is most intense during the morning and evening masses.

The painting is linked to the statue of Ludovica in yet another way. Hovering above the holy figures in the foreground, the charming cherubic infants in Baciccio's altarpiece are similar to the stucco cherubic heads on either side of the painting, who focus their attention upon the *beata.* Boldly foreshortened, the painted *putti* seem to pass through the frontal plane of the picture. They not only throw white roses upon the Madonna and Child with Saint Anne but also offer the illusion of strewing flowers on Ludovica, who lies beneath the altarpiece.

The visual evidence discussed above establishes that the statue of Ludovica, installed in the aedicule, is the focal point of a carefully orchestrated ensemble of painting, sculpture, and architecture; the altarpiece, the stucco decoration, the altar, the lighting, and the architectural space of the niche are all designed to create a setting for the *Ludovica* that is both lifelike and visionary. The sculpture of the *beata* is placed in a space reminiscent of a bedchamber, yet elements such as the hidden light source, the cherubic heads, the dove of the Holy Spirit, the flaming hearts, the decorative elements of the frame, and Baciccio's altarpiece all suggest a supernatural presence in the space inhabited by the *beata.*

While the statue recess was richly embellished, the chapel proper was left in the modest state in which Bernini found it.[29] The simplicity of the chapel was in keeping with the ascetic tastes of the Franciscan Observants at San Francesco a Ripa. Moreover, Bernini's patron, Cardinal Paluzzo, may have insisted that the decoration of the Altieri Chapel be kept within limits. The cardinal was undoubtedly aware of the sentiments of his uncle, Pope Clement X, who commanded in 1671 that the Altieri Chapel in Santa Maria sopra Minerva be rendered "più maestosa che ricca."[30] More important, by leaving unaltered the walls of the Altieri Chapel in San Francesco a Ripa, the sculptor was able to retain as much as possible the original appearance of this sacred space, which had been for more than one hundred years the center of Ludovica's cult.

Bernini's assiduousness in preserving the evidence of the *beata's* cult was a major factor in his campaign in the Altieri Chapel. He purposely retained such elements as the frescoes of the *beata,* the commemorative slabs, and the epitaph, all of which were cited in the *processi* as proof of the sanctity and longevity of Ludovica's cult. The image of the *beata* giving alms was employed not only in other frescoes[31] but also on liturgical cloths[32] and festival prints,[33] and was most certainly the subject represented in the print customarily placed in a beatification book.[34]

Strongly reminiscent of a sepulcher, the altar designed by Bernini (Fig. 12) reminds the viewer that the sacred remains of Ludovica, the focus of her cult, are preserved within it.[35] The center of the liturgical piece is pierced by a window offering a view of her casket. A light kept lit perpetually within the altar not only emphasized the presence of the holy relic of her body but also referred to the history of her cult.[36] Offering evidence of the longevity and continuity of Ludovica's cult, the *processi* inform us that a light always burned on her white marble sepulcher. Ludovica's biographer related that in honor of her beatification numerous silver candlesticks were placed on her tomb.[37] When her remains were exhumed and redeposited in the altar in 1675, the white marble sepulcher was dismantled. Preserving the evidence of Ludovica's cult, Bernini removed the ancient epitaph from the sepulcher and set it within the floor near the base of the altar, where it may be seen today. This inscription plaque, which dates from the year of her death (1533) and which refers to Ludovica as a *beata,* had been read as evidence of her cult at the ceremony of her exhumation in 1625.[38]

4

Visual Context

Bernini, who honored Ludovica's cult in the Altieri Chapel by preserving the physical evidence of her beatification, further commemorated the *beata* by the painted and sculpted elements of the altar recess, which, considered together, are reminiscent of funerary monuments. Although Rudolf Wittkower first suggested the *Ludovica's* resemblance to a *sepulcrum* in the 1950s, the connection of the ensemble to tomb sculpture has not been examined seriously.[1] My investigation of the relationship of the statue to the sepulchral tradition, as well as to other works of art, both clarifies Bernini's use of artistic sources and situates his masterpiece within the visual context of art history.

The installation of the statue in an aedicule over a sarcophagus altar, with the recumbent figure placed beneath a painted altarpiece, recalls a type of sepulchral monument common in Italy during the Middle Ages and the Renaissance. Characteristic of this genre of funerary monument are the tombs of Cardinal Matteo d'Acquasparta (d. 1302) in Santa Maria in Aracoeli (Fig. 36) and Bishop Giovanni de Coco (d. 1477) in Santa Maria sopra Minerva. Renaissance monuments of the Albertoni family, like that of Marco d'Antonio Albertoni (d. 1485) in Santa Maria del Popolo (Fig. 37), may also be associated with this type of tomb sculpture, although the Albertoni sepulcher omits the devotional image.

Bernini's unconventional placement of the *Ludovica* over the altar further relates the statue to funerary art. Sculptures of saints disposed in a prone position, such as Maderna's *Saint Cecilia* (1600) in Santa Cecilia in Trastevere, and Giorgetti's *Saint Sebastian* (c. 1672) in San Sebastiano (Fig. 40) were customarily placed in niches under the altar.[2] Prior to Bernini's installation of the *Ludovica,* only Menghini's *Saint Martina* (1635) of the church of Saints Martina and Luca (Fig.

41) was placed over an altar.[3] The statue of the female saint, however, is inserted within the recess of a retable whose large scale seems to dwarf the reclining figure. Dominating the niche in which it is placed, the semirecumbent figure of Ludovica more closely approximates such *demi-gisant* effigies as that of the monument of the *beata*'s relative, Antonio Albertoni (d. 1509), in the Albertoni Chapel in Santa Maria in Aracoeli (Fig. 42).

Specific motifs of Bernini's statue niche may be related to elements employed on Italian sepulchral monuments. The flaming torches embellishing the pilasters in the aedicule are commonly observed on Renaissance tombs, where they are used as symbols of the Resurrection (Fig. 51).[4] The double heads of the flaming torches flanking the *Ludovica* (Fig. 23) recall the funerary masks or Janus heads of Antique sarcophagi and are reminiscent as well of the heads decorating Bernini's tomb of Giovanni Battista Santoni in Santa Prassede (1610).[5]

Hovering over the figure of Ludovica, the stucco cherubs remind us of the angelic attendants in medieval and Renaissance tombs. Those in the funerary monument of Cardinal d'Acquasparta (Fig. 36), for example, stand guard attentively at the head and foot of the deceased as they patiently await the ascent of the soul. The angels in medieval tombs also aid in the transport of the soul to heaven, this function fulfilled by the celestial creatures on the canopy of the Archbishop Simone Saltarelli (d. 1342) sepulcher in Santa Caterina in Pisa.[6] Winged cherubs much like the heads in the Altieri Chapel are used in funerary art to evoke a heavenly presence, such cherubic creatures appearing, for example, on the archivolts of the tomb of Ludovica's relative, Marco d'Antonio Albertoni (Fig. 37).

The colored drapery beneath the *beata*'s bed in the Altieri Chapel (Fig. 17) recalls the cloth or burial shroud placed beneath the supine figure of the deceased in sepulchral monuments. During the Gothic period, this funeral cloth was often voluminous, nearly obscuring the sarcophagus over which it cascaded (Fig. 36). The shroud became less prominent in Renaissance tombs and in many cases was eliminated entirely (Fig. 37). Reminiscent of the funeral shrouds in Gothic sepulchral sculpture, the colored drapery beneath the figure of Ludovica also calls to mind the shroud used by Bernini in his contemporary tomb of Alexander VII in Saint Peter's (1672–78; Fig. 38). The burial shroud of the papal monument is made of Sicilian jasper and is energized by powerfully molded drapery folds, as the cloth now appears in the Altieri Chapel (the jasper version no doubt closely resembling the original of painted wood). While the colored cloth connects the sculpted image of the *beata* to the altar, the funeral drapery in Alexander's tomb links the kneeling figure of the pope with the door beneath it.

Standing in fictive niches on either side of the opening to the aedicule, the painted figures in the Altieri Chapel may be associated with sepulchral art, specifically with the virtues customarily placed in recesses flanking effigies (Figs. 13, 14, and 19). Allegorical figures referring to the character of the deceased are employed in Andrea Sansovino's tomb of Cardinal Ascanio Cardinal Sforza (1505) in Santa Maria del Popolo (Fig. 39). Similarly, elements in the Altieri Chapel recall Ludovica's virtues. The fresco of Saint Clare holding a monstrance may be associated with the theological virtue of Faith, shown in art with her attribute, the Host.[7] Although the allegorical figure of Charity is usually represented in the act of nursing twins, the fresco of Ludovica giving bread to a poor pilgrim presumably refers to this virtue frequently represented on funerary monuments.[8]

While these Italian examples offer numerous meaningful parallels, the single tomb that most closely resembles the *Ludovica* is a French sepulchral monument that Bernini saw in Paris. On 13 October 1665, Gianlorenzo visited the Orléans Chapel in the Church of the Celestines, where the tomb of Henri Chabot (d. 1655) was located. Accompanying Bernini on this excursion were his Parisian host and diarist, Paul Fréart de Chantelou, and François Anguier, the sculptor of the Chabot monument.[9] Since the tomb of Henri Chabot no longer exists, its appearance must be ascertained from an engraving (Fig. 43).[10] The architecture of the Chabot aedicule, its recess located above ground level, is not unlike Bernini's statue niche in the Altieri Chapel. Both the back wall and flat roof of Anguier's aedicule bring to mind Gianlorenzo's early sketch for the Altieri recess (Figs. 32 and 34).[11] The moldings of the French monument, like those in the Leipzig drawing, trace an arch on the back wall and articulate the junctures where the walls meet. Anticipating the disposition of the *Ludovica* in its chapel setting, the Chabot tomb offers a profile view of a semirecumbent figure (cf. Figs. 17 and 19). Lying on a sarcophagus, the figure of Chabot is attended by two *putti,* whose empathetic facial expressions foreshadow the cherubic heads of the Altieri Chapel. The billowing funeral cloth covering Chabot's lower torso and legs functions much like the colored drapery of the *Ludovica* by linking the statue in the recess to the space occupied by the viewer.

Gianlorenzo, then, was clearly inspired by sepulchral art. Notwithstanding, his figure of Ludovica is appreciably different from the sculptures just described. In fact, it is unique in the history of art, for no other sculpture combines so successfully the qualities of sublime surrender and active participation. While Ludovica's facial expression and posture suggest submission and ecstasy, her gesture of grasping her breast implies an active, voluntary involvement in the event portrayed. By placing this statue within the sculptural and pictorial contexts of art history, the originality of Bernini's vision becomes eminently clear. His inventiveness is best revealed by comparisons of the statue with various representations of dead, dying, and swooning figures, depictions that may be classified as "peaceful death," "death agony," "deathbed scene," "languid death," and "swooning Madonna and fainting saints."[12]

The *Ludovica,* whose impulsive grasping and turbulent draperies suggest the momentary, is substantively different from such representations of dead and dying figures as Maderna's *Saint Cecilia* (1600) and Menghini's *Saint Martina* (1635; Fig. 41). The saintly figures in the category of representation termed the "peaceful death" have already suffered the ordeal of martyrdom. Their pain over, nothing disturbs the stillness of eternal sleep.

Effigies of the deceased lying in state on tomb monuments may also be linked with the typology of the "peaceful death," an example of which is the stone *gisant* of Cardinal Matteo d'Acquasparta (Fig. 36). Of this type of statuary, only the figures with upraised praying hands seem to anticipate the *Ludovica* with its active gesture. Gianlorenzo may have been inspired by the praying *gisants* of Henry II and Catherine de' Medici of the Valois Chapel in Saint-Denis. During his trip to France, Bernini called the statues the most beautiful in Saint-Denis.[13] Perhaps he also recognized the shortcomings of these recumbent figures, whose vertically disposed hands are not well integrated with their inert prone bodies. Ludovica's vigorous gesture is wholly consonant with her semierect posture and energized drapery. In addition to these *gisant* figures, the *demi-gisant* effigies of tomb monuments also belong to the category of the "peaceful death." In contrast to the animated figure of Ludovica, such semirecumbent sepulchral figures as Andrea Sansovino's Cardinal Ascanio Sforza of Santa Maria del Popolo (1505; Fig 39) are characteristically quiet and contemplative.

It is also instructive to compare the statute of the *beata* with carved figures dramatizing the pain and suffering of death. Produced in 1685 by Francesco Aprile, a follower of Bernini, the statue of Saint Anastasia (Fig. 44), like the *Ludovica,* depicts the female saint with her head thrown backward and her draperies agitated. The resemblance to Bernini's sculpture, however, is only superficial. While the *beata*'s drapery rises up in buoyant folds suggesting the momentary, the folds of cloth of the *Anastasia* have just collapsed, implying that her travail, at this very moment, has ended. Unlike Ludovica, the young female saint has already crossed the threshold from life to death. The agony of her departure is implied by the stiffened, outstretched fingers of her right hand, a jarring reminder of her convulsive demise.[14] Attributed to Giovanni Battista Maini, the early eighteenth-century sculpture of Saint Anne in Sant' Andrea delle Fratte, like the *Anastasia,* suggests the agony of death (Fig. 45). Although closely based upon the *Ludovica,* it is not identical to its prototype. With a nearly grotesque wrinkled face, toes flexed in a violent paroxysm, the figure of Saint Anne appears harshly realistic when compared with Bernini's idealized image.

The figure of Ludovica, placed on a bed in a niche resembling a bedchamber, may best be associated with representations of the "deathbed scene," characteristically depicting a dead or dying figure with other figures in attendance at the bedside.

An artistic theme related to the "deathbed scene," the Death of the Virgin is based upon apocryphal legends.[15] These extrabiblical accounts inform us that when Mary was sixty years old, the apostles miraculously convened at the Madonna's bedside to ease her departure from the world.[16] As told in the legend, "Mary's soul went forth out of her body, and flew upward in the arms of her Son; and she was spared all pain of the body, as she had been from corruption from without."[17]

A Renaissance example of this subject is the Bruges *Death of the Virgin* by Hugo Van der Goes (c. 1481; Fig. 46). Lying in bed, surrounded by the apostles, Mary is portrayed at that moment before her soul leaves her body to join Christ. Her rolled-back eyes, like those of Ludovica, suggest a calm, painless transition from life to death, from earth to heaven. The Madonna is at peace, the whiteness of her pillow and veil seeming to remind us of the purity that earned her a good death. Hovering over the deathbed in a celestial glory, Christ awaits the reception of Mary's blessed soul.

Representations of the Virgin's peaceful demise nearly always included heavenly attendants floating above her bed. In fact, this element was essential in the rendering of the subject. Intended for the Cherubini Chapel of Santa Maria della Scala, Caravaggio's *Death of the Virgin* (c. 1604–5) did not include a swarm of angels, an element that seems especially lacking in the picture, owing to its high format.[18] The Carmelites who rejected Caravaggio's painting surely objected to the artist's omission of a heavenly glory.[19]

Thematically related to the Death of the Virgin, the death of the saints is also classified as a deathbed scene.[20] Typical of a seventeenth-century depiction of this subject is Andrea Sacchi's *Death of Saint Anne* (1649; Fig. 47). Here the quietly serene grandmother of Christ, lying upright on her deathbed is visited by the Madonna and Christ child, who, like the apostles in pictures of the Death of the Virgin, miraculously appear to ease the saint's departure from life. In the upper portions of Sacchi's painting, cherubs recalling the angels in Dormition scenes hover above Saint Anne. According to legend, the mother of Mary, like her daughter, Joseph, and other saints, is granted a good death for her holiness.[21]

Printed illustrations of popular manuals on how to die well, the *Ars Moriendi* (Figs. 48 and 49), include another type of deathbed scene.[22] The expiring figure, or Everyman, of the *Ars Moriendi,* unlike the Madonna and saints in their quiet deaths, is generally depicted as anxiety ridden. Holding a candle or crucifix, he is typically surrounded by mourners, devils to tempt him, a friar to hear confession and administer last rites, saints and angels to receive his soul, and Christ on the Cross with Mary and John. Among examples of three-dimensional statuary depicting deathbed scenes is Pierre Legros's *Blessed Stanislas Kostka* (c. 1703; Fig. 50), installed in the little room in Sant' Andrea al Quirinale where the Jesuit novice had died in 1568. The sculpture, rendered in different colored marbles, depicts the Polish Jesuit lying in bed, calmly awaiting his death. On the wall behind the dying figure is a nineteenth-century painting of the Madonna and angels by Tommaso Minardi that reflects the influence of the Altieri Chapel.[23] The saints in Minardi's picture, like the *putti* in Baciccio's altarpiece, seem to emerge from the painting, throwing flowers upon the semirecumbent figure of the young Jesuit. The statue's placement perpendicular to the wall forces the viewer to stand at Kostka's bedside and witness his death, much like a participant in a death scene. The tranquil expression on his face associates this figure with deathbed scenes of the Madonna and saints, while the crucifix and picture of Mary held by the young Jesuit bring to mind illustrations of the *Ars Moriendi* in which the dying person fixes his gaze upon a devotional image.

Of the painted deathbed scenes discussed above, the Death of the Virgin and its history, as well as the related theme of the death of the saints, had the greatest impact upon the Altieri Chapel decoration. The glory of angels, painted by Celio on the dome above Ludovica's tomb (Fig. 8) in about 1622, reflects this influence; God the Father at the apex of the vault, like Christ and the glory of angels in the Death of the Virgin, has appeared to receive Ludovica's soul rising from the white sepulcher that once stood in the middle of the Altieri Chapel, before Bernini's intervention.

The Altieri Chapel recess designed by Bernini is clearly indebted to artistic representations of the saintly deathbed. Most likely under the sculptor's advisement, Baciccio painted a swarm of angels that appears to break through the picture plane of the altarpiece to hover over Ludovica (Fig. 19). The miraculous appearance of a host of angels, the motif deriving from depictions of the Death of the Virgin and the death of saints, is also suggested in the chapel recess by Bernini's stucco cherubic heads. Baciccio's altarpiece, placed as it is behind the *Ludovica* in the Altieri Chapel recess, suggests the presence of the Madonna and Child with Saint Anne at the *beata*'s bedside. As in the case of Sacchi's *Death of Saint Anne* (Fig. 47), the holy personages have assembled to ease the dying figure's passage from life to death to everlasting life.

Through the imaginative integration of painting, sculpture, and architecture, Bernini was thus able to translate the pictorial qualities of the deathbed scenes to three-dimensional statuary. More important, the glory of angels and holy figures of the painted altarpiece, together with the statue of the *beata*, establish a visual link between Ludovica's demise and the ideal death of the Virgin and saints. Perhaps it is not irrelevant to mention that the Franciscan tertiary died at the age of sixty, the age at which the Madonna expired.[24] This coincidence, which could not have been ignored by Bernini and his patron, may explain in part why Ludovica's death was likened to Mary's.

The figure of Ludovica itself, however, is far removed from the Everyman of the *Ars Moriendi* and the saints of the deathbed scenes. With her head thrown backward and facial expression of sensual abandon, the *beata* may be associated with works depicting the "languid death." An example of a sculpture connected with this type of imagery is the Vatican *Sleeping Ariadne* (Fig. 51). Interpreted as a dying Cleopatra before the eighteenth century, the statue depicts a semirecumbent woman with her head sensuously tilted backward and to the side, her arm raised over her head.[25] The *Ariadne* or *Cleopatra,* a late Hadrianic or early Antonine copy of a Hellenistic work, entered the papal collection in 1512 and was moved to the *Stanza della Cleopatra* in the early 1550s, where it was set up as a fountain in a niche setting. Much admired by Renaissance artists, it was the prototype for the sensual sleeping nymphs of the sixteenth century. The critic Giovanni Battista Armenini in his treatise on painting (1586) ranked the *Cleopatra* as one of the finest sculptures in Rome, an opinion shared by Bernini, who (on 8 June 1665) claimed it was "among the finest pieces of sculpture in existence."[26] Apart from the Vatican *Cleopatra,* Gianlorenzo must have known Poussin's wax copy in the collection of his French host, Paul Fréart de Chantelou.

Also connected with the tradition of the "languid death,"[27] Michelangelo's so-called *Dying Slave* (Fig. 52) appears, at least indirectly, to have been a visual source for the statue of the *beata.* Bernini may have known this sculpture either from the original marble at Richelieu's estate in Poitou or from copies or engravings.[28] Chantelou's diary of 1665 informs us that the statue was discussed in Bernini's presence on 4 October, at which time the *Slaves* were referred to as "Michelangelo's best works."[29] The close relationship between the *Dying Slave* and the *Ludovica* may be discerned by comparing a top view of Bernini's *bozzetto* of the *beata* (Fig. 53) with

Michelangelo's sculpture. With the exception of the left arm and right leg, the posture of the *Ludovica* is nearly identical to that of the *Dying Slave.*

Its pose based on the *Dying Slave,* Giorgetti's sculpture of Saint Sebastian (c. 1672; Fig. 40) can also be classified with the "languid death." This statue, initiated about the same time as the *Ludovica,* may have been a more likely stimulus for Ludovica's posture than the *Dying Slave.* The close resemblance between Michelangelo's sculpture and Giorgetti's makes it difficult to determine which work, if not both, influenced Bernini. Although depicted as already dead, Saint Sebastian, with his head thrown back in surrender and his blissful facial expression, is reminiscent of the sculpture of the *beata.*

Ludovica's posture associates her with still another category of subject matter: the "swooning Madonna" or "fainting saint." It has been remarked that the *beata*'s pose is based on the fainting Virgin in Daniele da Volterra's *Deposition* (c. 1540) in the Orsini Chapel of Trinità dei Monti.[30] In fact, the *Ludovica* recalls any number of swooning Madonnas of the Renaissance and Baroque periods, examples of the latter being Giovanni Lanfranco's *Road to Calvary* in San Giovanni dei Fiorentini (Fig. 55) and Annibale Carracci's London *Pietà with the Three Maries* (c. 1606; Fig. 56). The posture of the fainting Virgin, often echoing that of the dead Christ, refers to the Madonna's mystical death on Calvary. Through her participation in her son's Passion, Mary assumed the role of co-redemptrix in heaven.[31]

It has been demonstrated that the swooning figure of Saint Francis, whose pose imitates that of the dead Savior, associates the Franciscan saint with Christ's sacrifice.[32] But the postures of fainting saints can also be related to that of either the dead Christ or the swooning Madonna. Thus the devotion of the saints to both the Son and the Mother is implied by their poses.[33] Some well-known depictions of saints whose fainting attitudes may be associated generally with that of Mary, Christ, and Ludovica as well, include Bernini's *Saint Theresa* (c. 1647; Fig. 57),[34] Giovanni Lanfranco's *Ecstasy of Saint Margaret of Cortona* (1618–20),[35] and Caravaggio's *Saint Francis in Ecstasy* (c. 1595).[36]

Another work of art that may be grouped with this type of subject matter is an engraving by Boethius a Bolswert from Hermann Hugo's *Pia Desideria* (1624).[37] This image, emblem 32 illustrating a line from *The Song of Songs,* depicts a young woman (the soul) who has collapsed on the ground, sick with love for God. Her posture, like that of the saints, parallels representations of the fainting Madonna and dead Christ. Thus Ludovica, her head thrown back in abandon like the swooning figures just described, seems to participate in the Passion of Christ, as did the Virgin Mary in her mystical death on Calvary.

The wide range of imagery discussed in this chapter provides the visual background to Gianlorenzo's masterpiece. The architectural design of the chapel niche, including its decorative elements, is related to medieval, Renaissance, and Baroque tomb monuments. Reminiscent of a bedroom, the recess in the chapel brings to mind a deathbed scene. The multiple representations of an angelic glory in the Altieri Chapel and the holy figures in Baciccio's altarpiece are linked to the visual tradition of the Death of the Virgin and its thematic variant, the death of the saints. Appreciably different from representations of the "peaceful death" and the "death agony," the figure of the *beata* is tied to subjects categorized as the "languid death" and "swooning Madonna and fainting saints." Three works from the former category—the *Cleopatra* (Fig. 51), Michelangelo's *Dying Slave* (Fig. 52), and Giorgetti's *Saint Sebastian* (Fig. 40)—are likely sources for the *Ludovica.* Yet, typical of Bernini, they have been so transformed that their role as prototypes for the statue of the *beata* is not immediately apparent. If I had not seen the *bozzetto* of the *Ludovica* from above, I might not have noticed the resemblance between it and the *Dying Slave* and/or *Saint Sebastian.*

Words of caution are in order: A discussion of the sources for the *Ludovica* should not overstate the impact of a few works of art. Rather, it is preferable to speak of the influence of *types* of subjects. To be more specific, the statue may be characterized as a synthesis of the sensuality of the languid strain with the yielding submissiveness of the "swooning Madonna and fainting saints." Yet even this descriptive statement cannot adequately explain the originality and freshness of Bernini's vision.

Even a work clearly influenced by the *Ludovica,* such as Baciccio's painting the *Death of Saint Francis Xavier* in Sant' Andrea al Quirinale (Fig. 54), is discernibly different.[38] Baciccio's dying figure of Saint Francis Xavier fails to possess the distinctive admixture of ardent involvement and yielding passivity characterizing Bernini's sculpture. Saint Francis has just expired; his grip on the crucifix has slackened, his draperies lie inert. In the sculpture of the *beata,* her active participation in the event portrayed is communicated by the energy of her draperies and the vigor of her grasping gesture.

The unique qualities of this masterpiece, however, may best be illuminated by investigating the complex meaning of the statue in its chapel setting. Close analysis of the *Ludovica* in the context of contemporary theological literature and literary accounts of the *beata's* life reveals this work of art as a visual demonstration of Catholic concepts of death and salvation in the age of the Baroque.

5

Charity and the Mystical Life

Her head is arched backward. Her mouth is open. Her eyes are rolled back within their sockets. Ludovica grasps her breast vehemently with one hand and presses against her abdomen with the other. Her draperies, animated by an unseen force, defy the laws of nature. Surely, there can be no dispute that the *beata* as depicted by Bernini is undergoing an intense spiritual experience (Fig. 17). Scholars have failed to reach a consensus, however, regarding the precise nature of the experience portrayed in the statue. While some authorities insist the Ludovica is shown in the throes of a painful death,[1] others propose that she is suffering from an intense heat caused by divine love,[2] or experiencing a mystical union with God on the day preceding her death.[3] The interpretation offered here proceeds from an examination of the sculpture in the full context of other works of art in the chapel, of written accounts of Ludovica's life and cult, and of devotional Catholic literature undoubtedly known to Bernini.

The statue and the other elements in the chapel are woven into a complex iconographic scheme whose layers of meaning, mutually interdependent and reinforcing, convey a unified conception of the *beata*. The *Ludovica* in its chapel setting represents the culmination of an ideal religious life, the reward for which is mystical union in death and eternal glory. As demonstrated in this study, the sculpture suggests the progress of the *beata's* mystical life to its very consummation, when she dies in union with Christ, departing from this world in an exquisite transport of divine love, her soul ascending to paradise.

Bernini's knowledge of the *beata* presumably derived from three major sources: the *processi* of Ludovica's cause read at the beatification ceremony in 1670 and published the following year;[4] the *Vita* of 1672 dedicated to Cardinal Altieri and written by Fra Pauolo, a descendant of the *beata* and the postulator of her cause;[5] and a panegyric to Ludovica, *I voli d'amore,* recited in San Crisogono in Trastevere in the spring of 1673 and published for this occasion with a dedication to Cardinal Altieri, who attended the event.[6] Written by the Carmelite Bernardino Santini, the panegyric begins with an ode to Ludovica and is followed by an oration. At the time in which *I voli d'amore* was read publicly, Cardinal Altieri was a Protector of the Carmelites, a fact no doubt explaining why a member of this order composed the work. Although the panegyric was presented after Bernini had already initiated the *Ludovica* (c. 1672), the sculptor most likely had advance notice of the ideas expressed in this literary work through his contacts with Cardinal Altieri, who may even have shown the text to the artist prior to its public recitation. This eulogistic oration, together with the testimony of the *processi* and the *Vita* by Fra Pauolo, are essential to the study of the levels of meaning informing Bernini's masterpiece.

Indeed, it is with reference to these sources that one of the most prominent motifs of the statue—Ludovica's ardent gesture of pressing against her bosom—may be interpreted.[7] Specifically, the gesture, which is at once one of reaction to an inner experience and of offering, affirms the *beata* as the embodiment of the theological virtue of Charity—precisely as do Pauolo's *Vita* and Santini's panegyric. Recurrent in these accounts of Ludovica's life is the theme that her heart was inflamed with the fire of charity,[8] the all-consuming nature of which is suggested by a passage from the panegyric: "She does not breathe other than the amorous exhalation of the flame nurtured in her bosom."[9]

Charity, the greatest of theological virtues, may best be described as the Christian concept of love, the two aspects of which are *amor dei,* love of God, and *amor proximi,* love of one's neighbor, the second manifested in good deeds such as almsgiving. The literary accounts of Ludovica's life emphasize that the fire of love burning within her encompassed both of these ideals. An entire chapter of Pauolo's *Vita* is devoted to the subject of the dual nature of the *beata*'s charity.[10] In describing the ascent of Ludovica's soul to God, *I voli d'amore* tells us in metaphoric terms that her flight to heaven is achieved by means of two wings: *amor di Dio* and *carità del prossimo.*[11] Of the former the panegyrist writes: "Ludovica offers her breast, gives her heart to the beloved, she rests on his chest."[12] And the writings affirm that the *beata*'s love for her neighbor was demonstrated by prodigious acts of charity, an example of which was the giving of bread, with pieces of gold and silver concealed within it, to the poor people of Rome.[13]

In the gesture of Ludovica's right hand Bernini dramatized these two aspects of the *beata*'s charity and their inseparability. Furthermore, the act of offering her bosom links Ludovica with the allegorical figure of Charity, who is often represented nursing a baby.[14] More specifically, the *beata* may be related to the figure of Roman Charity, who is commonly depicted as a young woman giving suck to her starving father.[15] A daughter of the Roman nobility, like the other pendentive figures in the Altieri Chapel (Saints Agnes, Cecilia, and Francesca Romana), the *beata* could have been viewed as an image of Roman Charity.

It has been suggested that Bernini's statue shows Ludovica lying in a faint precipitated by a seizure of the heat of divine love.[16] According to this interpretation, the colored drapery beneath the *beata*'s bed represents the blanket flung off as a consequence of the intense fire of *incendium amoris* (Fig. 17).[17] Although she is undoubtedly burning with love for God, it is untenable to think, as this reading of the statue implies, that the heat of divine love came upon Ludovica suddenly. The fire of charity, as her eulogists relate, burned always, and became more intense throughout her life. A momentary attack of *incendium amoris* impelling the *beata* to throw off her bed covering seems decidedly too literal and mundane an interpretation for a work by Bernini.

The level of the statue's meaning that refers to the greatest of theological virtues is reinforced by other works in the chapel. Ludovica's charitable acts on behalf of the city's needy described by Pauolo and Santini are expressed in unequivocal terms by the frescoes depicting her giving bread to a beggar (Figs. 8 and 13). The fresco of Saint Charles Borromeo likewise refers to the virtue of Charity (Fig. 11). The Milanese bishop, canonized in 1610, was "one of the heroes of active charity" of the seventeenth century;[18] however, the chapel fresco depicting the saint in fervent prayer clearly refers to *amor dei* rather than to *amor proximi.*

The virtue of *amor dei* is suggested further by Baciccio's altarpiece (Fig. 20) and by the engraving installed on the side wall of the chapel (Fig. 10). These works depicting the moment in which Saint Anne is about to receive the infant Christ from the arms of Mary are reminiscent of the rosary of Saint Anne, composed in the sixteenth century by Abbot Trithemius and still popular in the seventeenth century.[19] The prayers describe the relationship between the Madonna and Child with Saint Anne in tender, intimate terms, calling to mind the human warmth of Baciccio's rendering. In the third stanza, Christ's grandmother is exhorted to hesitate no longer, to take courage and hold the child "close to her heart." The prayer urges:

> You were not afraid to hold your daughter's hand,
> Before whom the sun and stars pale.
> Anne, what is keeping you from touching the
> Divine Child?[20]

The rosary then informs us that the infant is adorable and affectionate, and Christ's grandmother resists his charms no longer. She cares for him with tenderness:

> Anne, you nurse the Child with love,
> And with His rosey mouth
> He sips the nourishing milk,
> Making a delightful sound.

That Anne figuratively nursed the infant Christ may be implied in the print, in which the divine baby seems to be looking at Anne's breasts, her nipples protruding through her bodice (Fig. 10). Moreover, the image of suckling, used in the rosary as a metaphor of Anne's charity toward Christ, is analogous to Ludovica's gesture of offering her breast. As indicated earlier, the *beata* resembles Anne in dress and appearance. Ludovica may be compared with Mary's mother in other ways as well. The Franciscan tertiary had three daughters, and according to a legend condemned by the Council of Trent, Anne was widowed three times and had three female offspring. Like Christ's grandmother, who was the patron saint of motherhood and a widow, the *beata* was viewed as an exemplar for both mothers and widows.[21] Known as "Mother of the Poor,"[22] Ludovica may be likened to Anne, a model of charity, who gave one-third of her income to the Church and was said to have instructed Mary in charitable acts.[23] Thus the concepts of *amor dei* and *amor proximi* are reiterated in the Altieri Chapel.

The charity of the Franciscan tertiary is also recalled in another ecclesiastical site associated with the Altieri family, the chapel dedicated to Saint Joseph and Ludovica in Santa Maria in Campitelli. Commissioned by Don Angelo Altieri (d. 1706), brother of Cardinal Altieri, the chapel (completed c. 1706) was built on the site of Ludovica's house, a fragment of which was preserved on the altar wall.[24] A relief by Lorenzo Ottoni (1648–1736), the altarpiece of this chapel (Fig. 58), depicts the *beata* kneeling before an altar, above which appears a vision of the Madonna handing the Christ Child to Saint Joseph. Two pieces of bread shown in the foreground refer to Ludovica's almsgiving to the poor, this virtue noted by the angel who records her name in the Book of Life.[25]

According to Franciscan thought, the fire of charity was essential in achieving union with Christ and eternal salvation. Saint Francis de Sales (1567–1622), a Franciscan whose writings were admired by Bernini, stated that *amor dei* leads inevitably to *amor proximi* and to other perfections of the soul; charity, the universal means of salvation, stimulates, adorns, and gives the other virtues life, leading the soul to everlasting bliss.[26]

Contemporary devotional literature of the Jesuits and the Spanish mystics describes the way in which the love of God leads the soul to salvation. Popular Jesuitical writings such as *Cor Iesu amanti sacrum* trace through literary and visual images of the human heart the progress of the mystical life.[27] This work relates how the heart, pierced with the arrow of divine love by the infant Jesus, undergoes purgation and illumination, finally achieving the ultimate goal: unification with God. The Spanish mystics Saint Theresa of Avila (1515–82) and Saint John of the Cross (1542–91) also wrote of the union and transformation of the soul through the fire of *amor dei.*[28]

The concepts of the mystical life outlined above are not unique to the sources just discussed. Basic to Catholic thought in the seventeenth century, these ideas were unquestionably familiar to Bernini, who was learned in theological matters through his relationship with the Jesuits. He undoubtedly consulted the writings of Saint Theresa when working on the Cornaro Chapel and, as indicated, read with interest the devotional writings of Saint Francis de Sales. Also known to Bernini, it must be assumed, were the literary accounts of Pauolo and Santini, whose interpretations of the *beata*'s life conform to the aforementioned model of the mystical life.

More important, the sculpture of Ludovica may be viewed as a visual metaphor of the spiritual values expressed by the *beata*'s eulogists, as well as by other religious writers. The phases of the mystical life encompassing the concepts of purification, illumination, and divine union are each conveyed by the *Ludovica.* The purgation and illumination of the soul are implied in the statue by the effects of light and color. Intensified before the bright colors of the painted altarpiece, the extreme whiteness of Bernini's sculpture suggests the *beata*'s purity and divine knowledge (Figs. 19 and 33).[29] The light-infused marble statue seems to glow with a spiritual illumination, calling to mind Pauolo's description of the progressive purgation of her soul.[30] He reported that during the course of her lifetime "the light within her soul grew brighter," stimulating ever more rigorous acts of penitence.[31] The light within her was so intense at the time of her death that an aura miraculously appeared about her face when she was lying in state.[32]

Ludovica is also permeated with the light of sacred truth radiating from the dove of the Holy Spirit directly above her (Fig. 33). Writing of the progress of the mystical life, John of the Cross described how the darkness within the heart is driven away by purgation, until the soul is transformed in God and illumined with the light of divine wisdom.[33] The worshipper, kneeling before the altar in the semidarkness of the Altieri Chapel, looks toward the light-filled niche, from darkness to light, retracing in metaphoric terms the enlightenment of the *beata*'s soul (Fig. 3). Ludovica's special knowledge of sacred matters was celebrated by Pauolo and Santini. In the words of the panegyric: "[She] does not move a step without placing her foot on the pedestal of true wisdom."[34] Pauolo related that the book held by Ludovica in the frescoes in the Altieri Chapel (Figs. 8, 13) refers to her "highest contemplations."[35] Lying under the dove of the Holy Spirit with its gilded rays, the *Ludovica* brings to mind traditional representations of the descent of the Holy Spirit in which Pentecostal wisdom and inspiration descend as light and tongues of fire upon the Virgin and the apostles (Fig. 33).

Prepared by prayer, penance, wisdom, good works, and, most important, by charity, the most unitive of all these elements, Ludovica's soul soared to heaven, achieving the goal of the mystical life: union with the deity. The ascent of the *beata*'s "loving soul" to be joined with her divine Spouse is the recurrent theme of the panegyric whose very title, *I voli d'amore,* refers to her mystical flights.[36]

Viewed in conjunction with the panegyric and contemporary devotional literature, Bernini's statue is revealed as an image of Ludovica's union with Christ. The sculpture, in fact, calls to mind poetic images used by Santini, Theresa of Avila, John of the Cross, and Francis de Sales in their descriptions of the religious union. Thus Ludovica's gesture of pressing against her breast, in addition to visualizing the theological virtue of Charity, is suggestive of literary passages describing God's penetration of the soul (Figs. 17 and 18). The Spanish mystics explain that the soul united with Christ and Christ's will is a tabernacle or dwelling place for the deity. In describing the divine union, Saint John of the Cross spoke of God living "gently and lovingly . . . secretly and alone" in his bosom.[37] He related that the soul, whose deepest center is penetrated by God, is "like a crystal, clear and pure . . . like light itself."[38] Ludovica uniting her will to that of God, pronounced in the panegyric: "I will bind Him in my bosom, stamp Him in my heart."[39] This eulogistic account also informs us that "with the extinction of her [Ludovica's] sense of self, her spouse Jesus lives in her breast."[40] The *beata*'s bosom, within which the fire of charity flames, is thus the center of love for God, *and* of the deity's love for her, a place in which Christ dwells in mystical union with her loving soul.

The drapery folds of Ludovica's garments may be related as well to the *beata*'s union with Jesus (Fig. 17). Her veil near her right cheek and left hand and her gown in the vicinity of her vitals move upward, suggesting a force raising her toward God. The folds of her garments, meandering about her abdomen, arching upward in bunches about her navel, and flowing in thin, rushing streams to her foot, are reminiscent of the divine waters described by Francis de Sales, John of the Cross, and Theresa of Avila. According to these writers, the rivers of living water may be understood as the grace of God flowing through a soul united with the deity. "Men on earth are reflected in the living waters of God's love," Francis tells us.[41] John of the Cross explained:

> When a soul is enkindled with divine union,
> from its inmost part flow the rivers of glory,
> abounding in divine union and transformed through
> love in God, for it perceives that from its belly
> are flowing the rivers of living water which the
> Son of God said would flow from such a soul.[42]

The following discussion of the subject by Francis makes one think that Bernini may have been aware of this passage, or others like it, when he designed the folds of cloth moving like agitated water near the *beata*'s midsection, where they bubble up, radiating movement like a fountain:

> God makes a supernatural fountain well up at
> the apex of the soul's higher part.
> This we call grace. It includes faith and hope,
> of course; yet its essence is charity.
> This cleanses the soul from all its sins,
> adorns it with a wondrous beauty.[43]

The implied presence of both the fire of charity and the waters of God's love is another means by which the statue conveys the supernatural quality of Ludovica's experience. Saint Theresa described fire and water as coexisting and strengthening each other in the deepest center of the soul. This harmony of elements naturally antipathetic is viewed as a demonstration of the awesome power of the deity to reverse the laws of nature.[44] In Bernini's sculpture, as in the mystical writings of Theresa and John of the Cross, the fire of love for God burns with the divine flame of love, and the waters of God's love flow into the rivers of love for him. In sum, Ludovica's charity for the deity is answered by Christ's love and, thus, both his love for her and her charity for him unite in the flame and waters within her.

The drapery folds, facial expression, and pose of the sculpted figure of the *beata* together suggest that the *beata* is in the latter stages of her mystical union. Saint Theresa explained that in the early stages of the spiritual life, God slowly fills the basin of the soul with water, but in the advanced phases of union,

> . . . God, Who controls the sources of the waters and forbids the sea to move beyond its bounds, has loosed the sources whence water has been coming into this basin; and with tremendous force there rises up so powerful a wave that this little ship—our soul—is lifted up on high. And if a ship can do nothing, and neither the pilot nor any of the crew has any power over it, when the waves make a furious assault upon it and toss it about at their will, even less able is the interior part of the soul to stop where it likes, while its senses and faculties can do no more than has been commanded them: the exterior senses, however, are quite unaffected by this.[45]

This mystical occurrence seems to be recalled in the statue of Ludovica, the marble drapery suggesting an abundance of turbulent waters moving ceaselessly within her soul. Theresa described the influx of celestial waters as a sublime flight of the spirit granted by God in the latter stages of mystical ascent.[46] The *beata*'s expression, as well as the backward thrust of her head, imply a stage of ecstatic surrender wholly consonant with the raptures recorded by the female mystic:

> But when this most wealthy Spouse desires to enrich and comfort the Bride still more, He draws her closely to Him that she is like one who swoons from excess of pleasure and joy and seems to be suspended in those Divine arms . . . .[47]

At the same time, the gesture of clutching her breast demonstrates an active rather than a completely passive role. The coexistence in the sculpture of serenity and excitement, conveyed, respectively, by Ludovica's tranquil expression and agitated draperies, coincides with Theresan and Salesan descriptions of the highest form of union.[48] Francis de Sales explained that "the saints in heaven are restful in their activity, active in their response"; on earth, "when we try . . . to do acts of charity, we find rest in the outpouring of our hearts, we find movement in the repose of gratifying love for God—a foretaste of that future bliss on which our hearts are set."[49]

The sightlessness of Ludovica's eyes, her pupils rolled back within their sockets, may be associated with the Theresan concept that in the latter stages of union God speaks directly to the soul, imparting to it an "intellectual vision" not perceived by the senses (Figs. 17 and 18).[50] Even the presence of the deity is not seen, but felt by a soul in mystical union with Christ.[51]

The exalted nature of Ludovica's divine union is suggested further by the cherubs of the painted altarpiece (Figs. 3, 21, and 22), who seem to be celebrating the sacred event. These angelic creatures, who joyfully proclaim the mystical marriage of Mary and Christ by strewing roses, also seem to be showering Ludovica with flowers, in honor perhaps of her spiritual union. As a woman, Ludovica was considered most capable of reaching higher mystical states. According to Francis de Sales, holy women have a special aptitude for spiritual transport because of their great capacity for the fires of charity.[52] This characterization of religious women could well have been in Bernini's mind when he depicted Ludovica in ecstatic union with the deity.

6

The Good Death

In the statue of the *beata,* Bernini fused Ludovica's mystical union with her death, establishing without equivocation that she triumphed over her mortality. It is through death that Ludovica's soul is perpetually and everlastingly joined with God. Bernini's biographer Filippo Baldinucci reported in 1682, only eight years after the sculpture was completed: "[Bernini was asked] to make . . . a beautiful statue of the Blessed Ludovica Albertoni in the act of dying. . . ."[1]

Despite this statement, Anthony Blunt postulated an opposing interpretation based on Pauolo's description of the *beata*'s last days.[2] The *Vita* relates that Ludovica, suffering from a lingering illness, received the viaticum, and then demanded to be left alone in her room. A servant who later entered the bedchamber reported that the *beata* "was flushed, and seemed quite joyful, as if she had returned from paradise."[3] Ludovica died the next day, clutching a cross. Since Bernini did not depict the Franciscan tertiary holding a crucifix, Blunt argued that the sculptor represented the moment of divine union occurring on the day preceding her demise, and did not portray her death.[4] The scholar failed to notice, however, that neither the *processi* nor the panegyric mentions the use of a cross in Ludovica's last moments.

Blunt's theory is predicated upon Bernini's omission of the cross. Yet, one can reasonably explain why Gianlorenzo omitted this detail without challenging the interpretation that Ludovica is shown in the act of dying. The inclusion of the crucifix, for one thing, posed a major problem to Bernini. A cross was kept on the altar, and if the sculptor had employed a crucifix in his design, an unfortunate situation would have arisen in which two crosses would have been very close to each other.[5] This redundancy would have been a distracting note, upsetting the focused intensity of the *beata*'s sublime experience. Furthermore, if Ludovica had been shown holding a cross, then proper emphasis would not have been placed upon her gesture of clutching her breast, a major element of the composition referring to charity and divine union (Fig. 17).

In addition, Bernini may have left out the crucifix in order to emphasize certain theological concepts regarding the nature of death. Rather than focusing upon the moment of biological death with the Franciscan tertiary holding the cross, the sculptor stressed Ludovica's mystical union in death by placing emphasis upon her gesture of pressing against her bosom, the place in which Christ dwells in love. According to Catholic theology, a soul united with God cannot die; there is no death, only life in Christ culminating in perpetual union.[6] Francis de Sales says: "The soul that flows out into God does not die; death is alien to what is submerged in life."[7]

By excluding the cross, Bernini avoided situating Ludovica's death within a specific moment in time. Contemporary religious writers emphasized that death is not an instant, but is part of the continuum of the mystical life. The soul dies slowly to earthly life, living more and more in Christ, so that death itself is gradually overcome and replaced by eternal life. The panegyric devoted to Ludovica explains that there can be no division between life and death because the love of God is an unbroken thread.[8] Since the mystic is continuously in the process of dying, Baldinucci's statement that the *beata* is "in the act of dying" appears entirely appropriate. Thus Ludovica may be understood as existing within the continuum of spiritual time, by means of which she moves from life to death and from death to infinite life.

Influenced, no doubt, by accounts of Ludovica's blessed death, the figure of the *beata* conveys, through gesture, pose, and facial expression, the special nature of her departure from life (Figs. 17 and 18). The proceedings at her beatification hearing inform us that Ludovica died in "sanctity" and was "famed for the sign that she gave at the time of her death of her great charity for God," as well as for her willingness and desire to conform to the will of the deity and be joined with him in the afterlife.[9] Another account recorded in the *processi* describes the moment of her death: "With a devoted aspect, her eyes rolled back to heaven, [Ludovica] surrendered her spirit to her Creator."[10]

The sublimity of her death is evoked in both the sculpture and the panegyric *I voli d'amore*. Ludovica's facial expression of ecstatic fulfillment and quiet delight establishes in visual terms that she died a good death. As suggested by her "sightless" eyes turned upward, the Franciscan tertiary may be experiencing in her ascent to heaven a glimpse of the beatific vision, the glorious sight of the divinity awarded to the souls of paradise. Santini tells us that Ludovica stands "face to face" before Christ.[11]

A poetic view of Ludovica's death is expressed by her panegyrist: "Like a vapor attracted to the divine sun," the *beata* longed for Christ, her yearning so intense, that it was "sweeter dying than living without."[12] Referring to Ludovica's demise as "a sweet sleep," Santini quoted from the Psalms: "In peace I will both lie down and sleep; for thou alone, O' Lord, makest me dwell in safety."[13] Saint Theresa explained that in the latter stages of union, there is no involvement of the senses and consequently no bodily pain, although the soul suffers spiritually in longing for God.[14] According to the *Vita,* the *beata* was no longer burdened by her illness on the day of her death.[15]

The prototype for Ludovica's good death is the Virgin's joyful demise. Specific details of the *beata*'s death may be related to the legends of the Virgin. Ludovica, for example, died at the age of sixty, the same age at which the Madonna departed. The Franciscan tertiary, like Mary, experienced a heavenly vision shortly before death.[16] Recalling legends of the Virgin's Assumption, written accounts of Ludovica's exhumation report that her bodily remains smelled sweet like flowers.[17] Installed in a niche recalling a bedchamber, the statue of the *beata* itself is related to artistic representations of the Death of the Virgin.

The pose in which the Franciscan tertiary is rendered further associates her with the Madonna's mystical death on Calvary. It has been demonstrated that the motif of the fainting Virgin in scenes of Christ's Passion reflects a doctrine advocated by the Franciscans that Mary died a mystical death when her son suffered his martyrdom of the flesh.[18] Christ offered his body for the sins of man, and the Virgin, acting as co-redemptrix, sacrificed her own son in love. Francis de Sales offered a description of the Madonna's mystical death that calls to mind the experience Ludovica is undergoing in Bernini's depiction:

> . . . she [Mary] experienced there [at the foot of the cross] the most intense, most agonizing thrill of love you could possibly imagine. Extreme though this onset of love was, nevertheless it was at once strong but gentle, powerful but still.[19]

Ludovica's gesture links the *beata*'s charity with the Virgin's immolation of love on Calvary.[20] The touching of the Madonna's bosom refers to the Virgin's sacrifice at Christ's death, the gesture evoking charity and motherhood. Such a motif may be observed in Annibale Carracci's *Pietà with the Three Maries* (Fig. 56), in which one of the saintly women presses her fingers against the breast of the swooning Mother of Christ.[21] Bernini employed a variation of this theme on the reverse side of his drawing for the statue of Ludovica (Fig. 27). A preliminary sketch for the *Intercession of Christ and the Virgin* of the Gesù vault, this drawing refers to the *duplex intercessio,* by which Christ appeals to God by displaying his wounds, and Mary intercedes to her son by indicating the breast with which she nurtured him.[22] As explained by the Franciscans, the Virgin assumed the role of co-redemptrix, or intercessor to the Savior through her mystical death on Calvary.[23]

In light of the foregoing, Ludovica's death may be seen as an analogue of the Madonna's immolation on Calvary. Through the reiteration of Mary's swoon and gesture, the *beata* seems to be experiencing the Passion in the semblance of the Virgin. Ludovica has apparently been transformed by her charity and devotion, the mystical event of the Passion absorbed within her. Her gesture may have been stimulated as well by an inner vision of the crucifixion. A comparison may be drawn in this case to Bernini's monument depicting the good death of Sister Maria Raggi. In this cenotaph erected on a pier in Santa Maria sopra Minerva (1643), the nun's inner vision of the cross is implied by the crucifix above her head.[24] The same situation may be operative in the Altieri Chapel, where the cross on the altar may refer to an inner vision of the Passion. In any event, Bernini executed other figures that seem to anticipate *Ludovica*'s intense, consuming devotion to Christ and Mary. The *Saint Longinus* of Saint Peter's (1629–38), for example, implies by means of gesture the imitation of Christ's sacrifice on the cross.

Ludovica's eulogists report the *beata*'s devotion to the Virgin, whom she emulated. Santini described Ludovica as the woman of the Apocalypse [Mary] who is given the wings of an eagle,[25] and related that "her roses [Ludovica's] are grafted onto the Nazaren lily [Mary]"—a metaphor reflected in the vault decoration of the Altieri Chapel niche (Fig. 24).[26] The *beata*'s panegyrist and biographer also convey the notion that Ludovica was devoted to Christ and the Passion. "She embraced Jesus on the cross from which she could not be separated,"[27] and often meditated upon the suffering and death of the Savior.[28] Her *Vita* proclaims that she "died in the cross of Christ" on a Friday,[29] the same day of Christ's death on Calvary.[30] Ludovica's last words, "into thy hands I commend my spirit," are those uttered by Jesus at his passing.[31] Since the contemplation of Christ's suffering was a major devotional goal of the dying, Ludovica's posture and gesture, linking her by analogy to the Virgin's part in the Passion, clearly establish in visual terms the idea that she achieved the ideal Christian death.[32]

Ludovica's blessed death may be associated also with Saint Anne, the patron saint of the good death to whom the chapel is dedicated.[33] Bernini's sculpted figure of Ludovica resembles Anne as shown in Baciccio's altarpiece, and a number of iconographical connections have been drawn between these women. Further evidence that these holy women were linked is provided by an eighteenth-century sculpture of Saint Anne in Sant' Andrea delle Fratte—a near-replica of the *Ludovica* (Fig. 45)—attributed to G. B. Maini.[34] Anne's good death may be viewed as another way in which these religious matrons are extrinsically linked.

According to legend, Anne was able to assist the dying because her own death was soothed by the presence of Mary and Christ at her bedside. As demonstrated in Andrea Sacchi's painting of 1649, *The Death of Saint Anne* (Fig. 47), Mary's mother, surrounded by the apostles, is blessed by the Christ Child held in the arms of the Madonna. Winged angelic heads hovering above Saint Anne await the reception of her soul, while cherubs prepare the cloth that will convey her spirit to God.

Numerous elements in the Altieri Chapel recess announce Ludovica's triumph over death. The flaming torches of the pilasters, a decorative element commonly employed in Renaissance sepulchral art, symbolize the Resurrection (Fig. 21).[35] The colored cloth connecting the statue of Ludovica with the altar may also be related to the Resurrection. This jasper drapery, which calls to mind the palls or shrouds of Gothic tombs and, more specifically, the funeral cloth of Alexander VII's monument in Saint Peter's, repeats the configuration of Ludovica's form. By suggesting the contours of her sacred body, the activated drapery implies her resurrection from the sarcophagus altar where her remains are kept (Fig. 33). The pall or shroud was viewed as the cloth in which the soul was conveyed to heaven;[36] its function in sepulchral sculpture is reflected in Sacchi's *Death of Saint Anne,* in which drapery upheld by cherubs is most likely intended to carry the spirit of Saint Anne to paradise. A fifteenth-century fresco of the death of Santa Francesca Romana, a saint to whom the *beata* was likened, shows the soul ascending to heaven on a patterned cloth. While in the works discussed above the shroud is employed to convey the soul to paradise, the colored cloth repeating the shape of the *beata*'s form infers the deliverance of her body to life everlasting at the Second Coming.[37]

The statue in its chapel setting thus asserts that the *beata* prevailed over death itself through the sanctity of her mystical life. Ludovica's salvation is also confirmed by written accounts of her life and cult. The witnesses of the *processi* stated that the Franciscan tertiary went directly to paradise, performing miracles as intercessor immediately after her death.[38] God the Father, shown at the apex of the celestial glory in the chapel, awaits the arrival of Ludovica's soul (Fig. 6). A refrain of the panegyric, "I am going to Him Who sent me" (John 16:5), is a metaphorical comparison of Christ's departure to join his Father in heaven with Ludovica's ascent to God.[39] By purifying her soul through acts of penance, and willingly embracing her death, the *beata* apparently avoided the trials of purgatory.[40]

The means by which Ludovica triumphed over death is ultimately suggested by the spatial arrangement of the statue recess. Viewed by the worshipper in the chapel proper, the sculpture chamber functions as a visual demonstration of the pathway to salvation (Fig. 19). The frescoes flanking the altar and the perspective arch appear like an arched gateway leading to the statue recess. Paintings on the angled walls proclaim Ludovica's devotion to faith and good works, the means by which salvation is achieved. The picture of Saint Clare holding a monstrance refers to faith in the Eucharist and in Christ, and the image of Ludovica distributing bread is a sign of active charity.

Seen through an arch whose shape is repeated in the painted altarpiece, the figure of Ludovica appears to be lying within an intermediate space, between the "gateway" leading into the recess and the divine realm represented by the altarpiece. Infused with light suggesting a divine presence, the semirecumbent figure of Ludovica is poised between physical and spiritual states of being.

Her flesh is transformed by love to fire and water, the body becoming spirit, and the spirit of God penetrating and flowing through her. The *beata* ascends to the deity, while the divinity descends to her in the form of the flower-strewing angels of the altarpiece, the dove of the Holy Spirit, and light.

Ludovica is situated at the threshold of the illusionistic space of the painted altarpiece. To enter the celestial world of the painting, her soul must pass between the pilasters of the frame, the gateposts of a supernatural passageway. Pervasive in seventeenth-century religious literature is the concept of death as a door or gateway leading to the afterlife, an idea perhaps implied by Bernini in the door of the tomb of Alexander VII (Fig. 38).[41] The statue of Ludovica in its chapel setting thus seems to exist within a continuum in space and time, leading to eternal life, the heavenly world of Baciccio's Holy Family. This idea is reinforced by the serpents associated with the god Janus and by the Janus heads, motifs decorating the pilasters (Figs. 22 and 23).[42] The most holy and exalted of ancient Roman deities, Janus was the god of light who opened the gates of heaven in the morning and closed them at night.[43] As the god of entrance into a new division of time, he is also associated with the transition from one state to another, from life to death.

This ancient god is directly linked to Ludovica. The god of good beginnings, Janus is sacred to January, the month in which the *beata* died and (thus) of her feast day. In addition, the double-headed deity was the ancient god-king of the Janiculum, and San Francesco a Ripa is located at the base of this Trasteveran hill. In light of the foregoing discussion, the Janus heads flanking the altarpiece may be understood as guardians of the arched passageway to eternity, helping the *beata* complete the transition from life to death—to enter the spiritual world of the altarpiece, the final gateway of her mystical life.

As the god of auspicious beginnings, Janus assures Ludovica's passage to the celestial world, a pathway made accessible by the Holy Family depicted in the altarpiece. Commonly viewed as the Door to Heaven, the *Janua Caeli* of the litany, the Virgin Mary is considered the gateway to salvation, since she brought forth the redeemer and serves as intercessor to her son.[44] Bernini may have been thinking of this devotional reference to Mary when he designed the recess with its painted altarpiece. He may have been influenced also by the enframement used by Donatello in the Annunciation Tabernacle (c. 1428–33) in Santa Croce, Florence. The Janus heads on the pilasters of the tabernacle suggest that the frame functions as the gateway to eternity achieved through Mary. Another work of art that may have inspired the "gateway" in the Altieri Chapel is Sacchi's *Death of Saint Anne* (Fig. 47). In this painting an open arched doorway indicated in the background probably represents the pathway through which the soul of the deceased will pass.

The Altieri Chapel, suggesting the progress of Ludovica's soul to its eternal reward, thus embodies a complexity of interrelated ideas. Motifs within the statue of Ludovica itself often function on several levels, as demonstrated by the gesture in which she clutches her breast and by other aspects of her posture. The *Ludovica* also engages the participation of such other elements in the chapel as the lighting, the stucco dove of the Holy Spirit, the roses and lilies, the print of the Madonna and Child with Saint Anne, the colored drapery, perhaps the crucifix, the flaming torches, the Janus heads, the snakes, the arch-gateway, and the frescoes of Ludovica, Saint Clare, Saint Charles Borromeo, and the glory of angels with God the Father.

Some elements in the chapel function in more than one expressive or symbolic capacity, one example being Baciccio's altarpiece of the Madonna and Child with Saint Anne. In addition, the study of such other details as the flaming hearts, pomegranates, and cherubic heads demonstrates further the rich multiplicity of meanings interwoven in the Altieri Chapel. The flaming hearts on the windowsills (Fig. 25) and on the altar-sarcophagus (Fig. 12), the latter pierced in the center so that the light burning within it creates the illusion that the heart is actually on fire, refer to

Ludovica's charity and divine union. (A flaming heart, a symbol of love for the deity, is an attribute of the allegorical figure of Charity.)[45] Ablaze with large, darting tongues of fire, the hearts further establish that Ludovica is shown in an advanced stage of her mystical union. As John of the Cross explains: "The more intense the fire of union with Christ, the more vehemently issue forth the flames of love."[46]

The pomegranates depicted on the panel behind the *beata* may be related to Ludovica's charity, spiritual perfection, and salvation (Fig. 17). The fruit is symbolic of the perfect Christian, the rough outer skin representing humility, and the red juice and seeds charity and good works.[47] Commonly employed on sepulchral monuments, pomegranates are likewise funerary emblems alluding to immortality.[48] A symbol of the Virgin Mary, the pomegranate also refers to the charity and good works of the Madonna.[49] The pomegranates in the Altieri Chapel thus invoke the merits of both the Madonna and Ludovica.

The angelic creatures hovering above the sculpture of the *beata* (Fig. 33) may be associated with Ludovica's charity and purgation. These stucco cherubs most likely represent the celestial agents by which the flames of love and purification were ignited (Figs. 21 and 22). They are probably intended to function much like the angels of the highest order who burn perpetually with love for the deity, the cherubim and seraphim described by Dionysius the Areopagite.[50] Certainly relevant to this discussion, Saint Francis's heart was kindled with charity by a seraphic creature who also left the marks of the stigmata upon the saint's flesh. This ecstatic experience, for which Saint Francis was called the Seraph Saint, was represented in Cavalier d'Arpino's altarpiece in the choir of San Francesco a Ripa. Ludovica as a Franciscan tertiary was of the "Seraphic Order," and in a panegyric to her, Santini likened her ardor to that of Saints Francis, Catherine of Siena, and Theresa, all of whom were ignited by fiery angels.[51] Rejoicing, no doubt, in the reception of a blessed soul, the cherubic heads in the Altieri Chapel are also reminiscent of the angelic creatures in funerary sculptures who act as guardians of the spirit, escorting their precious charge to heavenly glory.[52] The same function seems to be performed by the celestial creatures in Sacchi's *Death of Saint Anne* (Fig. 47).

The interpretation of the *Ludovica* presented here is clarified by a comparison with an earlier masterpiece by Bernini, the *Saint Theresa* (c. 1647) of the Cornaro Chapel in Santa Maria della Vittoria (Fig. 57). This chapel, executed approximately a quarter century earlier, closely resembles the Altieri project in a number of significant ways. In fact, many of the theological ideas adumbrated in the earlier chapel were apparently recast in the *Ludovica.* According to Baldinucci, Bernini considered the *Theresa* his best work,[53] and it is not surprising, therefore, that this sculpture was still on the artist's mind in his old age.

As portrayed by Bernini, Theresa and Ludovica are undergoing similar religious experiences. Represented in the *Saint Theresa* is an event described in her autobiography: the transverberation or piercing of her heart by an angel who left her afire with divine love. The Spanish saint, like the *beata,* is inflamed with charity for God, an idea asserted emblematically in both chapels by flaming hearts. The sweet, compassionate angel smiling with joy at the saving of Theresa's soul, igniting her with his fiery dart of love, seems a precursor to the charming cherubic creatures who enkindled Ludovica.[54] Like the blessed one, the mystic of Avila is dying in union with the deity, since Theresa's transverberation is also her death, her mystical matrimony with God.[55]

It has been demonstrated here that Ludovica died in Christ, her posture implying an imitation of Mary's role in the Passion; Theresa's pose, as well, constitutes a visual analogue linking her to the suffering of Jesus. The posture of the saint, her arm hanging limply, her shoulder thrust forward, her head turned backward, is reminiscent of a dead Christ—for example, Michelangelo's *Pietà* in Saint Peter's (Fig. 59). Since the elements of Theresa's pose linking her to the Lamentation may not be traced to other depictions of the transverberation published in Irving Lavin's major study of the Cornaro Chapel,[56] one could reasonably assume that the visual connection with the *Pietà* was an innovation of Bernini's. In the artistic theme known as *lo spasimo,* the Virgin's mystical death at the Passion is implied by her pose imitating that of the dead Christ.[57] Theresa's posture, like that of Ludovica, may be related to the Passion, and to Mary's "immolation" on Calvary, thus suggesting by analogy that the Spanish mystic died on the cross, in union with her divine Spouse. This interpretation coincides with the credible theory that Theresa was a martyr who died of her intense love for Christ.[58]

The reiteration of Mary's and Christ's posture also links Theresa and Ludovica to Saint Francis of Assisi, to whom these holy women are frequently likened.[59] In fact, the flaming hearts in these chapels may be associated with Francis, who was said to have prayed to be inflamed with God's love so that he could die for the love of the deity.[60] Francis's ardor for Jesus, for which he suffered a martyrdom, is visually asserted by his pose imitating that of the Redeemer on Calvary.[61] In view of the above, Theresa and Ludovica, offering themselves in love in the semblance of Christ and Mary, may be associated as well with the saint of Assisi's imitation of Christ's Passion.

Despite these similarities, the event portrayed in the *Theresa* can be differentiated from that of the *Ludovica* in a number of ways. While the Carmelite is undergoing the transverberation, the *beata* has already been inflamed, the fire of charity and divine love burning within her soul. In the statue of Theresa (Fig. 57), the act of ignition is emphasized. The saint's spiritual transport is explained by the presence of a celestial creature whose delicate gesture of lifting the gown with one hand, poising the dart with the other, implies the repeated action of piercing the heart. The Spanish mystic informs us that the rapture of the transverberation causing both pain and pleasure to the spirit involved the body as well:

> The pain was so sharp that it made me utter several moans; and so excessive was the sweetness caused me by this intense pain that one can never wish to lose it, nor will one's soul be content with anything less than God. It is not bodily pain, but spiritual, though the body has a share in it—indeed, a great share. So sweet are the colloquies of love which pass between the soul and God. . . .[62]

As depicted by Bernini, Ludovica's experience is more internalized than that of Theresa, there being no visible external agent explaining the *beata*'s ecstatic rapture. While the figure of the Spanish saint is shown passively submitting to the act of transverberation, Ludovica, while wholly receptive, clutches her breast, demonstrably offering herself in love to the deity. Despite this gesture of active participation, the *beata* seems more serene, withdrawn, and ethereal than the figure of Theresa. Ludovica's facial features are softer, her face more feminine and gently rounded.[63] The horizontals and verticals in the Altieri Chapel setting create a quiet, stabilizing foil for Ludovica's garments, whose energetic movements suggest a miraculous intervention.[64] In contrast to Theresa's garments, at once ascending and collapsing in response to the transverberation, Ludovica's draperies are mellifluent, looping upward, rising in a meandering pattern, and flowing in a narrow, rushing stream across her body. The white marble of the *Ludovica,* absorptive rather than reflective, glows with infused light, the sculpture looming like an apparition above the altar, especially when viewed from the chapel entrance (Fig. 3).

Ludovica is depicted in a higher mystical state than her Spanish counterpart, a factor explaining many of the apparent differences between these works. The *beata,* inflamed with charity, is dying without bodily pain in an advanced phase of union, the waters of God's grace welling up within her. Since Theresa, according to her own account, experienced physical involvement in her transverberation, the saint depicted by Bernini must be in an earlier stage of her mystical life,[65] ignited by divine love, and transformed into the flames of love, the fires of which cause her demise. Although Theresa's death and salvation are implied in the tableau, the act of transverberation is the recurrent event of her life upon which our attention is focused.

In the *Ludovica,* however, its chapel recess resembling a sepulcher, emphasis is placed upon the theme of the good death and immortality. Perhaps the more pronounced ethereality of the sculpture of the *beata* reflects the concept that, depicted in the act of leaving this world in an ecstatic paroxysm of love, Ludovica is undergoing a spiritual transmutation from one state of existence to another; she is transformed in God, the deity indwelling her soul, her flesh becoming spirit, her soul ascending to paradise.

7

Image of Salvation

The sculpture of Ludovica, visually demonstrating a personal triumph over death, conveys, as well, the promise of salvation in universal terms. Through the sanctity of her pious life and sublime death, Ludovica is able to intercede in heaven on behalf of the sinner. Moreover, her mystical life serves as a model for the faithful, guiding them along the pathway to salvation. Bernini, who carved the statue in his old age, embodied the highest ideals of the Baroque period in this image of death and salvation. Associating the semirecumbent figure visually with the eucharistic rite, he emphasized Ludovica's special role in the process of redemption.

By placing the statue over, rather than under, the altar, Bernini imbued this work of art with a special liturgical function. Sculptures of recumbent figures were commonly positioned in niches under altars, some examples of which are the *Saint Cecilia* (1600) and the *Saint Sebastian* (c. 1672; Fig. 40). Even statues clearly indebted to the *Ludovica* were placed under the sacramental table: the *Saint Anastasia* (c. 1686; Fig. 44) and the *Saint Anne* (c. 1750; Fig. 45), for example.

In the recess of the Altieri Chapel (Fig. 19), the priest, standing on the steps before the altar/sepulcher, ceremoniously elevates the Host and chalice to the height of the sculpture. The statue is thus seen in relation to a liturgical act long considered the most significant moment of the mass, a ritual allegorized as the lifting up of Christ on the Cross. The idea of visually associating a work of art positioned over the altar with the celebration of the Eucharist was expressed earlier in Caravaggio's *Entombment* (1602–4), originally installed in the Vittrici Chapel of Santa Maria in Vallicella in Rome. As depicted in this altarpiece, the body of the dead Christ is intended to be seen as the counterpart to the consecrated bread and wine raised to the height of the painting during the service.[1] The theological connection between Christ's sacrifice and the sacramental offering is thereby demonstrated in concrete visual terms.

An analogous situation applies in the *Ludovica*, where the visual relationship with the mass implies a symbolic/spiritual connection as well. Through the juxtaposition of the statue with the elevated Eucharist and chalice, Ludovica's death "in the Cross" is seen in relation to Christ's sacrifice made present in the consecrated bread and wine. Just as Jesus died on Calvary for the redemption of mankind, Ludovica, like the Virgin, offers herself in love, thus becoming part of the "mystical body" of Jesus and thereby helping in the work of salvation.[2] The *beata*'s gesture of charity linking her to the Madonna's role as mediatrix implies Ludovica's own intercessory powers. As indicated earlier, the *beata* was famed for working miracles on behalf of the supplicants venerating her grave. Moreover, the achievement of the good death and eternal glory enabling her to intercede in heaven was accomplished through Christ's Passion embodied in the eucharistic rite.

The *Vita* informs us that the *beata* took communion frequently, at which times she would be overcome by rapture: "Burning with the ardent desire to be united with Christ, she goes to the altar taking the most Divine Bread, and having received it, is inflamed with divine love, her face, usually pallid from mortification, reddened and flushed."[3] Ludovica actually became a part of the sacramental rite in 1671, when she was raised to the altar at her beatification. In honor of this occasion, a special mass was said in her name to the Virgin Mary.[4] Now that she was a *beata* recognized officially by the Church, masses could thereafter be said in her honor by the Franciscans in Rome.[5] On 2 February 1672, Clement X granted plenary indulgences to those celebrating mass on Ludovica's feast day, thus enabling the faithful to draw upon the treasury of merits of Christ and the saints in the remission of the total temporal punishments of purgatory.[6]

The celebration of the Eucharist is also suggested by the Altieri Chapel fresco of Saint Clare holding a monstrance, a subject referring to the miraculous power of the Host (Fig. 14). According to an account in the *processi* of her cause (1253–55), Clare repulsed the Saracens from Assisi by frightening them with the sacred bread.[7] In the chapel, the subjects of the frescoes flanking the altar are both concerned with bread, the food consecrated on the *Mensa Domini.* With the image of the saint on one side of the altar and the painting of the *beata* on the other, the sacrosanct bread of everlasting life displayed by Clare is juxtaposed with the bread of earthly and spiritual sustenance distributed by Ludovica (Fig. 13). According to Pauolo, the bread given to the poor by the *beata* "not only healed the sick corporally, but spiritually as well," inspiring them to pursue the ways of holiness.[8] The cherubic heads floating above Ludovica in the Altieri Chapel may also be associated with the rite of oblation (Fig. 19). It was commonly believed that "at that time [when mass is said], angels surround the priest and the Heavenly powers sing aloud, and gather round the altar in honour of Him who is immolated thereon."[9] Perhaps in reference to this idea, Pauolo described the Host received by Ludovica as the "precious food of the angels."[10]

Other elements in the Altieri Chapel may be interpreted in light of the eucharistic service performed at the altar. Ludovica, offering herself in charity, united to God in death, is viewed in relation to the Passion of Christ, whose act of redemption is made present in the consecrated offerings. The theme of giving oneself in love expressed by this statue and embodied in Christ's sacrifice is also operative in Baciccio's painting (Fig. 20) in which Mary offers her son to Saint Anne, who reaches out to take him in her arms. The Virgin's gesture of lifting the Child is reminiscent of that of the priest offering the consecrated host to the celebrant. The Madonna offers her son, the Word made flesh, for the sake of mankind, and the worshipper receives the gift of redemption in Christ's body and blood. This theme of a spiritual offering of love is also expressed by Ludovica's gesture of charity referring to her acts of mercy in paradise; through *amor dei* and *amor proximi,* the *beata* as intercessor offers the prayers of the faithful to the Madonna and Christ. In addition, the disposition of the statue between the worshipper kneeling at the altar and the altarpiece depicting the Holy Family (Fig. 19) gives spatial expression to the idea that Ludovica is an intermediary to the Virgin and Son. Through her role as intercessor, the *beata* is therefore integrally connected with the subject matter of the altarpiece and the rituals performed at the altar, both of which are concerned with the promise of eternal life. The sculpture of Ludovica, as part of a network of meaning, is thus revealed to embrace the concept of the redemption of humankind.

It is possible that Bernini received assistance in formulating the complex iconography of the statue of the *beata* and its chapel recess, one likely adviser being Giovanni Pauolo. Undoubtedly well educated (as may be judged from his biography of Ludovica), Pauolo may have been engaged in scholarly activities at San Francesco, which since 1579 was a center for the study of philosophy and theology.[11] Furthermore, as we have seen, many elements of Bernini's project derive from the ideals of Saint Francis, whose presence was especially felt in San Francesco a Ripa. The strong emphasis in the *Ludovica* upon the concepts of *amor dei* and *amor proximi* reflects the Franciscan belief in the primacy of charity. More specifically, San Francesco a Ripa was, since the medieval period, a center of active charity for the poor pilgrims entering the city. Saint Francis himself, who like the *beata* was inflamed with *amor dei,* may be viewed as Ludovica's saintly prototype. The flaming hearts in the Altieri Chapel are emblems often associated with the Franciscan saint, and the *beata*'s transport of divine love may be likened to that of Francis, whose ecstasy was then the subject of the chief altarpiece of the church.

The sculpture of Ludovica and the altarpiece of the Holy Family and Saint Anne both reflect the influence of theological views advocated by the Franciscans. Baciccio's painting may be interpreted as a subtle reference to the Immaculate Conception, a belief vehemently supported by the Franciscans, who insisted that Mary was sanctified in Anne's womb. The pose of the *beata* and her gesture of clutching her bosom may be associated with the tenet advocated by the Friars Minor that the Virgin suffered a mystical death on Calvary, and therefore acts as co-redemptrix with Christ. Thus the iconography of Bernini's masterpiece may in part reflect the influence of Fra Pauolo, as well as other Franciscan scholars residing at San Francesco a Ripa.

Cardinal Paluzzi-Albertoni/Altieri, who commissioned the *Ludovica,* would certainly have had a voice in Bernini's project. By 1673, the cardinal was Protector of the Carmelites, a factor that could account for the Theresan qualities of the sculpture. There is no evidence, however, that Paluzzi was particularly sympathetic to Spanish mysticism. In fact, the cardinal was both worldly and ambitious.[12] A controversial figure, he was harshly criticized for having amassed great wealth for himself and his family, vast sums of which were spent on the building of the family palace, the most sumptuous in Rome.[13] In the early years of Clement's reign, Paluzzi, the adopted nephew of the pope, apparently sought to cultivate a public image of himself as a charitable leader; in 1670, a panegyric composed to Saint Francis of Assisi included an effusive dedication to Paluzzi in which the cardinal was praised for having the charity of Constantine, Solomon, Trajan, and others.[14] But the attempted deception failed and Paluzzi became increasingly unpopular in the years to follow: in 1674, a conspiracy organized against the cardinal was nearly successful.[15] This antagonism, probably in evidence around 1672, when the palace was under construction, may have been a motivating factor in commissioning the *Ludovica.* The cardinal would undoubtedly have recognized the advantages of glorifying his pious ancestor, who was famed for her life of poverty and charity. After all, Paluzzi's grandfather, the Marchese Baldassare Albertoni, known as "father to the poor," had already established a tradition whereby the family's reputation for charitable works was linked with that of Ludovica.[16] Baldassare had renovated the Altieri Chapel around 1622, memorializing his benefaction with an inscription plaque. With the example of the marchese probably on his mind, the cardinal, criticized for financial improprieties, resolved to glorify his family with a statue of his pious, ascetic ancestor—the blessed Ludovica—a motivation explaining the commission, but not the work of art. Our understanding of the sculpture of Ludovica is better served by examining the personal concerns of the artist in his old age, rather than the interests of the patron.

Bernini's biographers report that Gianlorenzo was assiduous in his preparations for death.[17] Like his contemporaries, the sculptor often meditated upon death. For forty years, he attended meetings of a Jesuit society, the Congregazione Spirituali della Buona Morte, whose goal was to prepare its members for the departure from life. He took communion at least once a week, and in his later years engaged in active charity, visiting the sick in the hospital and distributing alms anonymously through a servant. Affirming his faith that his sins would be washed in the blood of Christ, Bernini made a drawing, *Sangue di Cristo,* which he then had painted on a canvas and placed by his bed as a devotional image "in life and in death."[18] In order to ensure that he would be able to communicate in his last moments, the sculptor arranged a sign language with Father Marchese that ultimately proved useful.

Bernini's preoccupation with death in his old age may have been stimulated in part by the words of admonition in the *Imitation of Christ* by Thomas à Kempis (d. 1471), a devotional work much admired by Gianlorenzo.[19] This author urged the reader to prepare for death, warning that the older one gets, the greater the number of sins that must be purged.[20] The desire to achieve the good death was not unique to Bernini, however; in fact, it was a preoccupation of the seventeenth century, as it had been for centuries earlier.[21] The sculptor's contemporaries worried about the impossibility of predicting the moment of death, an anxiety that spurred the desire to prepare early for this inevitable event.[22] Accounts of the deaths of great personages and saints were read with great interest,[23] and meditation on death, advocated by Ignatius Loyola and Francis de Sales, among others, was a common practice,[24] often with the aid of a skull and cross.[25] Devotional works on the art of dying well in the tradition of the *Ars Moriendi* experienced a revival of popularity.[26] These guides, focusing upon the salvation of the soul, generally set forth five principles (known as Anselm's questions) pertinent to the "craft" of dying well:[27] a willing submission to death; the resistance to temptations; an affirmative response to the interrogations of faith; the use of Christ's Passion as a model; and the devotion to holy images.[28]

The achievement of the good death was also the focus of attention of the Congregazione Spirituali della Buona Morte, the confraternity to which Bernini belonged. The spiritual exercises and acts of penance practiced by the members usually culminated in the adoration of the holy sacrament displayed on the altar along with an altarpiece showing the Crucified Christ and the Madonna of Sorrows.[29] Preparation for the good death thus centered upon the honoring of Christ's sacrifice embodied in the Eucharist and Mary's role as mediatrix.[30]

The Sacrifice of the Mass and the Virgin's part as co-redemptrix, each implied in Bernini's *Ludovica,* are also recalled in Bernini's devotional picture *Sangue di Cristo.* This work, mentioned by the sculptor's biographers, is most accurately known through an engraving used as the frontispiece to Francesco Marchese's *Unica speranza del peccatore che consiste nel Sangue del N.S. Giesù'Cristo,* published in 1670 (Fig. 60). The print, engraved after Bernini's design by F. Spierre, depicts the Crucified Christ, his blood flowing profusely from his wounds to create an ocean beneath him. The Madonna kneeling at the feet of the Redeemer offers the precious blood to God the Father looming over the Cross. Inscriptions beneath the engraving refer to the redemptive powers of the blood of Christ[31] and to Mary's role as intercessor.[32] The book in which this engraving was published warns that there is much sin in the world, the only hope for mankind being the blood of the Savior dispensed by Mary as intermediary.[33] Its author (Bernini's nephew) urged frequent communion, explaining that the sacrificial offering "inflames the heart,"[34] offering the promise of a good death and eternal reward to the faithful.[35]

Integrated with the mass, and a metaphorical implication of the Madonna's role as mediatrix, the statue of Ludovica may thus be associated with Bernini's activities as a member of the Confraternity of the Good Death, as well as with his thoughts on salvation as expressed in the *Sangue di Cristo,* the latter stimulated by discussions with Father Marchese.[36] Furthermore, as an image of a dying person, this sculpture may be related to the popular manuals of the *Ars Moriendi* tradition; without doubt, both the *beata*'s complete submission to death and her death "in the cross," following the model of the Passion, reflect the ideals of these guides. Yet, as a monumental work of art, the statue and its chapel setting do not follow many of the conventions of printed illustrations of the *Ars Moriendi* (Figs. 48 and 49). For example, there is no figure of Death or devils to tempt her soul.[37]

As an image of a dying person, the *Ludovica* is, in fact, distinguished by its omission of negative references to death as a destroyer of life.[38] Although recollective of tomb sculpture, neither the statue nor its chapel setting includes representations of skulls, skeletons, or other emblems of death.[39] Rather, the sculpture of Ludovica offers a positive image of death as the crowning culmination of the religious life, a concept espoused by Theresa, John of the Cross, Francis de Sales, Pauolo and Santini, and others. In essence, Bernini viewed death in this sculpture as the *vitae testimonium,* the "witness to life," an idea earlier embodied in the tomb of Urban VIII.[40] The concept is expressed by Saint Jerome in his Commentary on Ecclesiastes (7:2): "It is known in death what kind of men we are. . . ."[41] At the same time, the *Ludovica* expresses dying as the supreme act of faith of the Christian soul *in extremis.* According to Christian thought, the moment of death is the moment of truth in which the soul chooses between Christ and the devil. Interestingly enough, Charles Borromeo, depicted in fervent prayer in the Altieri Chapel, emphasized the importance of the profession of faith at that final moment.[42]

As demonstrated earlier, the statue of Ludovica presents death also as existing within the continuum of the spiritual life leading to eternal glory. Moreover, the act of dying itself is shown in a positive light by Bernini, who was perhaps thinking of the words of the Jesuit theologian Roberto Bellarmino when he created the *Ludovica:*

> Truly blessed is the death of the saints, which by the command of the Heavenly King frees the soul from the prison of the flesh and conducts her to a celestial Kingdom; where just souls sweetly rest after all their labours, and for the reward of their good works, receive a crown of glory. On account of these excellent advantages, death to good men seems not horrible, but sweet; not terrible, but lovely.[43]

Bernini undoubtedly envisioned the *Ludovica* as the embodiment of the ideal death as described above. More prosaically, in view of the physical and emotional strains of the years in which he worked on this sculpture, one wonders if the master considered death an escape from the tribulations of life. Accused of being "the instigator of the pope's indulging in useless expenses in such disastrous times," Bernini was constantly under fire[44] and, as noted earlier, was burdened with the frustration of trying to arrange a pardon for his brother Luigi.[45] In August 1673 Bernini fell ill, and in the same year he suffered the loss of his cherished wife.

If Gianlorenzo in these years had in fact considered death preferable to life, it would not have been inconsistent with the thoughts of his contemporaries who viewed death as the "eternal life of summer" and earthly existence as the "winter."[46] This viewpoint is demonstrated in the libretto composed by Cardinal Giulio Rospigliosi (1600–1669) for the musical drama *Istoria di S. Alessio,* performed in Rome in 1632 and 1634.[47] After spending seventeen years living as a miserable beggar under his father's staircase, Alessio, the saintly hero of the play, welcomes the "sweet repose of death," a liberation from the pains, tears, and darkness of life.[48] In referring to his departure from this world, he sings, "If one can accompany the Sun [i.e., God], darkness [of life] cannot follow him."[49]

Perhaps at once fearful and desirous of his own departure from life, Bernini may have intended this image of Ludovica's rapturous death to be an inspiration and reassurance that a life of piety leads to salvation, the pathway set forth in the Altieri Chapel. Moreover, the demise of the *beata,* its exalted nature recalling the blessed deaths of saints as described in contemporary literature, serves as an exemplar for the layman.[50] At the same time, Gianlorenzo, by depicting Ludovica's death in accessible yet elevated terms, places her experience within the grasp of the faithful. The *beata* as rendered by Bernini is neither suffering a martyrdom of the flesh nor undergoing a miracle such as the transverberation; Ludovica is dying a holy death in bed. Moreover, through her ideal Christian death in the Savior, Ludovica plays a part in the redemption of humankind, offering the prayers of the supplicant to Mary and Christ in heaven.

Bernini in his old age must have located his own hopes for salvation within this work of art. The reference to hope in the *Ludovica* becomes clear if one envisions a penitent sinner kneeling in the chapel before the altar (Fig. 19). With the painting of Saint Clare representing Faith and the statue and fresco of Ludovica alluding to the two aspects of Charity, *amor dei* and *amor proximi,* the worshipper may be seen to represent Hope, often represented in art as a praying figure.[51] Thus the triad of theological virtues necessary for salvation seems to be completed by the faithful, among them perhaps Bernini himself supplicating before the sculpture.[52]

The statue of Ludovica Albertoni, with its inherent promise of salvation, must have been a personal votive for the artist in his late years—a personal prayer of hope for himself and for humankind.[53] He must have poured his deepest anxieties and fears into this project. Yet the result is an image of a sublime death; Ludovica, transformed by her love and God's love, becomes spirit, her loving soul ascending to paradise to be joined forever in union with Christ, who is love incarnate. The *beata,* through the power of love and Christ's sacrifice, triumphs over death to achieve everlasting life. Thus Bernini, perhaps viewing this sculpture as a personal offering of love, affirmed the Christian message of charity and redemption. He wedded his faith successfully to his art and, in so doing, created a masterpiece of profound beauty.

Appendixes

Appendix I

Ludovico da Modena, *Cronaca della Riforma dal 1519 al 1722. Fondazione e Riforma del Convento di S. Francesco a Ripa,* Archivio di San Francesco a Ripa, busta 12, fols. 227–31

Sopra la porta cui si va dalla chiesa in sacristia et vice versa vi è un nobilissimo antico Crocifisso dipinto in tela: ricopiato da quello che partò al nostro santo Padre in Assisi nel principio della sua conversione, conservato hoggi dentro il Monastero delle monache di S. Chiara, sotto si di cui piede si legge come segue, cioè- Vera crucifisci effigies qui sancteum franciscum est allocutus dicens. Vade francisce repara Dominum meum que Labitur.

Di cui vi è qualche tradittione sia l'antichissimo crocifisso levato dalla modernata cappella, promiscuamente detta B. Lodovica, edi S. Anna nomata. Non si sà veramente se il detto crocifisso fosse di rilievo, o di pittura, ma supposiato di pittura, i cosa credibile fosse il sopradetto.

Seguita nella medema tribuna il secondo Altare ò Cappella detta anticamente del Crocifisso, mercè che era al sommo Iddio che per noi pati morte di Croce, dedicata e seguito ad essere sotto questo nome venerata sino all'anno 1622, nel quale il Sig.^{r} Marchese Baldassar Paluzzi Albertoni Cavalier di S. Giacomo, e della Beata Ludovica Albertoni pronepote determino già che ivi era la prefata sua Avola sepolta, ristorare la Cappella e fare a quelle sante Reliquie un nuovo e più nobil deposito, il che fece eseguire con finissimi marmi e ben intesa architettura disegnata dal felicissimo ingegno di Giacomo Mola, dedicandola à sant'Anna; onde da quel tempo in qua, levato il crocifisso, la gloriosa S. Anna vi si adora.

Fu fatto il nuovo tumolo sollevato al quante da terra nel piano di detta cappella, ove riposano quelle sante Reliquie dentro una cassetta di odoroso cipresso foderata di seta sino all'anno 1675, nel quale anno alli 17 Gennaro, si fece la seconda traslatione con l'intervento di numerosa quantità di personnaggi de più riguardevoli di questa dominatrice del mondo, riponendo quell'ossa beate e di eterna veneratione degne, dentro un'altra cassetta di rame indorato di fuori e foderata di dentro con taffetta rosso et allocata poi dentro un'altra cassetta di pietra aperta d'avanti acciò possa vedersi l'indorata di Rame, e vi fu la seguente inscrittione scolpita, cioè, Corpus Beate Ludovice Albertonie.

Poscia fu il tutte dentro il nuovo altare accomodato quale ci fatto di finissimo diaspro di sicilia, et a foggia di nobilissima Urna, con un cuore nel mezzo, per dove si da alla lampana, che à tutte hore ivi riluce, il necessario sussidio e sopra quest'Urna si celebra l'evento sacrificio della messa.

In congiuntura detta prefata nuova traslatione l'emin^{0}. Altieri, che era in quei tempi del sovrano Pastore P^{o} ministro, e della nostra Beata amorevol parente, fece, oltre il nuovo tumulo, et oltre considerabile spese, una bellissima statua di bianco marmo, che in atto agonizzante la soprad^{a} Beata rappresenta, opera dell'eccellente scultore cavalier Bernini, e fu collocata sopra il predetto altare in sito guadagnato da ingegnati architetti fuori di esso altare con haversi anche posto un nobil quadro in tela, che in atto assai divoto la santissima Vergine, il Bambino Giesù e sant'Anna sua nonna rappresenta, colorito dal celebre pittore Baciccio Gaulli Genovese huomo di molto spirito nelle sue opere.

L'altre pitture sono del Cavalier Gaspare Celio celebre anch'egli ne suoi tempi racconta l'Abbate Filippo Titi nel suo nuovo studio di pit:, scoltura, et architettura. Il quadro che vi era di S. Anna, andò a la Palazzo d'Altieri. Questa cappella è rotunda con la sua cuppola tutta dipinta, et alle bande delle altare si vedono due antiche pitture fatte a fresco p. ordine del senato all'hor che la d^{a} Beata fu quivi sepolta; una delle quali, cioè quella che è dalla parte dell'Epistola, la nra B. Albertoni rappresenta, e l'altra S. Chiara d'Assisi sopra di che vogliono alcuni, che santa Fran^{a} Romana non S. Chiara, vi fosse nel principio dipinta. Sono in q^{a} medema nobilissima cappela tre epitafi passo al Palazzo del Sig.^{e}: Uno dalla parte del'Vangelo, ove è un nobil deposito con la seguente inscritto^{ne}: Quod senatus Populusq(ue) Romanus Beatam Ludovicam Petri Matthaei de Albertonibus Romanã singulari pietate prosequuturus, ultimum Ianuarii diem, quo felicissime convolavit incoelum, per curiam Capitolinam annua a Iudiciis cessatione celibrari, atque hoc sacellum solemni Pompa ut Mos est a Romano magistratu consueta Liberalitate adiri senatus consulto multis ab hinc annis iusserit, Balthasar Palutius de Albertonibus, grati animi monumentum pos. Ann. Iubilei 1625.

L'altro dalla parte dell'epistola nel muro come il primo, ove si legge: Sacellum hoc in quo ossa Beatae Ludovicae Petri Matthaei de Albertonibus Romanae, pie asservantur temporum iniuria collabascens Balthasar Palutius de Albertonibus, pio in gentilem suam obsequio, sacris ossibus sub veteri monumento repositis, antiquissima eius immagine proprio in loco restituta, (a) fundamentis erexit, ornavitq[ue] Anno iubilei 1625.

Sopra q^{o} deposito si vede come un'altarino, e visi conserva con il dovuto decoro l'immagine di S. Anna stampata in carta, quali teneva in stanza Fra Innocenzo da Chiusa, avanti di cui genufl:sso orava e confidentemente parlava, e quivi hoggi per degna memoria si conserva nel piano detta cappella in mezzo il Pavimento sopra l'antico sepolcro di q^{a} Beata si legge come segue et e il 3° epitaffio. Iacet hic B. Ludovica filia Stephani Petri Matthaei de Albertonibus, Uxor Iacobi et socrus

D. Nicolai Muti: Vixit annos 60 animam altissimo Creatori suo reddidit, die ultima Ianuarii 1533. Coelituum consors frueris quibus ocia posce. Ludovica tuis, nosque tuere malis. Da modo te facilem sanctissima numine dextro. quo miracla facis tot, pia, et affer opem.

Questa divota, e venerabil Cappella viene il senatore e magistrato Romano, con solenne pompa ogn'anno il giorno della sua festa di d^a^ Beata, che viene li 31 Gennaro e le porta in gratioso dono un calice d'argento, con la sua Patena e 4° torcie, honorandola come S. Romana.

Di q^a^ Beata scrivono molti de nri autori, tra quali il Gonzaga il Vaudingo; L'Autiro, et il Leguile et ultimamente scrisse dottamente il P.mR. Bonaventura Flagellotti di Roma, sotto nome del P. Gio: Pauolo di Roma data alle stampe.

Al sacro corpo di questa felicissima serva di Dio si è tenuta mai semp: La Lampana acessa, non ostante il Decreto di Urbano °8 in contrario nel quale mai si è tenuta compresa.

Serva questa divota e riguardevol cappella una balaustrata di finissimo marmo bianco con l'insegne dell'eccell^e^ casa Altieri.

In un pilastro che regge l'arco detta facciata di essa cappella si vede scolpita in pietra l'arma dell'eccell^ma^ casa Palutii, che sono alcune sbarre curve ce un Leone con tre cimieri.

Appendix II

Capitolo XVII
Morte della Beata Ludovica

From Fra Giovanni Pauolo, *Vita della B. Ludovica Albertoni* . . . , Rome, 1672, 227–34.

Il non esser potuto per tutto quel giorno entrare alcuna in camera di Ludovica, fù cagione, che niuno potesse osservar quel tanto ch'ella si fece. Ma lo pensi pure chi ha spirito. Io che scrivo l'historia, non devo inventarlo, questo solo voglio dir, ch'è verissimo. *A fructibus eorum cognoscetis eos.* Quando ella chiamò le serve, che entrassero, all'hora diè perfettamente à conoscere, che cosa havesse in quel segreto silentio operato. La ritrovarono tutta infiammata nel volto; ma così gioviale nel tratto, che parea fosse tornata dal Paradiso. Fece subito chiamar testimonij, e 'l Notaro, e disponendo più dell'anima; che del corpo: supplicò che facessero per lei celebrar molte messe; e la compiacessero in questo, cioè di seppellire il suo corpo nella Chiesa di San Francesco in Trastevere, nella stessa cappella, dove era sepolto Giacomo della Cetera suo Consorte. E benche nella Chiesa di Santa Maria d'Araceli, nella cappella di Sant'Antonio da Padoa, vi fosse, e sia la sepoltura delli Signori Albertoni Paluzzi; volle con tutto ciò esser sepolta in San Francesco per star anco doppo morte à suo marito vicina, acciochè quelli, i quali in vita havea Dio santamente congionti, non dividessero ingiustamente gl'huomini. Quindi aggiustati gl'interessi dell'anima, e quanto più parea espediente per il mantenimento della sua casa; dimenticatasi affatto di se stessa, e del mondo, assorta tutta in Giesù, fù veduta quasi fuor di se stessa per la vehemenza dell'amore, & acceso desiderio, che havea la Beata di andare à godere la beata visione di Giesù Christo.

Era già arrivata l'ultima hora di sua vita. Per lo che preso in mano un Crocifisso, e quello con occhi fissi guardando, molti gemiti sparse, e molte fiate gridò, misericordia Giesù, misericordia Giesù: & implorando l'aiuto della gloriosa Vergine Maria; liberatemi voi o Madre pietosa dalle insidie dell'inimico infernale, *nunc,* dicea Ludovica, *nunc, & in hora mortis mea,* e baciando con divotissimi affetti li piedi, e tutte le sagrate piaghe del Crocifisso, piangendo per compassione replicava ben spesso: *In manus tuas Domine commendo spiritum meum,* & in questi ultimi accenti con posatissimo animo *in oratione defixa* si addormentò nel Signore. Era la Beata Ludovica quando morì di anni sessanta, havendone ventisette consumati in continue penitenze, e mortificationi; che tanti appunto furono gli anni della sua vedovanza, in habito di penitente del terz'Ordine di San Francesco, essendo ella restata vedova nel trentesimo terzo della sua età nel 1506. Morì alli trent'un di Gennaio nel 1533, in giorno di Venerdì, non senza singolar providenza di Dio; acciochè Ludovica, che fu croce al mondo, e crocifissa del mondo; inamorata di Giesù Christo, e con tenerissimi affetti ligata alla sua santissima Croce; in quel medesimo giorno rendesse il suo beato spirito a Giesù Christo, nel quale il medesimo Giesù havea voluto spargere il proprio sangue per la redentione del genere humano.

Si divulgò per tutta la Città la gloriosa morte di Ludovica, e tutti a piena bocca diceano è morta la Beata, è morta la Santa. Fu grande il sentimento, & il dolore che tutti universalmente mostrarono per la morte di così divota Matrona. Ma molto maggiore in vero fu quello de'po, verelli, quali dirottamente piangeano la perdita di una tanta lor madre, e vera sollevadrice delle loro madre, e vera sollevadrice delle loro miserie. Correano a gara alla casa, per baciar quelle sante reliquie, & adorar quel corpo, ch'era stato tabernacolo di un'anima così pura. Furono però chiuse le porte, acciochè niuno molestrasse quelle pie Signore, le quali erano ivi restare in custodia di quel pretioso tesoro.

La santità di un'anima all'hora magiormente risplende, quando più si slontana. E quella semplicità, che vien delusa da certi savij del mondo, all'hora è in'ammiratione del mondo; quando che se'n fugge dal mondo. Quindi la Chiesa santa celebrai natali de'giusti, non quando nacquero essi alla luce (eccettuatene però quelli di Christo, della sua Vergine Madre, e del suo glorioso Precursor Giovan Battista) ma quando chiudendo gl'occhi alla luce, incominciano a vagheggiar la vera luce dell'eterno Sol di giustitia. Et all'hora invoca ciascuno il patrocinio di un'anima, quando sciolta da i legami del corpo, se'n vola trionfante alla gloria.

Fu cosa maravigliosa a vedersi il gran concorso del popolo, che compunto, e frettoloso correa alla casa di Ludovica per veder quel tesoro santissimo del suo purissimo corpo: e benche non potessero per all'hora sodisfar questo lor pio desiderio, per essere come hò detto serrate le porte; godeano con tutto ciò di contemplar quelle mura felici, che racchiudeano in se quelle beate reliquie.

Hebbero i parenti le visite di tutti i Principali di Roma, ne sò ben dirvi, se di congratulatione, ò condoglianza. Mercè santamente invidiando la santità della nostra beata; non sapevano ben determinare, se l'havessero veramente perduto, essendo morta; ò maggiormente acquistata, vivendo eternamente nel Cielo.

Terminate le visite; si preparò tutto quello, ch'era necessario per l'esequie della Beata. Non si curava Ludovica di pompa; ma non potendo far più resistenza nel mondo, mentre era già partita dal mondo: fecero i Signori Albertoni, Muti, Mattei, & Altieri quell'apparecchio maggiore, che somministrò loro la Pietà verso di una lor Matrona sì pia: E se la santità della loro Avola illustre, illustrava la lor famiglia, vollero essi correspondere in quel tanto puoternono, col farle fare nobilissimi funerali.

Appendix III

Letter of Carlo Cartari, 19 October 1674, Bibliothèque Nationale, Paris, Miscellanées III, Ital. 2084

Illmo e Rev^{mo} mio sig. Prone rive^{mo}

Viddi Martedi le quattro nuove operazioni del sig. Cavaliere, padri di N. Illma nelle quali, secondo gli oggetti, che rappresentano, non vi è che desiderari: Trio il Tabernacolo, La Beata Ludovica, il Sepolcro d'Alessandro Settimo, et il Re di francia. E certamento non potrà dissi senza molta maraviglia, che un Huomo di settantasei anni si sia mantenuta così vigorosa la vivezza dello spirito, che habbia intraprese, e condotte ad esquisito fine opere così vaste, e degne. Io me ne rallegro vivam^{te} con N. ILL^{ma} che se mi disse fin da Gennaro, che le opere dello stesso sig. Cavaliere erano giunte al numero di settanta, vi aggiungà hor questi di più, e spero, che ve ne aggiungera anche delle altri, essendo degno di vivere al Mondo un virtuoso, che lascia nel Mondo così belle memorie. Vorrei essere un Demostene, un Tullio, per encomiare un'Huomo cosi famoso nel secolo corrente; ma la mia penna è tarpata: e perciò valendomi dell'assioma, *qui per alios facit per se ipsum facere videtur,* lo trasmetto gl'annessi fogli, et assieme mi ratifico.

D.V. ILL^{ma} Rev^{ma}
Casa Li 19 Ottobre 1674

Divot.^{mo} S.^{re} osseq.^{mo}
Carlo Cartari

Appendix IV

Project Drawing for San Francesco a Ripa and the Altieri Chapel

The Uffizi plan, ascribed to Baldassare Peruzzi by Anna Menichella (126), is attributed here to the Milanese architect Onorio Longhi. Drawn in ink on vertically lined paper, the sketch represents a proposal for the renovation of San Francesco a Ripa. The project drawing calls for a portico consisting of orders disposed in pairs and a three-aisled nave with chapels on the left side. The use of coupled orders in the portico is taken up again in the left side of the nave. (An alternative solution calling for the employment of heavy piers in the nave is shown on the right.) A small sketch drawn along the right edge of the sheet further suggests a nave arcade of doubled columns. To the left of the arcade is a series of chapels whose entrances are flanked by heavy piers pierced by niches. The termination of the church on the east end is marked by a rectangular chapel with a small apse, and on either side of this space are two other chapels. The two entrances sketched on the plan, one leading to the central nave and the other providing access to the left aisle, are arranged to emphasize two focal points: the main chapel and Ludovica's sepulchral chapel in the left arm of the tribune.

The Altieri Chapel, the largest on the plan, is indicated with a width along the east-west axis of forty-seven palms. In Roman palms this dimension would be the equivalent of about ten and one-half meters. The width of the Altieri Chapel as it exists today is about five and one-half meters (5.45 meters). Thus, the design calls for a chapel twice the size of the present Altieri Chapel.

Menichella's attribution of this project drawing to Peruzzi (35) is not tenable, since the niches and double columns in the nave suggest a date of around 1600. H. Wurm (*Baldassare Peruzzi Architekturzeichnungen,* Tübingen, 1984, 519) also rejects the attribution. The plan was drawn by the Milanese architect Onorio Longhi, who redesigned the transept of the church around 1603. There are a number of parallels between the plan and documented works by Longhi and his circle. Martino Longhi the Elder's designs for the double columns in both the portico of Santa Maria Maggiore, which he restored for Pope Gregory XIII (1572–85), and in the courtyard of the Palazzo Deza-Borghese (1586–90) recall the plan for the nave and facade of San Francesco a Ripa. Ottaviano Mascherino (1524–1606), who worked in the orbit of Martino the Elder, used coupled columns in the nave and crossing of San Salvatore in Lauro (1594). Mascherino's plan for Santa Maria in Traspontina, preserved in the Accademia di San Luca, calls for a chapel in the left transept that recalls the plan indicated for the Altieri Chapel on the Uffizi sheet. For illustrations and for additional information, see Fagiolo (1982, 62–63); C. D'Onofrio, (99, 106, pl. 60); A. Cipriani and E. Valeriani, *I disegni di architettura dell'Archivio storico dell'Accademia di San Luca,* Rome, 1974, no. 2348; and Golzio (1929–30, 164–66).

Around 1603, Monsignor Lelio Biscia (1573–1638) commissioned Onorio Longhi to build an infirmary on the left side of the church and to reconstruct the east end of San Francesco a Ripa. A pertinent document is quoted in P. Degni's essay "Architettura Francescana e Riforma Cattolica a Roma . . ." (in *L'immagine di San Francesco nella Controriforma,* exhibition catalogue, Rome, 1982, 225–27): ". . . per la presente ordiniamo a voi P. Custode della Riforma dei Minori Osservanti nella provincia di Roma, che in fare la cappella dell'altar maggiore et il coro nella nostra chiesa di S. Francesco a Ripa dobbiate governarvi secondo il disegno fatto dall'architetto di Mons. Biscia . . . et in fare l'infermeria vi governerete secondo il disegno fatto da Messer Honorio Longo con fare il piano a volto e non a solaio . . . Di Casa 10 gennaio 1603. Il Cardinale Mattei Protettore."

Longhi's project for the transept involved the cardinal in a controversy with the friars at the church. The brothers were already angry with Longhi for his extravagance in vaulting the infirmary, rather than building it with a simple trussed roof. Apparently another design of Longhi, not preserved today, may have called for a large apse in the choir that would have necessitated the razing of the sacred cell of Saint Francis, a demolition deemed sacrilegious by the friars. Cardinal Mattei wrote to the *Custode* of the Reform, asking him to reassure the brothers that the Longhian project was not contrary to the Rule of Saint Francis. The *Custode's* letter proved to be ineffectual; the brothers were greatly distressed by Cardinal Alessandro Peretti's dreams in which Saint Francis appeared to warn the friars not to destroy his sacred cell. (An account of this incident may be found in Ludovico da Modena, fols. 166–67. The letter of 10 January 1603 is also discussed in Pesci [28 n. 59] and Escobar [68].) Cardinal Peretti's visions (earning him the title "Protector of the Cell of Saint Francis") were decidedly more persuasive than a letter from a high official of the reform. Thus, in spite of Cardinal Mattei's efforts in support of the project, Longhi's plan was ultimately modified to accommodate the wishes of the brothers.

The parts actually executed by Longhi are the central part of the transept, the *Cappella maggiore,* the dome, the lateral altars, and the arms of the tribune. In the latter area, Longhi apparently left intact such preexisting structures as the Altieri Chapel, the sacristy, and the corridors of the cemetery. The ambitious plan for the Altieri Chapel was never realized. See Menichella (50–52) and Ludovico da Modena (fols. 170, 349).

Appendix V

Selected Testimony from *Congregatione Sacrorum Rituum. Romana Canonizationis Beatae Ludovicae Albertoniae Tertij Ordinis Sancti Francisci.* Rome, 1671.

No. 3. Location of the fresco of Ludovica. Testimony of an aged friar.

". . . che prima fusse edificata la cappella nova non stava nel medemo sito, che stà hoggi, ma stava però dentro la medema cappella, e al presente l'effigie di detta Beata come sopra trasportata stà posta dalla banda dell'Epistola dell'Altare di detta Cappella di Sant'Anna e quella medema, che stava prima nell'istessa cappella . . ."

No. 4. Description of the sepulcher. Visitatio sepulchri praedictae Beatae, fol. 281. Testimony of an aged witness.

In primis. Avanti la detta Cappella una cancellata di ferro ferrata à chiave, in cima della quale in mezzo stà in alto elevata una Croce parimento di ferro, & à piedi di detta Croce è fisso in detta ferrata un ferro, che porge verso la Chiesa, dal quale pende la lampada d'ottone, che arde, e stà accesa.

Et aperta detta Cancellata con chiave portata dal detto Padre Sacristano si è proseguita la detta descrittione come segue, cioè.

Nel pavimento di detta Cappella in mezzo si vede, e stà un deposito di marmo scorniciato di lunghezza palmi otto, e mezzo in circa, di longhezza palmi quattro, e mezzo in circa, & altezza di palmo uno in circa, intorno al qual deposito equale al pavimento di detta Cappella vi è un'ornamento parimente di marmo bianco liscio di larghezza oncie dieci d'un palmo in circa, e nella parte superiore di detto deposito dalla parte verso l'Altare vi è una grata di ferro lavorato con un triangolo di ferro parimente lavorato elevato in alto, dal quale stà pendente una lampada parimente d'ottone accesa, e dall'altra parte di detto deposito verso l'ingresso di detta Cappella sopra marmo bianco vi è incisa la seguente inscrittione:

> Iacet hìc Beata Ludovica filia Stephani Petri Matthaei de
> Albertonibus uxor Iacobi Io: Iacobi, & Leonis Domini
> Nicolai Muti vixit annos sexaginta animam Altissimo
> Creatori suo reddidit die ultima Ianuarij millesimo
> quingentesimo trigesimo tertio.
> Caelituum consors frueris, quibus otia posce
> Ludovica tuis, nosque tuere malis.
> Da modò te facilem Sanctissima, Numine dextro, Qua
> miracla facis tot pia, & affer opem.

E sotto la detta grata di ferro per tutta la larghezza, e lunghezza d'essa, il cuperchio di detto deposito è più basso del restante circa oncie sette, e mezza d'un palmo, & è di porfido con cornice di marmo bianco con l'arme impressa in detto porfido, che denota un Leone sopra una sbarra attraverso, e sotto quella tre altre sbarre una sotto l'altra in angulo acuto.

No. 5. Exhumation and reburial. Testes deponentes de supulcro.

Primus Testis Fr. Eleutherius à Nursia Ordinis Sancti Francisci annorum 88 iuxtà 13. fol. 68. à tergo respondit. Io sò, che dal tempo, che io venni à questo Convento di S. Francesco à Ripa il corpo di detta Beata Ludovica Albertoni sempre è stato sotterrato nella Cappella, che hora è dedicata à Sant'Anna, che è dell'Eccellentissimi Signori Palutij, hoggi Altieri, e tengo per certo, che ivi fosse sepellita, perche era dell'Ordine Tertiario di San Francesco, e come hò detto, la Cappella è di detti Signori, & anco così è fama, che ivi fosse sepellita dopo la sua morte, e sò, che anche hoggi stà sepellita in detta Cappella, perche prima dell'anno mille seicento venticinque, se io non erro era detta Cappella dedicata al Santissimo Crocifisso, & era assai inferiore, e non così bella come hoggi, & in mezzo d'essa vi era una lapide, sotto la quale vi era una stanza grande quanto la medema Cappella, e non vi era altro dentro detta stanza se non le reliquie, & ossa di detta Beata Ludovica Albertoni, e questo io lo sò, perche dell'anno mille sei cento venticinque, volendo il Signor Marchese Baldassare Palutij far più alta, e più nobile la detta Cappella, doppo haverla finita ordinorno à me, & à Fra Bonaventura di Roma Muratore, che entrassimo dentro detta stanza sotterranea, come facessimo, e vi trovassimo una sola cassetta di quattro palmi, ò quattro palmi, e mezzo in circa dentro la quale vi erano l'ossa di detta Beata Ludovica, & anco dentro detta cassetta vi erano dui mattoni, nelli quali vi era scritto, non sò che, che io non seppi quello contenessero, perche subito cavata fuora la detta cassetta, e consegnatala al detto Signor Marchese, & alli Padri del Convento, che erano ivi con lui, mi partij dalla Cappella, & andai à fare quello dovevo, e poi sò, che nel medemo mezzo della Cappella è stato edificato il sepolcro alla detta Beata, che è più alto da terra nella maniera, e modo, che ivi si vede hoggi giorno, ne mai più è stata mutata la sua forma, e le dette ossa furono rimesse in una cassetta di cipresso foderata di materia di seta, che io la viddi mentre si levavano da quella cassetta che fù trovata sotto terra, e si riponevano in quest'altra, e se bene io non mi trovai presente quando fù riposta la detta cassetta nuova con l'ossa di detta B. Ludovica nel nuovo sepolcro edificatagli da detto Signor Marchese Baldassar Palutij, con tuttocio fù detto publicamente, & è publico, e notorio che la riponessero sotto detto novo sepolcro, e che ancora hoggi ivi si ritrovi, e ciò si tiene da tutti generalmente.

No. 6. Relics. Descriptio supellectiliũ sacrarum & tabellarum votiuarum facta à Iudice, fol. 276. Testimony of Fra Salvator a Forano, seventy-eight years old.

Quali paramenti, & altro come sopra descritti, sequita detta descrittione, furono dal medemo P. Sacristano riposti nell'istessi Credenzoni dove stavano e sono soliti ritenersi, e conservarsi.

Successivamente il medemo P. Sacristano aperta un'altra Credenza ne hà levati molti Calici d'argento, cioè quindici Calici, nel piede de quali dalla parte superiore vi è l'arme del Popolo Romano, in molti de quali vi è scritto B. Ludovica, & in uno B. Ludovica Romana 1614, & in un altro Beata Ludovica 1616, quali Calici, doppo descritti, furono dal medesimo Padre Sacristano riposti nell'istessa credenza, dove sogliono ritenersi, e da quella fù estratta dal P. Sacristano sudetto.

Una cassetta, che suole in detta credenza ritenersi, qual cassetta è di legno tinta in torchino con filetto d'oro, nel cuperchio della quale vi sono scritte à lettere d'oro le seguente parole.

Questo Camiscio l'hà filato la Beata Ludovica.

Qual cassetta si vede essere antichissima, perche tanto il colore torchino, quanto il filetto d'oro, che stà attorno, e le lettere sudette sono assai scolorite, e smontate, si come la chiave della medema cassetta, con la quale si serra, mostra l'antichità del tempo, che è stata fatta, poiche vedendosi essere stata tutta indorata, in varij luoghi è cascato l'oro, & è per tutto scolorita, & aperta la detta cassetta, dentro d'essa si è trovato riposto.

Un camiscio di tela finissima, e vecchia rotto, e rappezzato in più luoghi, & in piedi d'esso col filo ruzzo, che per l'antichità si è scolorito, e divenuto quasi bianco, à lettere maiuscole vi è la seguente Inscrittione:

Questo Camiscio l'hà filato la B. Ludovica.

E doppo riserrato detta cassetta, e riposta col detto Camiscio in detto Credenzone luogo solito, si sono trovati nell'istessa Sacristia molti Messali, nella cuperta de quali in mezzo vi è impressa in oro l'Imagine della B. Ludovica con raggi, e splendori in testa, in piedi della quale vi è la seguente Inscrittione:

Beata Ludovica

E sotto detta inscrittione l'arme del Popolo Romano.

No. 7. Description of paintings and plaques. Descriptio Imaginum praedictae Beatae cum radijs & splendoribus circum circũ caput & epitaphiorum in Cappella insculptorum, fol. 283. Testimony of Fra Salvator a Forano, seventy-eight years old.

Nell'Altare di detta Cappella ornato con Croce, e quattro Candelieri d'ottone, e due vasi di fiori parato con paliotto di seta pavonazzo, sue tovaglie e cuscini, vi è un quadro, nel quale è depinta l'effigie della Madonna Santissima, di Sant'Anna, e di Giesù Christo con la Corona d'argento nella testa di tutte trè dette pitture, & anche l'effigie di San Gioseffo, e San Giovacchino, e sopra dette pitture nella sommità di detto quadro vi sono dipinti alcuni Angeli.

Nel muro dalla parte dell'Evangelio di detto Altare vi è dipinta l'effigie rappresentante Santa Chiara in piedi con diadema in testa vestita con l'habito di San Francesco, e col velo nero in testa, tenendo nelle mani la figura del Santissimo Sacramento, qual pittura è di palmi nove in circa d'altezza, e larga quattro palmi, e mezzo in circa.

Incontro poi alla detta effigie di Santa Chiara dalla parte dell'Epistola dell'Altare nel muro vi è dipinta la figura, & effigie rappresentante una donna in piedi vestita con habito che da nel nero con cinta bianca in cintura, e vello bianco in testa, che cala lungo secondo il solito delle Tertiarie di San Francesco, quale copre il braccio sino alla mano sinistra, con la quale porge un pane al un povero, che sta inginocchioni con ginocchie ignude, e riceve detto pane con la mano destra, e con la sinistra stessa tiene un bastoncello per appoggio, vicino al braccio del quale parimente ignudo sino al gomito vi è dipinta una fiasca tonda, come di legno, e dalla parte della mano destra di detta donna vi è il braccio non poco scoperto con l'istesso habito di San Francesco, che tiene nella detta mano un libro à guisa di Breviario, & intorno alla testa vi sono li raggi, e splendori, ne piedi appariscono essere le scarpe nere.

E fuori di detto Altare, cioè in mezzo al sito di detta Cappella nel muro dell'istessa parte dell'Epistola vi è murata una cornice di marmo di colore nericcio mischio, in mezzo del quale vi è una lapide marmorea bianca di larghezza di palmi cinque, e di lunghessa palmi due, & otto oncie d'un'altro palmo in circa, nella quale vi sono incise l'infrascritte parole:

Sacellum hoc, in quo ossa
Beatae Ludovicae Petri Matthaei de Albertonibus Romanae
Pie asservantur, temporum iniuria collabescens
Balthassar Palutius de Albertonibus
Pio in Gentilem suam obsequio
Sacris ossibus sub veteri monumento repositis
Antiquissima eius Imagine proprio in loco restituta
A fundamentis erexit, ornavitque
Anno Iubilai 1625.

Sopra detta Inscrittione in marmo bianco di rilievo vi è scolpita un'Arme con la corona di Marchese in cima con la Croce di Cavaliere di San Giacomo, sotto detta corona un leone sopra una sbarra à traverso, e sotto questa tre altre sbarre in triangolo pontuto una sotto l'altra.

Dall'altra parte di detta Cappella nel muro incontro alla detta Inscrittione vi è un'altra lapide marmorea simile all'altra sudetta, nella quale è la seguente Inscrittione:

Quod Senatus Populusque Romanus
Beatam Ludovicam Petri Matthaei de Albertonibus, Romanam
Singulari pietate prosecuturus
Ultimum Ianuarij diem, quo faelicissime convolavit
in Coelum/ Per Curiam Capitolinam annua a Iudicijs
cessatione celebrari/ Atque hoc sacellum solemni pompa,
ut mos est/ A Romano Magistratu consueta liberalitate
adiri/ Balthassar Palutius de Albertonibus
Grati animi monumentum posuit Anno Iubilaei 1625.

Sopra poi detta Inscrittione vi è un marmo di rilievo con l'arme del Popolo Romano, cioè in mezzo la sbarra, le quattro lettere S.P.Q.R. con la corona in cima.

Nell'istesso muro sopra l'arme sudetta del Popolo Romano vi è appeso un quadretto in tela d'altezza di palmi quattro, e mezzo in circa, larghezza di palmi tre, e oncie quattro nel quale, cioè in cima è dipinta la Beatissima Vergine Maria col Bambino trà le braccia, & avanti alle dette imagini vi è l'effigie d'una donna, che hà intorno la testa la Diadema, quale stà inginocchioni vestita coll'habito, che da nel nero, & in testa stà col velo bianco, e sottogolo, & un manto giallo, quale donna tiene una mano sopra la spalla destra d'una putta vestita d'habito di voto con il cordone, che parimentre sta inginocchioni.

E sopra detto quadro è un'altro quadretto in quadro con cornice nera, nel quale vi è un'effigie d'huomo, che stà inginocchioni, & un'altro in letto, & in contro à quello vi è l'effigie della Madonna Santissima con Christo in braccio, e San Francesco, & alla spalla della Madonna un'effigie di Donna vestita coll'habito di San Francesco, manto bianco, e diadema in testa, & in piedi notate l'infrascritte parole.

Ex voto per gratia ricevuta 1622.

Nel muro poi di detta Cappella vi sono altre Tabelle votive dipinte in tela, e tavole di legno con simili effigie dipinte rappresentanti diverse gratie, e miracoli sino al numero di venti senza nome, & anno.

Sopra detta Cappella vi è una cuppoletta tonda, che risponde sopra il sopradescritto deposito, nella quale vi è la lanterna con diverse finestrelle, & invetriate, & in essa è dipinta la Gloria del Paradiso, & in piedi di detta cuppola dell'angolo dalla parte dell'Evangelio dell'Altare è dipinta la figura, & effigie di Sant'Agnese, nell'altro angolo dell'istessa parte è dipinta la figura, & effigie di Santa Francesca Romana, e dalla parte dell'Epistola incontro Santa Agnese è dipinta l'effigie di Santa Cecilia, e nell'istessa parte dell'Epistola incontro Santa Francesca vi è dipinta l'effigie di una donna vestita con habito di Tertiaria di S. Francesco col manto bianco in testa, e diadema intorno la testa come sono dipinte le tre Sante nominate, è dipinte di sopra, qual figura nella mano sinistra tiene un pane, che lo porge ad un povero, che sta ricevendolo inginocchiato, e nella mano destra tiene un libro à foggia di Breviario, e tutte le sopradescritte pitture in detti quattro Angoli di detta Cappella sono dipinte in guisa di stare à sedere, e tutte quattro le medeme figure sono di lunghezza di palmi sei in circa.

No. 8. Bellori's testimony on the paintings of Ludovica in the Altieri Chapel. Relatio Peritorum.

Primus Ioannes Petrus Belloni Pictor annorum 56. Interrogatus respondi. Si signore, che io conoscerei benissimo da chi Pittore fosse stata dipinta qualche Pittura, che io vedessi, quando però fosse di Pittore celebre, mà non essendo di celebre Pittore, saprò conoscere di che tempo in circa possa essere stara depinta [*sic*], e ciò per l'esperienza, che io ne hò.

Ex tunc Illustrissimus, & Reverendissimus D. mandavit per ipsum Deponentem inspici effigiem depictam in Pariete Cappellae praedictae Sanctae Annae à Cornu Epistolae Altaris.

Qui examinatus parendo mandatis praedictis se contulit praecisè in dicto loco ante dictam effigiem, illamque inspexit, & benè, ut dixit, & accuratè consideravit, &

Et successivè dixit Io hò già, per obedire à V.S. Illustrissima, visto, e ben considerato questa pittura, che stà in questo muro di questa Cappella à mano manca dell'Altare, che rappresenta la figura una donna in piedi velata di bianco, cioè col velo sopra il capo disteso frà le braccia vestita con cinta nel petto bianca, che con la mano destra tiene un libro à guisa di Breviario con coperta rossa, e con la sinistra porge un pane ad un povero, che in atto di riceverlo stende la mano, e stà inginocchioni, & havendola ben vista, e considerata, dico, che l'imagine di questa effigie è stata dipinta nel secolo passato, perche riconosco, che è nella maniera, e modo, che si dipingeva dopo che il famoso Raffaele morì, e saranno cento, e più anni, che fù dipinta, & anco dico, che il povero, che hò detto, è stato restaurato, perche si vede benissimo, che il pittore è stato assai inferiore à quello, che hà dipinta l'effigie di detta Donna, che si dice rappresenti la Beata Ludovica Albertoni, e vedo benissimo, che la figura di detta Beata è dipinta con raggi, e splendori d'oro in testa, e questi vi sono stati fatti dal tempo, che fù dipinta la detta figura, poiche mostrano l'istessi antichità, e tutte le sopradette cose io depongo, & atteso per verità per l'esperienza, che tengo nell'essercitio della pittura, e per essermi essercitato particolarmente nel sapore conoscere l'antichità, e modo di dipingere delli Pittori antichi, e moderni, e però ne stò anco hora mettendo alla stampa sopra di questo un libro.

Et successivè Dominus mandavit per dictum examinatum inspici aliam effigie consimilem praedictae depictam in angulo cuppulae eiusdem Cappellae, & ipsa inspectas referat à quo Pictore, & de quo tempore illa depictae fuit, & facta per dictum examinatum demandata inspectione, ut dixit.

Interrogatus fuit per dictum D. Subpromotorem, ut omnia, quae vidit, & recognovit, referat distinctè.

Respondit. Ho anco veduto l'altre effigie, che mi è stata indicata, che stà nel Peduccio della Cuppola di questa Cappela, cioè in uno de quattro peducci della cuppola, in uno de quali vi è dipinta S. Cecilia, nell'altro Santa Agnese, nell'altro Santa Francesca, e nell'altro l'effigie della medema, che habbiamo veduto nel lato dell'Epistola dell'Altare, qual Imagine, & effigie stà à sedere, con la mano destra tiene il libro come l'altra, e la sinistra porge un pane ad un povero, e che hà in testa un velo bianco, che cade sopra l'habito nero, & in testa vi è la diadema, & havendola ben vista, e considerata per le ragioni, che hò dette, e per l'esperienza, che hò della pittura, dico, che questa effigie, & Imagine con il detto Povero sono state dipinte di fresco, cioè saranno quarant'anni fà in circa, e dovrà essere quando fù restaurata la Cappella.

No. 9. Paintings of B. Ludovica and Saints Agnes, Cecilia, and Francesca Romana in the chapel of San Antonio in Santa Maria in Aracoeli. Visitatio Cappellae Sancti Antonij de Padua in Ecclesia Aracoelitana.

Relatione facta comparuit in supradicta Cappella Sancti Antonij de Padua in Veñ Ecclesia Sanctae Mariae de Aracaeli coram illustrissimo, & Reverendissimo D. Marco Antonio Vicentino Episcopo Fulginateñ Iudice subdelegato, praesentibus, & interuenientibus illustrissimo, & Reverendissimo D. Alexandro Columna Prothonotario Apostolico à Sac. Rituum Congregatione specialitèr deputato & . . .

In Primis una cancellata di ferro avanti detta Cappella, & omissis alijs demandato dicti Illustrissimi, & Reverendissimi D. Iudicis subdelegati sopra detta Cappella vi è una cuppoletta, nella quale vi è dipinto il Padre Eterno in gloria d'Angeli, e nelli peducci di detta Cuppola, cioè nel primo à mano dritta dell'ingresso vi è l'effigie, ò figura di Santa Francesca Romana in forma di sedere con l'Angelo à lei vicino, & à piedi di essa l'infrascritte parole, e lettere descritte *S. Francesca R.* nell'altro peduccio dell'istessa parte vicino l'Altare, che è la parte dell'Epistola l'effigie di Santa Cecilia nell'istessa forma di sedere con la seguente inscrittione sotto il suo piede *S. Cecilia V. e M.* Nell'altro peduccio di detta Cuppoletta vicino l'Altare dalla parte dell'Evangelio l'effigie, ò figura di S. Agnese nell'istessa forma di sedere, con la seguente inscrittione alli piedi *S. Agnese V. & M.* e nell'ultimo Angolo, ò Peduccio à mano sinistra nell'ingresso di detta Cappella l'effigie della Beata Ludovica Albertoni col manto bianco in testa parimente informa [*sic*] di sedere, & in atto di dar l'elemosina con la mano sinistra ad un povero, che al medemo lato sta ricevendola inginocchioni, e nell'altra mano destra tiene un libro come un Breviario, vestita con habito come nero, & à piedi di lei vi sono le seguente lettere, e parole: *B. Ludovica R.* quali quattro figure in detti Peducci esistenti, e come sopra descritte hanno tutte intorno la testa la diadema, e splendori tutte uniformi, nel resto della cappella diverse figure, e pitture rappresentanti li miracoli fatti da S. Antonio di Padova, & anco vi sono in detta Cappella diversi depositi, e sepolchri degl'Antenati dell'Eccellentissima Casa Palutig &c.

No. 10. Testimony of Bellori and Baciccio regarding the attribution and dating of the paintings in the chapel of San Antonio. Relatio Peritorum super antiquitate Imaginis dictae in fornice d. Cappellae inter alias Imagines Sanctarum.

Relatione facta comparuit in supradicta Cappella Sancti Antonij de Padua in Veñ Ecclesia Sanctae Mariae de Aracaeli coram illustrissimo, & Reverendissimo D. Marco Antonio Vicentino Episcopo Fulginateñ Iudice subdelegato, praesentibus, & interuenientibus illustrissimo, & Reverendissimo D. Alexandro Columna Prothonotario Apostolico à Sac. Rituum Congregatione specialitèr deputato & . . .

Primus Ioannes Baptista Bellori Peritus Interrogatus respondit. Io hò veduto, e fatto diligente consideratione, e riflessione nella figura, sotto della quale vi è scritto *B. Ludovica R.* che stà dipinta nel primo peduccio nell'ingresso di questa Cappella di S. Antonio à mano sinistra, e dico, e riconosco benissimo, che la pittura è antica di sopra settant'anni, e credo anco, che il Pittore sia stato uno, che si chiamava il Navarra, perche io riconosco benissimo tanto dalla medema figura, quanto dall'altre tre figure, che stanno nell'altri tre peducci di detta Cuppola, cioè di S. Francesca Romana, di S. Agnese, e Santa Cecilia, che è il modo di dipingere, che osservava il detto Navarra, e vedo, che in tutte quattro dette figure in testa vi è la diadema, e raggi dipinti in essi nel tempo, che le pitture furono dipinte, e si conosce anco benissimo, che quelle figure sono molto più antiche di quelle, che sono dipinte à S. Francesco à Ripa nella Cappella di S. Anna nelli Peducci di quella cuppoletta, e sicuramente quelle sono state fatte ad imitatione di queste quattro, che stanno in questi peducci, mà quella, che stà al lato sinistro dell'Altare di S. Anna in S. Francesco à Ripa, e molto più antica di queste, perche supera li cent'anni, come dissi in quell'altro mio esame, e tutto ciò dico, attesto, e depongo per l'esperienza, che io tenga nella cognitione delle pitture, e delle loro antichità, & essermi io particomente esercitato in questo, come dissi in d. altro mio esame.

Secundus Ioannes Baptista Gaullus Ianuen Pictor Peritus Interrogatus respondit lo vedo, & hò considerato benissimo la figura, che è in questa Cappella di S. Antonio di Padova, che stà nel primo Peduccio della cuppola à mano sinistra nell'entrare in detta Cappella, sotto la quale vi è scritto *B. Ludovica R.*, e dico, e conosco essere stata dipinta da sopra settant'anni, & anco riconosco, e credo certamente essere stata dipinta da un tale pittore, che si chiamava Navarro, e questo io conosco, perche tutte le altre tre figure di Sante esistenti nell'altri tre peducci di detta Cuppola sono della simile mano, nelle quali vi riconosco la maniera, che eggli usava, & anco perche sono dell'istessa maniera, e mano d'altre pitture, che sono dell'istesso Pittore in SS. Apostoli di Roma . . .

No. 11. Antiquity of the physical evidence of Ludovica's cult. Testes deponentes di praedictis Imaginibus depictis cum radijs, & splendoribus. Testimony of Fra Io: Baptista a Roma, sixty-two years old.

Idem 10 iuxta 19. fol. 227. respondit. Io sò, che nella Chiesa di San Francesco à Ripa, cioè nella Cappella dedicata à sant'Anña vi è l'effigie della B. Ludovica Albertonia dal lato dell'Epistola dell'Altare nel muro dipinta incontro all'effigie di santa Chiara, che però è stata posta in quel luogo come Santa, e Beata, & anco sò, che è effigiata nelli parati, pianete, & altre suppellettili Ecclesiastiche, che sono à S. Francesco a Ripa, & ivi sono stati posti, perche sono stati fatti del prezzo de'Calici, che suol presentare ogn'anno il Senato, e Popolo Romano nella sua festa in honore di detta Beata, & anco sò, che è stata stampata in carte, che si distribuivano a quelli, che concorrevano nel giorno della sua festa, & anco mi pare d'haverla veduta in altri luoghi, che hora non mi sovvengono, e la sua imagine, che è dipinta nella Cappella di sant'Anna nel muro, come hò detto, hò inteso dire dal P. Frà Vincenzo di Roma, che era vecchissimo, quando io entrai in Religione, che quella era la medema effigie, che stava nella Cappella vecchia, e che si ricordava sempre d'haverla veduta, perche vi era molto prima, che lui entrasse in Religione, come intese dire dalli vecchi, che trovò esso quando entro nella Religione.

No. 12. Votives on Ludovica's sepulcher. Testes deponentes de retentione Tabellarum votiuarum in praedicta Cappella Albertonia. Testimony of Fra Petrus Paulus, seventy-five years old.

Idem Tertius iuxta 17. fol. 110. Respon. lo sò, perche si vedono publicamente, & universalmente, che al sepolcro di detta Beata Ludovica Albertoni vi sono appese tavolette, e voti in segno delle gratie, che hanno ricevuto quelli, quali si sono raccomandati all sua intercessione non posso però dire il numero di essi perche non ne hò contati, ma si potranno vedere se si fara la visita della Cappella, e ve li hò veduti tutto il tempo, che io mi ricordo, & anco mi dicevano li vecchi Religiosi, che io ritrovai nel Convento, quando da Chierico vi habitai, che vi l'haveano sempre vedute, e ciò come hò detto di sopra, sara stato, e seguito con scienza, e toleranza de Sommi Pontefici, poiche benche cosa publica, e notoria, non è stato mai commandato, che si levino.

No. 13. Burning lamp. Testes deponentes de lampade accensa ad sepulcrum. Testimony of Fra Petrus Paulus, seventy-five years old.

Idem Tertius iuxta idem fol. 110. a tergo Respondit. Io hò detto di sopra, che tutto il tempo, che io mi ricordo, e che sono stato Religioso, hò veduto accesa la lampada al sepolcro de detta Beata Ludovica Albertoni, e parimente li vecchi Religiosi, che erano nel detto Convento di san Francesco quando io vi cominciati à stare, come hò detto, mi decevano, che anche loro ve l'havevano veduta tutto il tempo, che loro si ricordavano, e questo anco si deve credere, che sia stato con scienza, e toleranza de Sommi Pontefici per le ragioni dette di sopra.

No. 14. Veneration of Ludovica's cult. Testes deponentes de concursu, & veneratione sepulchri & reliquarum praedictae Beatae. Testimony of Fra Zaccharias of Rome, seventy-five years old.

Idem sextus iuxta 15. fol. 157. à tergo respondit. Io sono andato più, e più volte dal tempo, che hò havuto notitia della detta B. Ludovica à visitare il suo sepolcro, & inginocchi armi avanti ad esso, & à fare oratione à detta Beata, come fò à gl'altri Santi, perche io tengo sicuro, che sia in Paradiso, e che possa intercedere per me appresso Sua Divina Maestà nelli miei bisogni, & hò veduto ancora, che altre persone d'ogni qualità, e conditione, nobili, & ignobili si sono parimente inginocchiate al sepolcro di detta Beata, e farui oratione, con farui altri atti di veneratione, cioè baciare il detto suò sepolcro, toccar corone dentro la gratella sopra detto sepolcro, inchinarui il capo, e farui altri atti di veneratione, che sogliono farsi all sepolcri dell'altri Santi, e Beati, e ciò non solamente hò io veduto questo concorso di Popolo, e veneratione alla detta Beata al suo sepolcro, mà anco hò inteso dalli vecchi, che io ritrouai in detta Religione, che sempre era stato il medemo, nel tempo, che loro si ricordàvano, & anco, che così havevano essi sentito, che si era fatto anticamente, e havendo essi così ritrouato, e sentito, quando entrono nella Religione, e di tutto questo ne è stata, & è publica voce, e fama, e publico, e notario, nè mai è stato detto, fatto, ò sentito cosa alcuna in contrario.

No. 15. Sanctity of Ludovica's death. Ex praeolaris illius virtutibus semper vixit, & obijt cum fama Sanctitatis. Testimony of Fra Eleutherius, eighty-eight years old.

Super primo fol. 79. dixit. E la verità, che la detta Beata Ludovica Albertoni morì quì in Roma, mà dell'anno preciso io non me ne ricordo, e che morì con gran fama, & opinione di Santa, e gran Serua di Dio per l'heroiche virtù, e sante sue attione, con che visse, e per il segno, che diede nel tempo della sua morte di gran carità verso Iddio, e che il concorso al suo funerale fù grandissimo d'ogni sorte, e conditione di persone, & in particolare de Signori grandi, e gente nobile, e che fù sepellita nella Chiesa di questo nostro Convento di S. Francesco à Ripa nella Cappella della famiglia Albertoni, dove anco al presente le sue reliquie riposano con la venerazione, che hò detto di sopra, & anche perche ne è publica voce, e fama, contro la quale non è stato detto, fatto, ò sentito cosa alcuna in contrario questo medemo hò sentito dire dalli più vecchi di questo Convento, come hò detto di sopra, e quelli dicevano haverlo sentito dire dall' altri più vecchi, e Religiosi prima di loro in detto Convento, e per essere il tutto publico, e notario.

Testimony of Fra Iacobus a Cantalupo, eighty-one years old. Io hò inteso dire, che la detta Beata Ludovica morì in Roma, e così bisognò, che fosse necessariamente, mentre le sue Reliquie, & il suo Corpo sta sepellito nella Chiesa di S. Francesco à Ripa nella Capella dedicata à S. Anna, & anco la fama della sua morte fù di gran Santa, perche ancora adesso è da tutti stimata tale, e che sia in Paradiso da tutti si crede . . .

Testimony of Fra Bernardinus a Preneste, seventy-two years old. La detta Beata Ludovica Albertoni sò, che era Romana per haverlo letto nelle sue Inscrittioni, e sò, che è morta in Roma per essere stata sepellita nella nostra Chiesa di S. Francesco à Ripa, e per conseguenza bisogna, che habbia habito in Roma mentre visse, e la fama di lei mentre visse fù d'una gran Serva di Dio, e di gran Santità, & in particolare hò sentito dire, che era grand'Elemosiniera, e questo sò non solamente per haverlo inteso dire, mà anco perche l'effigie sua si dipinge in atto di dare l'elemosina, e di souvenire alli Poveri, e così è dipinta nella Cappella di Sant'Anna à S. Francesco à Ripa dove è sepellita, & anco si dipinge in certe carte, quando si distribuiscono nel giorno della sua Festa, & anco si è dipinta, ò effigiata nelle Pianete, Paliotti dell'Altare, e Piviali, che sono stati donati alla nostra Chiesa di S. Francesco dal Sign. Marchese Baldassar Palutij, & anco la medema effigie si ritrova nelle Tunicelle, e la fama della Santità della detta Beata Ludovica in vita, come hò detto, hebbe origine dal suo vivere virtuosamente, e fù sempre continua, nè mai interrotta, nè mai è stato detto, ò fatto cosa alcuna in contrario, e le dette cose io le sò di certa scienza, e per esserne stata, & esserne publica voce, e fama respettivamente.

Testimony of Fra Zaccharias a Roma, seventy-five years old. . . so bene che morì con grand'opinione di santa, e che quest'opinione fù concepita da tutti, non solamente perche visse con heroiche, e Christiane virtù, ma anche perche nell'ultima sua malatia diede gran segno di conformarsi con la volontà del Signore, e del suo grand'amore verso Sua Divina Maestà, e del desiderio, che haveva di andare à godere la Gloria del Paradiso . . .

No. 16. Ludovica the Blessed One. Testes deponentes de veneratione dict. Beatae, & titulo Beata a die opsius obitus. Testimony of Fra Bernardinus a Preneste, seventy-two years old.

Et super quinto fol. 119. dixit. E anco la verità, che sempre d. Beata Ludovica è stata chiamata col titolo di Beata, poiche tutto il tempo, che io mi ricordo l'hò sentita nominare con questo titolo, & anco me dicevano li vecchi, che io trovai nella Religione, che sempre in tempo loro l'havevano sentita nominare, e chiamare con il medemo titolo, e che havevano sentito dire dall'altri loro maggiori, che sin doppo la sua morte cominciò ad essere nominata col detto titolo, essendo anche à me note tutte le sudette cose per essere publiche, e notorie, e per altre cause dette di sopra nell'interrogatorij.

No. 17. Honoring Ludovica's cult by the Magistrates. Decreta Senatus Populique Romani super praesontatione Calicis, & Cereroum die dictae Beatae cum indicatione teriarum in Capitolio inaugmentum cultus, & venerationis eiusdem.

Ex codem S.C. attenta sanctitate, ac dignissimis meritis Beatae Ludovicae Albertoniae de Cithara Romanae praedefuncte existentis in Ecclesia S. Francisci in Transtyberim de Vrbe in cappella Dominorem de Cithara, & adhoc ut magis cognito sanctae vitae praedictae Beatae Posteris innotescat, decretum est, quod in posterum singulis annis in die festivitatis suae, quae est ultima Ianuarii ad similitudinem Beatae Franciscae Romanae offeratur unus Calix cum quatuor Intortitiis Ecclesiae supradicti sancti Francisci in Transtyberim, in qua existit corpus praedictae Beatae, & quod Magistratus illius temporis maiori, quo potuerit, decore, & concomitatu dictam Ecclesiam, & corpus praedictae Beatae visitare ac supradictum munus praesentate debeat omni meliori modo.

No. 18. Celebration of Ludovica's feast day. Testes deponentes de dicta praesentatione, & solemni festiuitate dictae Beatae cu celebratione Missae die anniuersario illius obitus. Testimony of Fra Zaccharias a Roma, seventy-five years old.

E anco la verità, che l'ultimo giorno di Gennaro nella Chiesa sudetta di S. Francesco à Ripa si solennizza la festa di detta B. Ludovica con gran corcorso di Popolo, & il Senato, e Popolo Romano vi porta à presentare un Calice, e quattro Torcie, come fà ad altre Chiese in occasione de festività de Santi, e posso anco dire d'avantaggio, che hò sentito dire, che nella nostra Sacristia si conservino in una Cassetta di legno un Camice, che fù filato dalla detta B. Ludovica, e che questo con occasione della festa di detta Beata da certi Sacrestani è stato esposto sopra il suo sepolcro, e tutto quante le cose, che hò detto di sopra le sò per le cause dette di sopra negl'Interrogatorij, e per essere publiche e notarie.

No. 19. The fame of Ludovica's cult. Testes deponentes de fama cum suis requisitis. Testimony of Fra Bernardinus à Virgoleta, sixty-three years old.

Idem nonus iuxta idem fol. 209. à tergo respondit. La fama è quella, che si dice da tutti publicamente, e la fama della santità di detta Beata Ludovica è stata universale, e commune di tutti, & ha havuto origine dalle sue sante, e virtuose attioni, e da Persone nobili, Letterate, e degne di fede, & è stata sempre continua, nè mai interrotta, nè mai contro di lei è stata detta, fatta, ò sentita cosa alcuna in contrario.

No. 20. Passages from Angelo Bernarbo's biography of Ludovica. Testimony of R. Suor Antonina Casalia Monialis, seventy-nine years old.

Nel Libro intitolato *Leggendario delle Vergini,* stampato in Roma l'anno 1655. per Angelo Bernabò al foglio 281. vi è segue.

Leggenda della Beata Ludovica de Albertoni Vedova Romana, la cui festa si celebra all'ultimo di Gennaro.

Nacque in Roma la Beata Ludovica nell'anno 1473 e fù figliuola di Stefano di Pier Matteo Albertoni, e di Lucretia Tebaldi nobili Romani, dalli quali fù maritata à Giacomo figliuolo di Gio: Iacomo della Citera nobile giovane Romano, dal quale ella generò tre figlie femine denominate Camilla, Silvia, & Antonia, che maritorno la prima ad un'altro della medema Famiglia Albertoni, la seconda à Nicola Muti, l'ultima à Curtio Mattei, il tutto lo pone Alessio de Peregrinis Notario Capitolino 7. Maggio 1510.

L'anno 1506 passò all'altra vita Giacomo suo marito, e Ludovica desiderosa di dedicarsi tutta à Dio, e servissi di tale occasione, si diede totalmente al dispregio del Mondo. Vestiva poveramente, era di molt'astinenza, e penitenza impiegandosi in molte opere di carità dispendando tutto quello, che mai poteva à i poveri, restando povera per divenire poi ricca in Cielo, visitava di continuo le Chiese, e sacri luoghi di Roma, impiegando il tempo in orationi, e meditationi, e nella frequenza de'Divini Sacramenti in amare Dio & il prossimo per amor suo, & era il specchio, & il modello delle Vedove Romane.

Così finalmente come piaque à S.D.M. nell'ultimo di Gennaro l'anno 1533 nel Pontificato di Clemente Settimo di anni sessanta in circa doppo molti giorni della sua infermità con divoto aspetto havendo gli occhi rivolti al Cielo rese l'anima sua al suo Creatore, e saputasi la sua morte, quasi tutto il popolo di Roma la pianse, in particolare li poveri, quali dicevano di haver persa la loro Madre, che li souveniva nella loro povertà, e con gran devotione il suo corpo fu portato à San Francesco à Ripa, dove gli furno fatte honorate essequie con l'intervento di tutto il sacro Collegio de'Cardinali, e molti di essi vi celebrono la santa Messa con il concorso di tutta la Città à vederla, come con pie autentica si può vedere negli Annali di quel tempo nella Biblioteca Apostolica in Vaticano. Si dipinge la detta Beata con un pane in mano dandolo ad un povero, e perche havea in uso di fare alcuna pizza di pasta, dove metteva dentro diverse monete di oro, e d'argento, quelle benediceva, & offeriva à S.D. Maestà, acciò si compiacesse esso, al quale era noto il maggiore, e minore bisogno de'poveri, di date quelle monete secondo la necessità di detti poveri, e così ne dava à sorte un poco petuno di quel pane, quale anco giovava à guarire gl'infermi, & altri tribolati, ciò perche fù trovato nel pane, che dava alli poveri delli pezzi di oro . . .

Notes

Introduction

1. "Nel discorrere col Cavaliere di cose spirituali gli faceva di mestiere di un'attenzione tale, come se andar dovesse ad una Conclusione." See Bernini, 171.
2. Many artists were employed in the execution of Bernini's design for Alexander's tomb. For documentation of this project, see Golzio, 119–47.
3. J. Pope-Hennessy, III, pt. 3, 114.
4. See discussion in chapter 5.

Chapter 1

1. For information on the history of the church, see Menichella. San Francesco a Ripa is also discussed in Golzio and Zander, 83–85, and in Pesci.
2. The conventual complex, taken over by the army in 1870 and used as barracks (*caserma dei Bersaglieri*), is now uninhabited and undergoing renovation under the auspices of the Soprintendenza per i Beni Ambientali e Architettonici del Lazio.
3. Destroyed in the campaign of 1683, the paintings, datable around 1285, are attributed to Cavallini. See Ghiberti, 39; G. Vasari, *Le vite de'più eccellenti pittori, scultori ed architetti* (1550–68), Florence, 1878, 535–43; and Celio, no. 29. For further information on the church during this period, see Ludovico da Modena, *Cronaca della riforma dal 1519 al 1722, fondazione de conventi,* in *Fondazione e riforma del convento di S. Francesco a Ripa.* Archivio di San Francesco a Ripa, busta 12, fols. 154, 272; and Menichella, 22, 23.
4. For information on the *Popolo Romano,* see Partner, 65–70 and Nussdorfer.
5. *Congregatione,* (see Appendix V) and Pauolo. Other biographies of Ludovica are found in Gonzaga, 178; Wadding, 386–90; L. Iacobelli, *Compendio della Beata Ludovica,* Foligno, 1641; P. Arturi du Monstier, *Martyrologium Francescanum* 44; Arturi du Monstier, *Sacrum gynecaeum amplissimum; G. Alveri, Roma in ogni stato,* 1664, Biblioteca Nazionale, pt. 2, fols. 32–33; G. Díaz Vara Calderón, 476–77; B. Mazzara, 145–55; *Breviarium Romano-seraphicum,* Rome, 1882, 711–12; Guerin, II, 155–56; Boncampagni, IV, 425–81; and *Martirologio romano.*

6. Holy women living outside a cloister are known in Italy as *pinzochere* or *mantellate* (the latter term referring to the veil worn by these pious women). The *pinzochere,* who were in many cases widows and married women, dedicated their lives to acts of penance and charity. They visited sacred sites, took communion frequently, and cared for the sick. Some of these women were famous for their mystical experiences and became the objects of cults, for example: Margherita Colonna, Rosa of Viterbo, Catherine of Siena, Rosa of Lima, and Bridget of Sweden. Ludovica Albertoni and Francesca Romana are viewed as the most famous of the *pinzochere* in Rome (see R. Guarnieri, "Pinzochere," in *Dizionario degli Istituti di Perfezione,* VI, 1722–49.

7. Pauolo, 151–53, 231.

8. Ibid., 83–127.

9. Ibid., 215–26.

10. Ibid., 220.

11. Ibid., 225.

12. Ibid., 227.

13. Ibid., 228. See also Boncampagni, IV, 461–62. Ludovica's will of 7 May 1520 is preserved in Rome, Archivio de Stato, *Notari Capitolini Alexius de Paregrinis,* busta 1257, fols. 199–200. Ludovica drew up a will on 15 January 1496, in which she asked to be buried in the church of Santa Maria in Campitelli. The will is preserved in Rome in the Archivio di Stato, *Archivio dei Notari Capitolini,* busta 1181, (1470–99), carte 674v, 733r (Pacificus de Pacificis).

14. Pauolo, 229. See Appendix II.

15. Ibid., 229–30. See Appendix II.

16. Two of Silvia and Niccolò Muti's children, Girolamo and Giovanna, married into the Altieri family. Girolamo married Drusiana Altieri, and Giovanna became the wife of Ottavio Altieri. See Pauolo, 49, and Visconti, 559–60.

17. See Palladio; *Le cose maravigliose di Roma,* Rome, 1561; *Le cose maravigliose . . . ,* Rome, 1566, 10; F. Cavalli, 27; Alveri; and F. Franzini.

18. *Congregatione,* 20–21, no. 12. See Appendix V.

19. In his will, Giacomo asked to be buried in the church of San Francesco a Ripa, "nella cappella nuova ove è sepolto suo padre." Giacomo commanded that Ludovica be paid her share of the estate on 2 March 1507. Her brother-in-law refused to pay, however, and Ludovica subsequently became involved in a lengthy, bitter lawsuit that was not settled until 1520. See Boncampagni, IV, 453–55.

20. The document was discovered by Anna Menichella. Much additional information may be culled from this document, the relevant pages of which are transcribed here in Appendix I.

21. Appendix I. An earlier account by Pompeo Ugonio offers a slightly more detailed picture of the chapel. In his description of 1588, Ugonio called it a "sacellus novus cum duobus altaris," the first altar of which was surmounted by a wooden cross, the second by a picture of the Madonna and saints. The fact that Ugonio refers to the chapel as new suggests a renovation shortly before 1588. See P. Ugonio, *Pompeii Ugonii theatrum Urbis Romae. Compendium rerum memorabilium Urbis Romae. Antiquitates Urbis.* Cod. Vaticano Barb. lat., busta 1994, fols. 550, 556, 557 (quoted in Menichella, 37–38).

22. *Congregatione,* 4–9, no. 4. See Appendix V.

23. The floor pavement of the chapel, as it appears today, is delineated by pavement stones that trace a circle repeating the shape of the dome. Set into the pavement within this circle are a removable marble slab (presumably leading to a burial chamber beneath the floor), a small porphyry plaque with the Albertoni arms, and a white marble epitaph with a partially worn inscription on it. The three slabs are arranged in a straight line leading to the altar. Another barely legible inscription slab was found in the pavement at the far left of the chapel. The inscription is recorded in Forcella, XIII, 418, no. 1007: "DOM Hic Requiescit Corpus P.F. Deodati AB Albano Sacerdotis Strict. Observ. S.P. Francisci Qui in Hoc Conventu Decessit die XXIV Novembr. 1741. Aetatis Suae/ Vero 62 Mens. 8 Die 7. Pie Ac Liberali Concessione Illimi Et Excemi Principis D. Hieronymi de Alterys Huis Sacelli Patroni." This inscription of 1741 is cut off at the right side, suggesting that the pavement at the center of the chapel was redone after the plaque was set into the floor. L. Cipriani (*Ludovica Albertoni,* Rome, 1973, 17) reported that the pavement was renovated in 1969.

24. The inscription is recorded in Forcella, IV, no. 939. It reads in translation: "Here lies the blessed Ludovica, daughter of Stefano Piermattei Albertoni, wife of Giacomo, and mother-in-law of D. Niccolò Muti. She lived sixty years and gave back her soul to her creator on high the last day of January 1533. Ludovica, pray for the peace that thou enjoyest as consort of the heavenly ones, for thy people; and guard us from evil. Most holy woman, only make thyself propitious with that favorable spirit whereby, pious one, thou workest so many miracles; and give succour."

25. *Congregatione,* no. 4. See Appendix V.

26. Pauolo, 224, and Ludovico da Modena. See Appendix I.

27. *Congregatione,* 13–16, nos. 8, 9, 10. See Appendix V.

28. Gabinetto dei Disegni e delle Stampe, Disegni de Architettura, Florence, n. 1643A. The drawing is published in Menichella, 126. The first to notice the relation between this sketch and San Francesco a Ripa was R. Lanciani, *Storia degli scavi di Roma e notizie intorno alle collezione romane di antichità,* Rome, 1902–12, I, 242.

29. For a full discussion of this drawing, see Appendix IV.

30. Pauolo, 255.

31. An architectural project in Spoleto suggests that the splayed walls of the Altieri Chapel were designed by Giacomo. The architect's brother, Giovanni Battista Mola (d. 1665), with whom Giacomo collaborated, designed a niche in 1626 for the Chapel of the Holy Icon in the Cathedral of Spoleto, which also used angled walls as a perspective device, leading the worshipper's attention to the recess beyond the altar. (For additional information on this chapel, see K. Noehles, *Roma l'anno 1663 de Giovanni Battista Mola,* Berlin, 1966.) The beveled walls, pierced with statue niches, anticipate the angled walls of the Altieri Chapel, also depicting figures set into niches, although the recesses of the latter are fictive, the figures painted rather than sculpted. The motif of the perspective arch was already well absorbed into the architectural vocabulary of the period by 1622. For example, Carlo Maderno (1556–1629) utilized a perspective arch in the opening at the foot of the staircase of the Palazzo Mattei (1598–1618).

32. An aged witness testified at the *processi* that the fresco of Ludovica was moved during the restoration of 1622 from another location within the same chapel (*Congregatione,* 15, 16, no. 11, See Appendix V). The removal and resetting of the fresco may have caused damage to the picture, which was later repaired. Baciccio states in the testimony of the *processi* that the figure of the poor pilgrim, inferior in quality to that of Ludovica, was repainted at a later date (*Congregatione,* 16, no. 8; see Appendix V). The cropping of the column on the left side of the fresco was probably done to accommodate the painting to its new location.

33. The inferior quality of the paintings of Borromeo and of the holy women on the pendentives of the vault, when compared with the fresco on the dome, suggests that the former works were done by Celio's assistants. Borromeo's fresco is not mentioned in the *processi* probably because the picture was covered by votives. A description of the numerous devotional pictures hanging on the left wall above the inscription plaque appears in *Congregatione,* 12, no. 7; see Appendix V.

34. The brothers at San Francesco a Ripa demonstrated their devotion to Saint Charles Borromeo on 22 June 1614 by marching in a procession honoring the saint. The document recording this event may be found in Gigli, 29. Borromeo was a Protector of the Brothers Minor of the Conventuals from 1564 to 1584. For additional information on the saint, see Réau, III, pt. 1, 298–99.

35. "La Madonna con S. Anna e il Cristarello pittura di altare ad olio, nella Cappella della Cetera, del Cavalier Gasparo Celio." See Celio, 15.

36. Pesci, 54. A document in the Archivio Segreto Vaticano records an official apostolic visit to San Francesco a Ripa on 26 June 1625. The Visitatio (*S. Visitatio Apos.* II, Miscellanea Arm. VII, 112, fol. 84v) mentions the tomb of Ludovica with its burning lamp.

37. Among the Franciscans devoted to Saint Anne were the preacher Bernardino da Busti (d. 1500) and Pelbart von Temesvar, who wrote in favor of Saint Anne in the fifteenth century, and Jacob Polius, a Friar Minor of the Strict Observance, whose treatise, *Exegeticum historicum S. Anne,* was first published in Cologne in 1640. The infirmary at San Francesco a Ripa, constructed around 1660, was dedicated to the Virgin and Child with Saint Anne. (See Ludovico da Modena, fols. 166, 299.) The cult of Saint Anne is discussed in Kleinschmidt; Künstle, I, 329–30; and Mâle, 346–53.

38. Kleinschmidt, 301.

39. "Si conserva parem te quivi e con singolare riguardo un dente di S. Anna Madre dtta S^{a}s V.M^{a} nra sig^{ra} donato l'anno 1621 al divotiss^{o}. Religioso e gran servo di Dio fra Innocenzo di Chiusa, dall'emin. sig. Cardinal Francesco [illegible word] Titolare di S. Maria in Trastevere." See Ludovico da Modena, fol. 209; see also *Elenco SS. Reliquie,* Archivio di San Francesco a Ripa, busta 261, undated, 67, which records "un corpo del braccio di S. Anna con carne Madre di Maria Vergine estratto dalla Basilica di S. Paolo fuori delle mura il giorno 30 aprile 1641."

40. F. M. Nicolini da Collamato. *Vita de'Servi di Dio Francescani dal 1630–1685,* Archivio di San Francesco a Ripa, busta 16, fol. 327.

41. Ludovico da Modena reported (fol. 40) that the painting was transferred to the Palazzo Altieri. My investigations of the palace holdings failed to locate the picture.

42. Gabinetto dei disegni, nos. 11826, 11827, and 11795. The Celio drawings were first published by Emma Zocca (see Celio, n. 3).

43. *Congregatione,* 10, no. 7. See Appendix V.

44. For additional information on the theme of Anna Selbdritt, see Künstle (330), Kleinschmidt, Mâle (491–92), and Carol, March and June 1943, 5.

45. Recalling Andrea Sansovino's statue grouping in San Agostino, the print (c. 1610, circle of Cavaliere d'Arpino) mentions the churches Santa Maria Maggiore, Sant' Andrea delle Fratte, Santa Maria in Via Lata, Santa Maria in Aracoeli, Santa Maria della Pace, and Santa Maria della Consolazione.

46. Innocenzo da Chiusi died in 1631 (Ludovico da Modena, fol. 340). According to Ludovico (fols. 233–34), his tomb in San Francesco a Ripa was commissioned of Giovan Battista Mola in 1643. In 1494 Pope Alexander VI granted indulgences for deadly and venial sins for those who said the prayer on these prints of Saint Anne (see Kleinschmidt, 163).

47. The translation: "Hail Mary, full of grace, the Lord is with thee. May thy grace be with me. Blessed art thou amongst women. And blessed be your mother Anne, from whom the Virgin Mary came forth without stain or sin.

And from her womb was born Jesus Christ, the son of the living God." In 1678 this prayer to Saint Anne was forbidden in Italy (see Kleinschmidt, 302).

48. The inscription is recorded in Forcella, IV, no. 992.

49. The sepulcher is described in *Congregatione,* 3–8, nos. 4, 5. See Appendix V.

50. Pauolo, 259, 288–98.

51. *Congregatione,* 4, no. 4. See Appendix V.

52. Cardinal Giovanni Millini, Vicario Generale of Rome, presided over the exhumation. According to Boncampagni (IV, 482), the Rogito of the exhumation preserved in the Archivio Altieri (Arm. B4.9.4) records the inscription on her tomb plaque.

53. Pauolo, 256–58. The legends of the Virgin relate that Mary's corpse smelled sweet like fragrant flowers. See *The Apocryphal New Testament,* 208. In artistic representations of the Virgin's Assumption, Mary's tomb is often shown with roses and lilies in it. For example, see Raphael's *Assumption* or *Coronation of the Virgin* (1502) in the Vatican.

54. The procession and the reburial on 31 January 1626 is described in Boncampagni, IV, 482.

Chapter 2

1. The designation "Senate and the People of Rome" is an ancient epithet that, in the Renaissance and later periods, refers to the Roman nobility involved in the government of the city of Rome at the Palazzo dei Conservatori. It does not, as one might think, refer to the Senate. The latter body could consist only of nobles from cities outside Rome.

2. Pauolo, 248–52; *Congregatione,* 42–43, no. 17. See Appendix V.

3. One of the functions of a conservator was to make appearances at chapels and offer chalices and candles in the name of the *Popolo Romano.* See Nussdorfer, 35.

4. Forcella, IV, no. 991 (in translation): "Seeing that the Senate and People of Rome, in order to honor with singular devotion the Blessed Ludovica of Rome, daughter of Piermattei Albertoni, have ordered by a resolution that for many years to come the last day of January, on which she most fortunately ascended to heaven, shall be celebrated by an annual suspension of the law courts in the Capitoline Curia, and that this chapel shall be visited in solemn pomp by a Roman magistrate with the usual generosity, as is customary, Baldassare Paluzio Albertoni erected this monument in gratitude in the year of the Jubilee 1625."

5. Information pertaining to the history of this chapel is published in Pecchiai, *Il campidoglio nel cinquecento,* 175–81. Investigation of the Fasti Consulares Capitolini in the Palazzo del Conservatori reveals that "Ant. Palutii De Albertonib" was a governmental official in 1645 and 1646 (the dates indicated are 1 October 1645 and 1 January 1646). One might speculate that this descendant of Ludovica played a role in commissioning this painting of 1645 honoring Ludovica. The inscription beneath the picture is published in Boncampagni, IV, 484–85.

6. Members of her mother's family, the Tibaldi, her father's family, the Albertoni and the Altieri, and her husband's family, the Della Cetera, were high-ranking officials on the Capitoline (see Boncampagni, IV, 427, 428, 430, 431, 435, 446, 451; III, 28; and Visconti, 492, 500, 535, 536, 556, 564, 569, 579). Ludovica's son-in-law, Curzio Mattei, is listed as a conservator in 1550 (Visconti, 498); a descendant of her other daughter's family, Alessandro Muti, is recorded as having the high rank of *maestro delle strade* in 1611 (Visconti, 575).

7. During a grave illness of Pope Julius II in August 1511, Marcantonio organized a meeting of the *Popolo Romano* on the Campidoglio, where he delivered an oration urging the nobles to put aside their personal differences and sign an oath of political unity. When Julius died in 1513, Marcantonio delivered a long speech to the conclave, in which he voiced the grievances of his class regarding the number of foreigners holding office in the papal See. Consult Boncampagni, III, 14–27.

8. *Congregatione,* 20, no. 11. See Appendix V.

9. Pauolo, 104.

10. Ludovico da Modena, fol. 229, and Pauolo, 244.

11. For information on this chapel, see Vichi.

12. The papal bull of 19 November 1532 is mentioned in Boncampagni, IV, 464, and is discussed by Ludovico da Modena, fols. 13–22.

13. Mâle, 98.

14. The *Popolo Romano* spent 19,000 *scudi* to finance the celebration of her canonization in 1608. Thirty years later the conservators met with a church official to discuss ways of sponsoring a procession in honor of the recently discovered body of the saint. See Nussdorfer, 70–71, 102 n. 186.

15. The pontiff set up a fountain along the street connecting San Francesco a Ripa with San Callisto, and built another connecting link between the church and the Porta Portese and the Ripa. Paul V originally intended to extend the street leading to San Callisto to Santa Maria in Trastevere. See the plan published in Fagiolo dell'Arco, 1982, 35, and the discussion in Menichella, 48–50, and E. Taramelli, R. Albertazzi, A. Draghi, "Un documento sulla Roma di Paolo V," *Ricerche di Storia dell'Arte,* I–II, 1976, 129–48.

16. The inscription is recorded in Menichella, 61 n. 8. Ludovica's daughter Silvia married Niccolò Muti, and their daughter was wed to Ottavio Altieri (1538). Alessan-

dro Muti Altieri, who was *maestro delle strade* in 1611, may be the son or grandson of this union.

17. Menichella, 50. A cistern in the large courtyard of the convent bears the crest of Paul V and Cardinal Scipione Borghese in commemoration of this act. The inscription is recorded in ibid., 61 n. 12.

18. Urban's act was preceded by that of Gregory XV, who had granted indulgences on 30 March 1622 to those who worshipped at San Francesco a Ripa. See *Guida storico-artistica della chiese . . .*, 115. According to Visconti (115), Pope Gregory was "assai amorevole agli Albertoni."

19. Baldassare was appointed *maestro delle strade* by Pope Gregory XV. The two persons who held this position were the highest-paid officials on the Capitoline; see Nussdorfer, 62–63. According to Visconti (504–5), Urban VIII awarded Baldassare "la metà del castello di Rasina."

20. Pauolo, 259. The bull of 13 March 1625 is published in *Magnum Bullarium Romanum,* IV, 1673, 83–84. According to testimony at the *processi* (*Congregatione,* 23, no. 13; see Appendix V), the burning lamp was kept on Ludovica's grave with the full "knowledge and toleration" of the papacy.

21. The papal bull issued in 1634 is published in *Magnum Bullarium Romanum,* IV, 196–98.

22. For additional information on the career of Cardinal Paluzzi-Albertoni/Altieri, see Stella, in *Dizionario biografico degli italiani,* II, 561–64, s.v. "Altieri (Paluzzo degli Albertoni), Paluzzo": Pastor, 442–45; C. Bertini, *La storia delle famiglie romane di Teodoro Amayden,* I, 20–22; A. M. Trivellini, *Il Cardinale Francesco Buonvisi nunzio a Vienna (1675–89),* Florence, 1958, 4, 12–24; and Visconti, 517–24.

23. Visconti, 595–600.

24. An account of this conclave is recorded in De Bildt, and Pastor, 431–41.

25. *Miscellanea Famiglie.* "Altieri," 1672, busta 9. The document is a written agreement of Clement X regarding rights of primogeniture and consequential obligations owed to Paluzzo, Angelo, and Gaspare Altieri.

26. See Visconti, 598–600, and Pastor, 442.

27. A petition for Ludovica's beatification was made by the "Senate and the People of Rome." See Pauolo (283), Visconti (616), and Boncampagni (IV, 488).

28. Mazzara, 155.

29. Additional information on rules of beatification and canonization may be found in Holwick, XIX–XXIV, and Brinktrine.

30. *Congregatione,* 10, no. 6. See Appendix V.

31. Ibid., 16–17, no. 11. See Appendix V.

32. See Summary of Testimony, ibid., 1–11.

33. The papal bull is published in Wadding, XXVI, 388–89.

34. This celebration is described in Boncampagni (IV, 488–90) and Mazzara (154–55).

35. The brief is mentioned in *Guida,* 115. A plenary indulgence of fourteen years had been granted previously by the pope on 24 January 1671 to those who celebrated the feast day of Ludovica. See Wadding, XXXII, 78–79.

36. Cardinal Altieri arranged for his nieces to be wed to the sons of aristocratic families. The marriage of Ludovica Altieri with the duke of Gravina is mentioned in Pastor, 446.

37. See Schiavo, *Palazzo Altieri,* 172.

38. Baldinucci, *The Life of Bernini,* 64, and D. Bernini, 164.

39. The scandal is documented in Martinelli (1959, 204–27).

40. The nasty quip about the mounting of the stable boy was stated in the *avviso* of 17 February 1674. See note 44 below.

41. See Martinelli (1959, 206).

42. Archivio di Stato di Modena, letter of 20 December 1670, quoted in Martinelli, 209.

43. The *avviso* of 27 December 1670 (Archivio Vaticano, Cod. Barb. lat. 6405) is quoted in Martinelli, 209.

44. Archivio Vaticano, Cod. Barb. lat. 6411, quoted in Martinelli, 213. The reference in this *avviso* to a "concorsi" is not to be taken literally, but was probably sarcastic and intended to insult Gianlorenzo. The author implies that the selection of Bernini was assured by the artist's offer to work without compensation. The *avviso* also states that the cardinal desired a sculpture in "basso relievo." One might speculate that Paluzzo initially contemplated an effigy of Ludovica carved in relief like the Albertoni tomb of Marco d'Antonio in Santa Maria del Popolo (Fig. 37). Bernini, however, probably rejected this idea immediately after receiving the commission.

45. Bernini, who recommended Gaulli for this project, was responsible for the "invention" of the designs. Lavin (1972, 169) first mentioned the relationship between this drawing and the Gesù dome. See also Ostrow (in Lavin et al., *Drawings,* 310–14). Brauer and Wittkower (166–67) erroneously related this study to Bernini's drawing for the *Sangue di Cristo.*

46. The license is referred to in a papal brief in the Archivio Segreto Vaticano (Sec. Brev. 1585, fols. 337–38).

47. The letter is preserved in the Bibliothèque Nationale, Paris (cod. Ital. 2084, fol. 114). Wittkower (237) claimed that the letter was written by Bernini's assistant, Giulio Cartari, and cited the date as 14 October. See Appendix III.

48. F. Titi, *Studio di pittura.*

49. Ludovico da Modena, fol. 288ff. A papal brief of 11 December 1674 in the Archivio Segreto Vaticano (Sec. Brev. 1585, fols. 337–38) gives permission for the body to be reburied under the altar. Other papal briefs of 1672 and 1673 give permission for the effigy of Ludovica to be placed over the altar. See the Archivio Segreto Vaticano (Sec. Brev. 1584, fols. 51–53).

50. This statement is made in a letter of Giovanni Battista Muzzarelli written to Count Geronimo Gratiani. The correspondence is preserved in the Archivio di Stato in Modena. Fraschetti (396) quoted from the letter but did not mention the date of this correspondence. D. Bernini (164) mentioned that Gianlorenzo's son was promoted to the post of Secretary of the Congregazione del'Acque.

51. Bernini, 164, and Ludovico da Modena. See Appendix I.

52. Carlo Cartari praised Bernini in his letter of October 1674, quoting the axiom (translation from Latin, see Appendix III for original text): "He who does it through others appears to be doing it through himself."

Chapter 3

1. Blocking the right window of the niche, a small structure attached to the outside east wall was probably added later, since its roof tiles seem much newer than those covering the aedicule. This addition serves as a means of access to the roof of the oratory of the Third Order. Bernini had previously designed an architectural recess with a concealed light source in the Raimondi Chapel (1638–48) of San Pietro in Montorio, the Cornaro Chapel (1644–51) of Santa Maria della Vittoria, and the Scala Regia, where the sculpture of Constantine, begun in 1654, had only recently been installed and unveiled in 1670.

2. See Ludovico da Modena and Appendix I.

3. For information on the history of the theme of *Anna Selbdritt,* see Künstle, I, 329–30, and Kleinschmidt.

4. Hibbard (220) notes that the cherubs seem to enter the chapel on beams of light. Bernini had previously used a host of angelic figures in the arch of the vault of the Cornaro Chapel of Santa Maria della Vittoria and in the base of the lantern of Sant' Andrea al Quirinale.

5. Lavin (1980) was the first to consider in any depth the relationship between painting, sculpture, and architecture in Bernini's work.

6. For a discussion of this drawing, see Brauer and Wittkower, 165–66, and the catalogue entry by S. Ostrow in Lavin et al., *Drawings,* 302–9.

7. Ostrow (see ibid.) reported that the sketch is trimmed on the left vertical side. The top horizontal edge is apparently also cropped.

8. The relationship between the *Ludovica* and the cenotaph of Maria Raggi is discussed in chapter 6.

9. Lavin (1967 and 1978) discussed Bernini's working methods in general; see also Matzulevitsch.

10. A number of other terra-cotta statuettes of the *Ludovica* have come to light, among them a clay statuette in the Hermitage in Leningrad (see Kosareva). The folds of cloth in this piece, although similar to the marble sculpture, are not identical to it. The cloth around Ludovica's midsection is not as buoyant and lies closer to her body in folds that are more stylized and ornamental. The drapery offers no sense of the body beneath the cloth. The veil framing her head is fuller and nearly square, and the part of the mantle that flares upward is longer. The Hermitage statuette, lacking the freshness of an autograph *bozzetto,* was probably executed by an assistant. It is difficult to imagine Gianlorenzo contemplating a flat, straight-angled base for the statue. Even the mattress he designed for the *Hermaphrodite* in 1620 was softly rounded by tufting (illustrated in Wittkower, 180, fig. 12). Both the clay sculpture in the Hermitage and another in a private collection (the latter published by V. Martinelli in *Le XVII siècle européen,* Rome, 1956–57, fig. 84) lack the vibrancy of an original work. The drapery folds are stiffly faceted, without the softness and fluidity of the cloth in the Victoria and Albert *bozzetto.*

11. Ludovico da Modena (229) see Appendix I. One may safely assume that the original version of the drapery in wood was painted to simulate Sicilian jasper. Bernini used this type of stone for the shroud cascading over the door in the tomb of Pope Alexander VII (see documents published in Golzio, 1939, 119–22). Another addition to the Altieri Chapel by Angelo Altieri in 1702 was the while marble balustrade bearing the Altieri crest at the chapel entrance.

12. Bernini had previously designed recesses in which sculpture is installed in the Raimondi Chapel of San Pietro in Montorio (1638–48) and in the Cornaro Chapel of Santa Maria della Vittoria (1644–51).

13. Black chalk on white paper, 177 by 206 mm, trimmed. This drawing is discussed by Brauer and Wittkower, 166, pl. 93a, and Ostrow, in Lavin et al., *Drawings,* 304.

14. Scholars agree that the sketch is a study for Bernini's project for the Altieri Chapel. The light entering the space from the side, the winged cherubs, and the curved lines suggesting the enframement of the altarpiece are elements in the drawing that establish its close relation to the chapel recess. According to the traditional interpretation (Brauer and Wittkower, 166), the drawing depicts a vaulted space, the cluster of curved lines in the sketch representing one section of the vault and the triangular section illustrating another. The vertical and horizontal lines drawn along the left and upper edges of the sheet are said to represent moldings of the cross-vault. It is difficult, however, to imagine the triangular segment or spandrel terminating at the left and top in a straight line.

15. The emblematic frieze is illustrated in Lavin (1980, pls. 24, 26). A document mentioned by Lavin (206) re-

cords that approval of funds for the gate of the Cornaro Chapel was given on 31 March 1659.

16. The staircase leading to the Cappella Segreta was executed by the German carver Antonio Chiccari (Kicker). See Gonzalez-Palacios.

17. See Fagiolo dell'Arco. 1967, pl. 82.

18. The painting was most likely installed late in 1674, since it is not mentioned in Titi's guidebook of that year. See also Titi (1686).

19. This dating is based on Cartari's letter and Titi's guidebook entry.

20. It is logical to assume that the work was completed before the exhumation and reburial. Once the new altar had been installed, it would have been extremely difficult to gain access to the recess.

21. Ludovico da Modena, 1698, f. 40.

22. Ibid.

23. Ibid.

24. The sketch is mentioned in Wittkower, 237.

25. Baciccio's picture is discussed in Enggass (142). A drawing related to this painting is published in D. Graf, *Kataloge des Kunstmuseums Düsseldorf: Die Handzeichnungen von Guglielmo Cortese und Gio. Batt. Gaulli,* II, Düsseldorf, 1976, fig. 261.

26. Naldini's painting in San Isidoro in Rome is illustrated in A. Daly, *S. Isidoro,* from the series *Le chiese di Roma illustrate,* Rome, 1971, 44. This picture was first suggested by Mâle (352) as a source for Baciccio's altarpiece. Johns's (46) suggestion of Giuseppe Puglia's *Madonna and Child with Saint Anne* (1631) of San Girolamo degli Schiavoni as a source for Baciccio's altarpiece is untenable. Naldini's painting, with its activated figures, flying *putti,* and robust Christ Child reaching for his grandmother, is much closer to the painting in the Altieri Chapel than is the Puglia composition.

27. Palma Vecchio's *Sacra Conversazione* is illustrated in S. J. Freedberg, *Painting in Italy, 1500–1600,* Baltimore, 1975, 161, and Titian's *Virgin with the Rabbit,* in the Louvre, is reproduced in J. Wilde, *Venetian Art from Bellini to Titian.* Oxford, 1974, 156.

28. The resemblance between the *Ludovica* and Saint Anne was discovered simultaneously by myself and by Johns. See Perlove, 1984, 12, and Johns, 43–47.

29. Scholars have neglected to consider why, despite the elevated status of the patron, the chapel proper was left starkly plain.

30. *Avviso* from the Barberini Archives published in Enggass, document 33, 179. For discussion of the chapel in Santa Maria sopra Minerva, see ibid., 8.

31. Partially hidden by layers of plaster, a painted medallion of Ludovica has been discovered by this writer in the sixteenth-century cloister of San Francesco a Ripa. This picture, depicting the *beata* giving bread to a pilgrim, is apparently part of a fresco cycle of thirty-eight medallions and thirty niches, all of which portray important religious persons of the Franciscan orders. Both pictures and their accompanying inscriptions, now covered by plaster, are recorded by Ludovico da Modena (busta 12, fols. 300–340). The Franciscan chronicler, who lists the painting of Ludovica as the eighth medallion (fols. 333–34), reports that the cycle, originally executed by an artist whose identity is no longer known, was repainted in 1654 by another painter whose name has also been forgotten. When the northern end of the cloister was demolished around 1683 in the reconstruction of Matthia de' Rossi, the courtyard was rebuilt, and the artist Fra Emanuele da Como (1625–1701) was apparently called upon to fresco the new walls in continuity with the preexisting cycle and to repaint the old frescoes remaining on the eastern, southern, and western walls of the courtyard (see Menichella, 80, 85, n. 13). The frescoed medallion of Ludovica, located on the east wall near the southern end of the cloister, most likely belongs to the latter category of works executed by Emanuele.

32. For a description of these cloths, see *Congregatione,* 9, 10, no. 6, and Appendix V.

33. The prints are discussed in *Congregatione,* 16–17, no. 11, and Appendix V.

34. During beatifications, effigies of the blessed one are displayed in Saint Peter's. Although prints used for Ludovica's beatification have not come to light, these images most likely depicted the *beata* distributing bread to a poor pilgrim. Pauolo (Appendix II, 286) mentioned a book printed with an image of Ludovica that was displayed in San Francesco a Ripa on her feast day in 1672.

35. *Congregatione,* 26–31, nos. 13, 14, and Appendix V. Sarcophagus-type altars are uncommon in the Eternal City. See Braun, I, 242. See also Lavagnino et al.

36. See chapter 2. For a general discussion of the use of lights, see Rushforth, 164.

37. Pauolo (286).

38. Boncampagni (IV, 478) reports that the plaque was read on 4 March 1625 by Odoardo Tibaldeschi, secretary of Cardinal Millini, Vicario of Pope Urban VIII.

Chapter 4

1. Wittkower, 237–38.

2. These sculptures are discussed by D. Malignaggi in "La Cappella Altieri in S. Francesco a Ripa e alcune interpretazione della B. Ludovica Albertoni," *Rassegna d'arte,* II, 1973, 14–28.

3. For additional information on the statue and the saint, see Honorato; Montenovesi; and Noehles (1970).

4. For example, that of Bishop de Coco (d. 1477) in

Santa Maria sopra Minerva. For a discussion of the use of lights in sepulchral art, see Rushforth, 149–64, and Jacob, 45, 156.

5. See the Antique sarcophagus incorporated into the tomb of Guglielmo Fieschi (d. 1256) in San Lorenzo fuori le mura. For further information on the Santoni monument, see I. Lavin, "Five New Youthful Sculptures by Gianlorenzo Bernini and a Revised Chronology of His Early Works," *Art Bulletin* 50 (1968), 233–48.

6. The Saltarelli tomb is illustrated in E. Panofsky, 1964, fig. 336.

7. The use of Virtue figures in tomb monuments is discussed in Panofsky, 1964, 74–76, and Jacob, 209–10.

8. The figure of Charity appears, for example, on Bernini's papal tombs of Urban VIII (1628–47) and Alexander VII (1671–78) in Saint Peter's.

9. Chantelou, 14 October, 297–98. Bernini admired the tomb of Admiral Chabot (attributed to Pierre Bontemps), which is in the same chapel as the sepulchral monument of Henri Chabot.

10. The effigy of Henri Chabot, however, does survive and is in storage at Versailles. Unfortunately, it is inaccessible and cannot be photographed.

11. See the discussion of this drawing in chapter 3.

12. This classification has been devised to facilitate the discussion of the visual context for the *Ludovica*.

13. On 15 September Bernini visited the Valois Chapel and admired the sculpture of Henry II. His comments are recorded in Chantelou's diary (15 September; 202). On his second excursion to Saint-Denis (29 September; Chantelou, 237–38), Bernini admired the quality of the marble from which they are carved, saying they were "the most beautiful thing in Saint-Denis."

14. The statue was finished by Ercole Ferrata after Aprile's untimely death. Hibbard (227) saw an ambiguity or "loss of clarity" in this work. He believes it is uncertain whether the saint is alive or dead, an interpretation contrary to that offered here.

15. Some representations of this theme include the tympanum of the cathedral in Strasbourg; Giotto's *Dormition of the Virgin*, Gemäldegalerie, Berlin; Dürer's *Death of the Virgin* from the engraved series *Life of the Virgin*. See reproductions in W. Friedländer, *Caravaggio Studies*, New York, 1972, 197.

16. The apocryphal legends are recorded in *The Apocryphal New Testament*, 195–220 (Coptic texts); Jacobus de Voragine, 449–65; and Jameson.

17. Jacobus de Voragine, 451.

18. For a complete discussion of the commission of this work, see Parks, 438–48. Representation of the Death of the Virgin in the period of the Counter-Reformation was controversial. The theologian Johannes Molanus deemed it inappropriate to depict the Madonna on her deathbed, since she left the world without suffering. Sandinus questioned both the appearance of the apostles at her deathbed and her Assumption. The monastic orders, however, perpetuated the legends of Mary's death. The most popular artistic subject from the legends of the Dormition was the Virgin's Assumption to heaven, a scene in which the miraculous nature of the Madonna's death was asserted both by her empty tomb and her elevation to heaven. See discussion in Mâle, 359–63.

19. Of course other explanations for the rejection have been suggested. See the remarks of the contemporary critics Giovanni Baglione and Giovanni Pietro Bellori, who focused upon the Madonna's bare feet and swollen body. Another seventeenth-century critic, Giulio Mancini, maintained that Caravaggio used a common whore as the model for the Virgin. (See quotations in W. Friedländer, *Caravaggio Studies*, New York, 1972, 195.) E. Borsook ("Documents Concerning the Artistic Associates of Santa Maria della Scala in Rome," *The Burlington Magazine*, 96 [1954], 270–75) convincingly demonstrated that the rejection of the painting had nothing to do with the artist's style, since the Carmelites at the church had commissioned other works by Caravaggesque painters. The problem, other scholars suggest, lies in its lack of decorum in depicting the Virgin dead rather than dying (Hinks, 12, 13; Florisoone; and Hibbard, 202, 204). Yet there is a rich tradition for the representation of the deceased Madonna that includes Byzantine, medieval, Renaissance, and Baroque art, and there is no problem of "decorum" in these depictions. Important Renaissance examples are Mantegna's painting of 1460 in Madrid and the mosaic *Death of the Virgin* of 1443 in Venice (Mascoli Chapel, San Marco) attributed to Andrea del Castagno and Michele Giambono. The Baroque artist Carlo Saraceni often showed the Virgin dead (see examples in A. Ottani Cavina, *Carlo Saraceni*, Milan, 1968, nos. 66, 67, 69, 84, 121). The rejection of Caravaggio's *Death of the Virgin* will be the topic of a future article.

20. The deathbed scene of the saint is based on depictions of the Madonna's death; for example, see Giotto's *Death of Saint Francis*, a fresco in the Bardi Chapel of Santa Croce, Florence, c. 1317–24; *Death of Santa Francesca Romana*, a fresco in the Tor dei Specchi, c. 1440; Andrea Bergondi's altar of San Alessio in SS. Bonifacio e Alessio; and Baciccio's *Death of Saint Francis Xavier* in Sant' Agostino, c. 1685.

21. Mâle (323–24) observed that the death of Saint Joseph was a popular subject in the Baroque period. An account of the saint's death is found in the Infancy Gospels (*The Apocryphal New Testament*, 85).

22. The *Ars Moriendi* is discussed in chapter 7. Bernini admired Poussin's painting of a death scene, *Extreme Unction*, during his trip to France in 1665 (Chantelou, 79).

23. For additional information on this subject, see Giachi, xx.

24. Jacobus de Voragine (449) reported that Mary died at the age of sixty.

25. The statue was interpreted as a dying Cleopatra because of the snake bracelet on her left forearm. For

information on the history of this sculpture, see Brummer, 154–84, and Haskell and Penny, 184–87.

26. Chantelou, 8 June, 25.

27. The Barberini Faun, which to my knowledge has never been interpreted as a dying figure, may be classified as "languid." The Antique statue (a copy of a Pergamene bronze of the late third or early second century B.C., or perhaps an original) was in the Barberini collection at least from 1628 until the nineteenth century. Displayed on its back (c. 1642–79), this sensual figure may have had an impact upon the *Ludovica*. The traditional idea that it was restored by Bernini has been questioned by Haskell and Penny, 202–5.

28. The *Slaves* of Michelangelo were in the collection of Cardinal Richelieu from 1632 to 1749. Chantelou does not mention an excursion to Richelieu's estate.

29. Chantelou, 4 October, 250.

30. Barolsky, 1–2, suggests that the *Ludovica* was influenced by the figure of the Virgin without discussing the subject any further.

31. See chapter 6 for further discussion.

32. Askew.

33. The point must be considered seriously in any study of Baroque imagery. The interconnections of the images examined in this category illuminate the importance of the Passion of Christ and Mary in the lives of the saints.

34. See discussion of the *Theresa* in chapter 6.

35. See reproduction in G. Bernini, *Giovanni Lanfranco (1582–1647)*, Parma, 1982, pl. 59, 221.

36. For an illustration, see Hibbard, 1983, 57, pl. 30.

37. Sommer (33–34). claims that this engraving is a visual source for the *Ludovica*. The print is not a specific source, and in fact is more like the *Theresa*.

38. The kinship with the statue of the *beata* may be explained in part by Bernini's role as adviser to Baciccio at Sant' Andrea al Quirinale. The expression of ecstatic submission on the face of the dying Jesuit and the position of his head are recollective of the *Ludovica*. The juxtaposition of a dying figure with a glory of angels was also inspired by the Altieri Chapel, its statue of Ludovica situated beneath an altarpiece whose upper reaches are populated by angelic creatures. Two works closely related to this painting are Baciccio's *Death of Saint Francis Xavier* in Sant' Agostino (c. 1685) and Carlo Maratta's rendering of the same subject (1679) in the Gesù. These pictures depict the saint as already dead.

Chapter 5

1. Among the scholars who advocate this point of view are: Menichella, 58; H. Hibbard, "Ludovica Albertoni: Art and Life," text of a public lecture, 1983: Weibel, 89; and Fraschetti, 397. V. Martinelli (1953, 165–66) claims that Ludovica's death is tormented.

2. Sommer, 30–38.

3. Blunt, 79–81.

4. *Congregatione*. The Apostolic Brief is traditionally read at beatification ceremonies. See Brinktrine, 47.

5. Pauolo.

6. See Santini.

7. Bernini's early interest in this motif is demonstrated in the Leipzig sketch. See chapter 3.

8. See Pauolo, 56, 57, 61, 134, 156, 162, 183, 190, 217, and Santini, 11, 12, 24, 27, 32.

9. Santini, 11.

10. Pauolo, chap. 10, 156–77.

11. Santini, 13, 33, 37.

12. Ibid., 7.

13. Ibid., 34, and Pauolo, 176.

14. There are numerous seventeenth-century representations of Charity as a nursing mother. (See examples in Tapié.) Bernini depicted Charity as a woman with two babies in the tomb of Urban VIII (1628–47), and as a mother with a single infant in the tomb of Alexander VII (1671–78).

15. The theme of Roman Charity, extremely popular in the seventeenth century, is based on Valerius Maximus's ancient Roman tale of filial piety, in which Pero saves her imprisoned father from starvation by nursing him. Roman Charity appears, for example, in Caravaggio's *Seven Works of Mercy* (1606) in Pio Monte della Madonna della Misericordia in Naples (illustrated in Hibbard, 1983, 214, fig. 138; 218, fig. 143).

16. Sommer, 30–38.

17. Ibid., 35.

18. Mâle, 87.

19. For additional information on Trithemius, see Kleinschmidt, 142, 150ff. The touching sentiments of this rosary are echoed in the writings of Jean Thomas de Saint-Cyrille (*Mater honorificato, sancta Anna,* Naples, 1655, 125). Mâle (352) stated that the altarpiece in San Francesco a Ripa reflects the influence of Jean Thomas.

20. The rosary is published in German in Mâle, 311–13.

21. The cult of Saint Anne was extremely popular in the seventeenth century. Among theologians who wrote in favor of honoring Mary's mother was Jean Thomas de Saint-Cyrille and the Franciscan of the Strict Observance Jacobus Polius (*Exegeticum historicum S. Annae,* Cologne, 1640). The *processi* (53, no. 19) reports that the *beata* was the "mirror and model of Roman widows." See also Santini, 34–35.

22. Pauolo, 156–77, 231, and Santini, 34.

23. Anne and Joachim gave one-third of their income to the church, one-third to the poor and kept the remainder. Saint Ignacio de Loyola (*The Spiritual Exercises,* 153) cites Anne and Joachim as examples of almsgiving. See

also A. Dunbar, *A Dictionary of Saintly Women*, I, London, 1904, 65–67. For additional information on the education of the Virgin, see Mâle, 350–51. A discussion of seventeenth-century confraternities devoted to Saint Anne may be found in Piazza, 554–55.

24. Erra, 47. See also Visconti, 617–18, and Schiavo, 193. The chapel was open to the public in 1705, and one year later Giambattista Vaccondo composed an ode praising it (*I pregi dell'architettura,* Rome, 1706).

25. Santini (13) spoke of a book used by Saint Michael in the Last Judgment to determine the fate of the resurrected dead.

26. For example, Bernini was known to be fond of Francis de Sales's *Introduction to the Devout Life* (1956; first published in 1609). Bernini's admiration for this treatise is recorded in Chantelou, 139. Gianlorenzo told his French host that this excellent book was preferred by the pope (Alexander VII).

27. This text is discussed in Praz, 152–54.

28. See, for example, Juan de la Cruz, 1945, and Theresa of Jesus, 1957.

29. Enggass (25) remarks that the colors of the altarpiece become richer and brighter against the *Ludovica*, and the whiteness of Bernini's statue is intensified before the strong hues of Gaulli's painting.

30. The biographer related that Ludovica, inflamed with the fire of charity, was spiritually cleansed by prayer and penance. The progress of Ludovica's mystical life may be traced in the following chapters in Pauolo: "Della grand'Humilità di Ludovica," chap. 5, 64–82; "Purità del Cuore della Beata Ludovica," chap. 6, 83–96; "Stimando molto la B. Ludovica il tempo, & essendo inimica dell'otio, occupava se stessa in continovi essercitij spirituali," chap. 7, 96–110; "Dell'Oratione, e meditatione della B. Ludovica," chap. 8, 111–41; "Quanto gran zelo havesse la Beata Ludovica della salute dell'anime," chap. 9, 142–55, and "Della Carità della B. Ludovica verso iddio, & il prossimo," chap. 10, 156–77.

31. Ibid., 49–83, 96–110, 111–41, 142–55, 178–87.

32. Ibid., 60; see also 4, 6, 8. Santini (frontispiece) referred to Ludovica as "refulgent" in a caption beneath a print of the *beata*.

33. Juan de la Cruz, III, 1945, 30. Theresa ("Interior Castles," II, 1957, 330) explains how the darkness is driven out of the soul, which, having achieved a state of grace, is filled with light. The female Spanish saint ("Way of Perfection," II, 1957, 86) also described the pathway to God as the pathway to light.

34. Santini, 11.

35. Pauolo, 264–65.

36. Santini, 12–14, 27, 29, 33, 36.

37. Juan de la Cruz, III, 1945, 104.

38. Ibid., 25–26.

39. Santini, 35–36.

40. Ibid., 28–29.

41. Francis de Sales, *Devout Life,* 70.

42. Juan de la Cruz, III, 19.

43. Francis de Sales, *Love,* 478.

44. In Theresa's world, the fire of love does not consume with its flames, nor is it extinguished by water. The images of fire and water are employed by the Spanish mystics as a metaphor of the divine union, since fire merges imperceptibly and completely with fire, and water unites with water. Petersson (27, 32, 41–42) discussed the use of the metaphor of fire and water in Theresa's writings; for examples, see Theresa, "Way of Perfection," II, 1957, 79–81, and Juan de la Cruz, III, 1945, 64–65.

45. Theresa, "Interior Castles," II, 1957, 294. The Spanish saint is describing the Sixth Mansion (the highest level being the Seventh Mansion).

46. For example, see Theresa's discussion of raptures granted in the Sixth Mansion ("Interior Castles," II, 1957, 293–97). See also "Way of Perfection," II, 1957, 86, and "Life," 101.

47. Theresa's "Conceptions of the Love of God," II, 1957, 384. This work, written between 1571 and 1573, is based on the love poetry of the Canticles. Sommer (33–34) claims that Ludovica's pose was borrowed from Hermann Hugo's *Pia Desideria* (1624), a Jesuit devotional work based on the Song of Songs. The posture of the *beata* is also reminiscent of Theresa's description of the third degree of prayer (the highest level of prayer being the fourth) ("Life," I, 101): "In this state it is well for the soul to abandon itself wholly into the arms of God. If He is pleased to take it to Heaven, let it go."

48. See Petersson (93, 129) on Theresa's use of the combination of excitement and quiescence.

49. Francis de Sales, *Love*, 189.

50. Theresa ("Interior Castles," II, 288–91, 295–97, 310, 315–22, 331–35) describes the "intellectual vision" in the Sixth and Seventh Mansions. See also "Life," I, 110–11, 130, 333.

51. Theresa, "Interior Castles," II, 332–33.

52. Francis de Sales, *Love,* preface, xxviii, and also 227–29.

Chapter 6

1. Baldinucci (1948), 130: ". . . la bella statua della B. Ludovica Albertoni in atto di morire, la quale si ammira oggi della suntuosa cappella in S. Francesca a Ripa." C. Engass (Baldinucci, 1966, 64) translated "in atto di morire" as the "throes of death." D. Bernini (164) also uses the words "atto di morire" in characterizing the sculpture. See also Ludovica da Modena, f. 40, and Appendix I.

2. Blunt, 79–80.
3. Ibid.
4. Ibid.
5. According to the *processi* of 1672 (10, no. 7), a cross, four brass candlesticks, and two vases of flowers were kept on the altar in the Altieri Chapel. King, (100) informs us that a cross, having an image of the crucified Christ turned toward the celebrating priest, is placed on every altar on which mass is said. According to Jungmann, a crucifix has been prescribed for the altar since the eleventh century.
6. "If we have died with him [Christ], we shall also live with him" (2 Timothy 2:11–12). For additional information on Catholic concepts of death, see Rahner; Didier; and Delumeau, 48.
7. Francis de Sales, (*Love*, 252, see also 545–46).
8. Santini, 29. Theresa's life was a daily dying, by which her soul died to itself to live in Christ. See Petersson, 20.
9. Ludovica's death is discussed in *Congregazione*, 32–38, no. 15. See Appendix V.
10. Ibid., 53, no. 20. See Appendix V.
11. Santini, 28. The Church has always believed that the saints go directly to heaven to share in the joys of the beatific vision. According to Catholic doctrine, a purified soul united with God is immediately received into heaven, where the triune deity may be seen face to face. As intercessor in paradise, Ludovica must have experienced this joyous sight, since the power to act as intermediary is granted through the beatific vision.
12. Ibid., 13, 29. Theresa ("Life," I, 119) says: ". . . the Lord gathers up the soul, just (we might say) as the clouds gather up the vapours from the earth, and raises it up till it is right out of itself (I have heard that it is in this way that the clouds or the sun gather up the vapours) and the cloud rises to Heaven and takes the soul with it, and begins to reveal to it things concerning the Kingdom that He has prepared for it." This passage probably inspired Santini's description of Ludovica's ascent to God.
13. Santini, 29.
14. Theresa related that there is no physical pain in the fourth degree of prayer ("Life," I, 105–11) and in the Sixth and Seventh Mansions ("Interior Castles," II, 325–28, 341–43). There is a great deal of spiritual torment, however, in the Sixth Mansion. Francis de Sales (*Love*, 280) also speaks of the suspension of the faculties occurring when the soul is united with God.
15. See Pauolo, 215–28, and Appendix II.
16. See Coptic texts in *The Apocryphal New Testament*, 195–220.
17. Ibid., 208–9 and Appendix V, no. 5.
18. For a discussion of Mary's role in the Passion, see Carol (both March and June 1943). In the first article Carol discusses the doctrine advocated by the Franciscans that through Mary's sacrifice on Calvary the Virgin satisfied *de congruo* for the sins of mankind, just as Christ accomplished redemption *de condigno* through his Passion, the Madonna assuming the role as co-redemptrix with her son. Perhaps this concept is best summed up by the Spanish exegete Jerome di Guevara (quote from ibid., 6–7): "Whatever has come to men in the form of grace because of the death of Christ the same thing [has come to them] because of Mary's Passion." Hamburgh asserts that the posture of the swooning Virgin constitutes a reiteration of Christ's pose. This motif in which the Madonna's posture repeats that of the suffering Jesus is also employed in seventeenth-century paintings of the Lamentation. Mary's role in redemption was challenged by Adam Widenfeld (1618–78) in 1673 in *Monita salutaria Beatae Virginis Mariae ad cultores suos indiscretos*. Widenfeld's publication was officially condemned on 19 June 1674, and among his opponents was the Jesuit Paul Segneri, who wrote a treatise expressing his views on the subject, *Il divoto di Maria*, published in Bologna in 1677. For a discussion of this controversy, see Guibert, 381–82.
19. Francis de Sales, *Love*, 310. Another description of Mary's martyrdom by Francis de Sales (*Love*, 307–9) is worth quoting: "[Mary contemplated Christ] until the fire of God's love consumed her utterly—a holocaust of sweetness. In other words, she died of love, her soul enraptured, transported into the embrace of her Son's love. How lovingly her love led to death! . . . she died consumed with charity—a perfect holocaust for all the sins of the world."
20. Mary is traditionally viewed as the embodiment of charity. See Francis de Sales, *Love*, 134.
21. Hibbard (see chapter 5, note 1, above) notes this detail and mentions this work as a possible source for the *Ludovica* but does not discuss the meaning of the gesture.
22. See E. Panofsky, 1927, 290–94. Brauer and Wittkower (166–68) considered this drawing to be a sketch for Bernini's *Sangue di Cristo*, dated to 1670. The theme of the double intercession was popularized by the devotional work *Speculum humanae salvationis* of 1324, based on a passage from a book by Ernaldus Abbot of Bonneval (d. 1156). The passage translated by M. Meiss ("An Early Altarpiece from the Cathedral of Florence," *Bulletin of the Metropolitan Museum of Art* 12 [1954], 306) reads: "O Man, you . . . have secure access to God when the Mother is before her Son, and the Son before his Father. The Mother showed her breast to her Son, the Son showed his wounds to his Father: there where the proofs of love are so many no one can be denied."
23. Carol, June 1943, 155.
24. Lavin, 1980, 69.
25. Santini's description (13) refers to Apocalypse 12:1–2. The wings possessed by Ludovica are those of *amor dei* and *amor proximi*. Pauolo (112, 114, 118–19) also speaks of the *beata*'s devotion to Mary.

26. Santini, 7. This passage was taken from the Ode to Ludovica.

27. Ibid., 27.

28. Pauolo, 112–16, 118, 120, 122. In the seventeenth century, the emphasis was upon the presence of the Virgin and Christ in one's life, especially the mother and son of the Passion. Widely practiced in the Baroque period, the Spiritual Exercises (1548) of Saint Ignatius Loyola called for meditations upon the life of the Madonna and Jesus, with emphasis upon the sacrifice on Calvary. Catholic devotion emphasized the importance of adopting Mary and the Savior as models of holiness, the imitation of whom led to salvation.

29. Ibid., 57.

30. Ibid., 230.

31. Ibid., 229–30. Her last words were taken from Luke 23:46. According to Francis de Sales (*Love,* 298, 301–2, 387, 394–95), these words signify a complete submission to the will of God.

32. P. Kelly (in *New Catholic Encyclopedia,* IV, 695, s.v. "Preparation for Death," 1967) informs us: "There is no better way to prepare for death's sacrifice than to associate with Christ's Passion."

33. For additional information on the dedication of chapels to Saint Anne, see Kleinschmidt, 426.

34. The attribution of this sculpture is problematical. See M. D'Onofrio, 56, and Malignaggi, 25–26.

35. The motif may be seen, for example, in the quattrocento tomb of Bishop de Coco in Santa Maria sopra Minerva. See chapter 4.

36. Jacob, 121.

37. Saint Thomas Aquinas believed that the soul aids in the resurrection of the body. See discussion of this theological concept in Michel, "Resurrection," 2557–71. According to M. Redle (in *New Catholic Encyclopedia,* IV, 193, s.v. "Beatific Vision," 1967), the beatified soul gives life to the glorified body of the Resurrection.

38. *Congregazione,* 29, no. 14, and also 34, no. 15. See Appendix V.

39. Santini, 11, 13, 14, 17, 18, 21, 24, 29, 33, 36, 37.

40. According to Duns Scotus (1265?–1308), a resignation to one's death can lessen the trials of purgatory. See O'Connor, 31. Ludovica's suffering during her illness may also be considered purgative. According to Catholic thought, sickness is viewed as a time of great spiritual travail, a kind of purgatory in which one's pain takes on the dimensions of that of Christ on Calvary. For example, Cornelio Musso in the sixteenth century declared that those who do not receive "qualche purgatorio" in this life are most unfortunate. A similar sentiment was expressed by Girolamo Cacciaguerra (*Lettere spirituali,* Venice, 1584), who urges the sick not to call upon the services of a doctor because the more one suffers in life, so much the less will be the punishment of purgatory. For a discussion of concepts of purgatory in the fifteenth and sixteenth centuries, see Tenenti, 319–26. The seventeenth-century Jesuit writer Biverius addresses this concept in his history of ancient and modern martyrs, *Sacrum sanctuarium crucis et patientiae,* Antwerp, 1634. The book is dedicated "to the sick and to those who in suffering learn how to live and die well" and advises the afflicted to endure "with the patience of a martyr, but with the joy of being associated with the Passion of the Saviour." See Mâle, 148–49.

41. E. Panofsky (1964, 228) remarked that the idea that death opens the door to a better life is pervasive. In describing death, Bellarmino (1847, preface, xii–xiii) referred to the "gate leading from prison to a Kingdom." and Marchese (91) to the "door of our salvation." In Eustachius de Rosario's print of the *Ars Moriendi,* the art of dying well (Augsburg, 1677), a skeleton enters the sickroom through a doorway inscribed "Aeternitatis aditus." See Brisemeister, fig. 163. For the *Ars Moriendi,* see chapter 7. The meaning of the arcade in tomb sculpture is discussed in K. Cohen, *Metamorphosis of a Death Symbol: The Transi Tomb in the Late Middle Ages and the Renaissance,* Berkeley, 1973, 7.

42. Hall (286) reported that in Late Antiquity the snake was interpreted as a symbol of eternity and was thus associated with Saturn, the personification of time, and Janus, god of the new year.

43. For general information on the ancient deity, see *The New Century Classical Handbook,* ed. C. Avery, New York, 1962, 611, and *The Oxford Classical Dictionary,* ed. N. Hammond and H. Scullard, Oxford, 1970, 561.

44. M. Lavin (1981, 198–200) interpreted the Virgin in Filippo Lippi's *Madonna and Child with Two Angels* (Uffizi, Florence) as the *Janua Caeli.* According to Dobias (70), the altarpiece of the Fonseca Chapel is related to the Gate of Salvation of the litany.

45. For example, Andrea dell'Orcagna's figure of Charity holds a flaming heart in one hand while nursing a baby. Orcagna's tabernacle relief in Or San Michele is illustrated in Tapié, 32. The motif of the flaming heart is discussed in Hall, *Dictionary,* 146, and Praz, 151ff. According to H. Roeder (*Saints and Their Attributes,* Chicago, 1956, 192–93), flaming hearts are attributes of Saint Augustine (d. 430) and Saint Catherine of Jesus (d. 1594). See also G. Roeder, *Dizionario illustrato dei simboli,* Milan, 1922.

46. Juan de la Cruz, III, 21.

47. M. Levi D'Ancona, 312–16, 317, 318. The pomegranate is also a symbol of the elect in heaven (316). It might be noted that Giotto's figure of Charity in the Arena Chapel (c. 1306) holds a basket of roses and pomegranates and hands one of the fruits to God. See illustration in J. Stubblebine, ed., *Giotto: The Arena Chapel Frescoes,* New York, 1969, pl. 58.

48. The symbolism of the pomegranate in sepulchral art is mentioned in Cohen, *Metamorphosis of a Death*

Symbol, 177, and S'Jacob, 49, 164. In speaking of the *Ludovica*, Hibbard (222) states: "The frieze of pomegranates signifies the immortality to which her soul is passing."

49. Alanus de Insulis speaks of the fruit's connection with Mary: "The pomegranate is red outside and has many seeds in one fruit; so we can contemplate the multitude of good works of the Virgin Mary enclosed by her faith in our Lord's Passion" (quoted in Levi d'Ancona, 315 n. 47).

50. Since seraphs are traditionally depicted with six wings and cherubs with four, it would be difficult to identify the angelic heads in the Altieri Chapel specifically with either one or the other of these divine creatures. Seraphs, however, are often associated with the element of fire. (See G. Davidson, *A Dictionary of Angels,* New York, 1967, 267.) Cherubs and seraphs are viewed as agents of fire and purification by Dionysius the Areopagite (25–29, 35–42, 52, 56–57).

51. Santini, 25. Pauolo (54) states that Ludovica was "filled by God with a spirit wholly seraphic."

52. Jacob (115) mentions this function performed by angels in sepulchral monuments.

53. Baldinucci, *Vita di Bernini,* 101.

54. The smiling angel of the Cornaro Chapel is discussed in Lavin (1980, 112, n. 14).

55. Lavin (1980, 113–18) convincingly interprets her transverberation as her death, offering as evidence the hymns composed to Theresa by Urban VIII.

56. See Lavin (1980), figs., 263–88.

57. See Hamburgh.

58. Lavin (1980, 114) explained that Theresa is a martyr "not in the physical sense of dying for her faith, but in the spiritual sense of dying of her faith." Theresa ("Life," I, 123–24) described her own spiritual pain as a martyrdom. The Spanish mystic ("Thoughts and Maxims," III, 269) quoted Saint Chrysostom on the subject of martyrdom: "Perfect martyrdom is not accomplished by the shedding of blood alone. Martyrdom also consists in true abstinence from sins and in the practice and observance of the commandments of God."

59. Lavin (1980, 106) mentioned Theresa's resemblance to Saint Francis.

60. Flaming hearts also appear in the Raimondi Chapel of San Pietro in Montorio. Saint Francis is associated with the flaming heart because, according to a prayer said to have been composed by him, he asked to be inflamed with God's love so that he could die for the sake of the deity's love. This prayer is quoted in Lavin (1980, 49, n. 94). J. Reymond (*Le Bernini,* Paris, 1911, 63) and Kauffmann (145–46) both note a resemblance between a study for the *Theresa* (Leipzig 7882v) and Francesco Baratta's *Ecstasy of Saint Francis* (1642–46) in the Raimondi Chapel.

61. See Askew, 280–306. Francis de Sales (*Love,* 263) related: "He [Francis of Assisi] experienced a martyrdom in his flesh through the enkindling of his soul."

62. Theresa, "Life," I, 192–93. Theresa's pain is a martyrdom, the trials of which she desires always to suffer. S. Warma ("Ecstasy and Vision: Two Concepts Connected with Bernini's *Teresa,*" *Art Bulletin* 66, no. 3 [1984], 508–11) proposed that the posture of the *Theresa* reflects that the Spanish saint is experiencing a vision, as well as an ecstatic transport.

63. Hibbard, 222.

64. Wittkower (13) claimed that the emphasis upon verticals and horizontals in the *Ludovica* is typical of Bernini's late style.

65. Blunt (78) postulated that Theresa is shown in the second stage of prayer and Ludovica depicted in the fourth. Hibbard (see chapter 5, note 1) claimed that Ludovica was experiencing bodily pain.

Chapter 7

1. Wright.

2. According to P. Molinari (in *New Catholic Encyclopedia,* XII, 972, s.v. "Saints, Legends of the," 1967), the saints, having died in Jesus, complete the work of redemption as members of the "Mystical Body of Christ."

3. Pauolo, 203–4. For another description of her communion, see also 131–33. The enkindling of the heart at mass was a *topos* in the biographies of contemporary saints. See Marchese, 1671, 55, 114, 135, 138–39. This description calls to mind the communion of Bonaventure in which the Host was said to have entered not his mouth but his heart. (See Mâle, 484).

4. Boncampagni, IV, 488–90, and Mazzara, 154–55.

5. The papal bull is published in Wadding, XXVI, 78–79.

6. Plenary indulgences may be granted only by a pope. For further information on indulgences, see Pohle and Preuss, 253–59.

7. For information on Saint Clare, see A. Iacovelli, *Vita di Santa Chiara d'Assisi,* Assisi, 1975, 130–36.

8. Pauolo, 176. This description reminds one of a passage from the Scriptures (John 6:35): "I am the bread of life: he that cometh to me shall never hunger. . . ."

9. Quoted from Saint John Chrysostom in Bellarmino, *Art of Dying Well,* 105. The passages from Bellarmino quoted in this study have been checked for accuracy of meaning with a seventeenth-century Italian edition (see Bibliography). For additional discussion on angels and the mass, see Francis de Sales, *Devout Life,* 72, and Mâle, 301.

10. Pauolo, 131, 139.

11. See Rome, Roma Calcografia, 228.

12. The offices held by Paluzzi include Treasurer (*Camerlengo*) of the Holy Church, Secretary of Briefs, Prefect of Propaganda, Protector of the Augustinian and Dominican Orders, Legate to Avignon and Urbino, and Governor of Tivoli. See Stella, 562.

13. Paluzzi had great ambitions for his family. In 1674 he made an unsuccessful attempt to place his nephew Gaspare on the throne of Poland. The cardinal, receiving an annual income of more than 100,000 *scudi*, was not only criticized for his excessive salary but was also accused of procuring large profits for the Colonna and Corsini, powerful families to whom the Altieri were now allied through marriages arranged by Paluzzi. See Stella, 562–63; Trivellini, 4; and Pastor, 445.

14. G. Gizzi, 3–6.

15. Stella, 563. The cardinal had also incurred the resentment of Christina of Sweden, who was slighted in 1674 at the Opening of the Holy Door and the benediction of the Agnus Dei. After the death of Clement X on 22 July 1676, Cardinal Paluzzi was no longer a powerful force in Rome. His will (Rome, Archivio di Stato, *Stato dell'Eredità della Ch. me. del Cardinal Paluzzi,* busta 1, 20 June 1698) reveals that his wealth by this date was not excessive.

16. Boncampagni (IV, 481) and Bertini (25) inform us that Baldassare helped the orphans and prostitutes of Rome, contributing to such charitable institutions as Santa Croce della Penitenza on the Lungara and the hospice of Trinità dei Pellegrini e Convalescenti.

17. The accounts of Bernini's biographers are quoted in English and Italian in Lavin, 1972, 160–62, 184–86. An insightful investigation of this subject is offered by Lavin (1972, and 1973, 729–36), to whom I am most indebted.

18. See Baldinucci's account quoted in Lavin, 1972, 160.

19. Bernini recommended this book to Chantelou. See Chantelou.

20. Thomas à Kempis, 50.

21. Nor, of course, was this preoccupation unique to the seventeenth century. For a discussion of concepts of death in the Baroque period, see Vovelle. See notes 26 and 27 below.

22. See Vovelle, 65, and Costanzo "Mors victa," in *Il gran teatro del mondo,* 70. Francis de Sales (*Devout Life,* "Fifth Meditation: Death," 30–31) says: "Consider the uncertainty of the day of your death. One day, my soul, you must depart from this body. When will it be? In winter or summer? In town or country? During the day or night? With or without warning? As the result of illness or accident? Shall I have a chance to go to confession? Shall I be assisted by a priest? Unhappily I know none of these things: only one thing is certain, I will die, and sooner than I imagine."

23. Vovelle (67–68, 96–97). Among the works cited by this scholar are *Pensez-y bien, ou réflexions sur les quatre fins dernières,* Paris, 1737; L. Grignion de Montfort, *Oeuvres complètes,* Paris, 1966; and Lalemant.

24. See Ignacio di Loyola, 76–77, and Francis de Sales, *Devout Life,* 30–38. See also Vovelle, 68–70. Describing heaven, hell, and the Last Judgment in graphic terms, literary works may have been employed as aids in meditation upon death. For example, see Giovanni Battista Manni (first moderator of the Jesuit Congregation of the Congregazione Spirituali della Buona Morte), 1670 and 1673, and *Il tribunale intolerabile di Dio Giudicante,* Venice, 1671.

25. On the use of the skull and cross, see Vovelle, 67–68. Pope Alexander VII (1655–67) is said to have kept a skull for this purpose in his bedroom.

26. These devotional guides, popular from the fifteenth to the mid-sixteenth century, declined in number in the late sixteenth century, and increased in the early seventeenth century. Lavin (1972, 163–71, 183–84) demonstrates that Bernini's own demise was in some respects a "literal enactment" of the *Ars Moriendi.* For additional information on the *Ars Moriendi,* see Tenenti, 80–138, O'Connor, and Rudolf, *Ars Moriendi.*

27. In English guides the words "crafte," "art," or "cunnynge" were used. See Lavin, 1972, 163. Extended versions of the *Ars Moriendi* consisting of the six parts mentioned here were used in Italy. See O'Connor (157 n. 28) and Lavin (1973).

28. An excellent example of a seventeenth-century devotional work of this type certainly known to Bernini is *De arte bene moriendi* (1620) by Roberto Bellarmino, a theologian whose portrait was carved by the master in 1622. This guide is distinguished by the fact that it was written by a Jesuit who was decidedly more worldly than the monkish authors who preceded him in this genre of literature.

29. See Lavin, 1973, 164. For additional information on the activities of this society, see Piazza, 684–87, and Pecchiai, 1952, 314.

30. Lavin, 1973, 164.

31. The inscriptions are reported and interpreted in Lavin, 1973, 159, 167–68. Taken from Paul's Epistle to the Hebrews, the inscription reads: "The blood of Christ, who offered himself without spot to God, will purge our conscience."

32. The inscription is quoted from Maria Maddalena de'Pazzi (V. Puccini, *Vita della Madre suor Maria Maddalena de'Pazzi fiorentina,* Florence, 1609, 241ff.; cited in Lavin, 1973, 168 n. 27): "I offer you, Eternal Father, the Blood of the humanity of your Word: I offer it to you yourself, Divine Word: I also offer it to you, Holy Spirit; and if anything is wanting in me, I offer it to you, Mary, that you may present it to the Most Holy Trinity."

33. Marchese, *Unica Speranza,* 3–24, 24–30, 82–91.

34. "The Blood of Christ inflames the heart to embrace the Truth." Ibid., 116, and 117–25.

35. Ibid., 91–102.

36. Bernini's design and Marchese's book were apparently intended to complement one another. See Lavin, 1980, 166–67.

37. Also missing is the lighted candle often represented in the hand of *moriens,* the dying man. The skeleton of death is shown sitting on the bed in the illustration accompanying Girolamo Savonarola's *Predica dell'arte del bene morire* (1496). See Tenenti's discussion (444–51) of the use of the skeleton in Italian representations of the *Ars Moriendi.* Kauffmann (330) saw the *Ludovica* as an example of the saintly death in the *Ars Moriendi* tradition, citing such features as her "nearly fainting" posture, "weary upturned eyes, open mouth," and her "attitude of longing for paradise in penitent humility." The statue in its recess is associated with the *Ars Moriendi* by Lavin (1972, 171 n. 43), who proposed that the altarpiece functions as a devotional image to the *Ludovica* beneath it. See also Lavin, 1973, 171. Although the sculpture must be understood in the context of the ideal death and the *Ars Moriendi*, the *beata* does not, in my opinion, resemble the relatively prosaic demeanor of *moriens* (cf. Figs. 48 and 49). Unlike *moriens,* the figure of Ludovica does not look at the devotional images. Moreover, the dying person in the *Ars Moriendi* does not use a picture of the Holy Family as a devotional aid but as an image of the Crucifixion. However, the Virgin and Child do appear in these illustrations as apparitions (see Tenenti, fig. 33). Lavin (1973, 171) demonstrates that the Mater Dolorosa who assists at the bedside and the image of the Crucifixion—both elements appearing in prints of the *Ars Moriendi*—are combined in Bernini's *Sangue di Cristo,* the devotional image contemplated by the artist at his bedside.

38. After 1650 allegories of death, such as skulls and skeletons, were prominent features of tombs and funeral catafalques (see Huxley, 167–73).

39. Bernini used skeletons in the papal tombs of Urban VIII (1628–47) and Alexander VII (1671–78), and in the sepulchral monuments of Alessandro Valtrini (San Lorenzo in Damaso, c. 1639) and Ippolito Merenda (San Giacomo alla Lungarna; c. 1640).

40. This concept of death is discussed in reference to Urban's tomb by Panofsky (1964, 221–36) and in terms of the *Theresa* by Lavin (1980, 129–33). Panofsky demonstrates that the skeleton of death inscribing the pope's name in a book is not a "destroyer of life" but rather a means by which the pope's fame will be immortalized.

41. The passage is quoted in Panofsky, 230. n. 42.

42. Borromeo's ideas on this subject were taken up by Vincenzo Auruccio (*Rituario per quelli che havendo cura d'anime . . .*). See discussion in Tenenti, 344, 347.

43. Bellarmino, 1847, preface, xii–xiii.

44. *Avviso* of 2 August 1670, published in *Roma* 18 (1940), 95; quoted in Haskell, 162.

45. See chapter 2.

46. Tenenti, 344.

47. *Il S. Alessio,* music by Stefano Landi, libretto by Giulio Rospigliosi (the future Clement IX), presented to Alessandro Carlo di Polonia, published by Paolo Masotti in 1634.

48. Ibid., Act 2, scene 10.

49. "Chi puo seguir' il Sol, l'ombra non segua." Ibid., Act 2, scene 9.

50. See the account of the death of Saint Rosa of Lima in Marchese, 1671, 148. See also the demise of Santa Francesca Romana reported by the Jesuit Virgilio Cepari (*Vita di santa Francesca fondatrice dell'Oblate di Torre de'Specchi,* 1675, busta 1697, fols. 345–57, Biblioteca Angelica, Rome).

51. The figure of Hope in Renaissance art is usually depicted with her eyes raised and her hands clasped in prayer.

52. Hibbard (227) remarks that the dying Ludovica "seems to exemplify faith, hope, and love of God" but does not elaborate. In Eustachius de Rosario's print of 1677 of the *Ars Moriendi*, the dying man is accompanied by three allegorical figures: Faith, shown with a cross, chalice, and Host; Hope, with an anchor; and Charity, with a child and a flaming heart. See Briesemeister, fig. 163.

53. Bernini had earlier recorded his intention that the *Sangue di Cristo* serve as a personal offering "useful to everyone." See dispatch to the court of Modena, published by Imparato, 142; Fraschetti, 420; and Lavin, 1973, 164 n. 17. Lavin (181–84) demonstrates that Bernini's last work, the bust of the Savior, embodied the master's personal faith in Christ as a "mediator in the process of salvation."

Bibliography

Apocryphal New Testament, trans. M. Rhodes James. Oxford, 1966.

Argan, Giulio Carlo. "S. Maria in Campitelli." *Commentari* 2 (1960), 74–86.

Arisio, E. *Memorie sulla vita di Clemente X.* Rome, 1863.

———. *Guide de Roma.* Rome, 1887.

Arturi du Monstier, P. *Martirologium francescanum* ... Paris, 1653; Venice, 1899.

———. *Sacrum gynecaeum amplissimum.* Paris, 1657.

Askew, Pamela. "The Angelic Consolation of S. Francis of Assisi in Post-Tridentine Italian Painting." *Journal of the Warburg and Courtauld Institutes* 32 (1969), 280–306.

Auruccio, V. *Rituario per quelli che havendo cura d'anime.* Rome, 1611.

Baglione, Giovanni. *Le vite de'pittori scultori et architetti dal pontificato di Gregorio XIII del 1572. In fino a tempi di Papa Urbano Ottavo nel 1642.* Rome, 1935.

Baldinucci, Filippo. *Vita di Bernini (1682).* Milan, 1948.

———. *The Life of Bernini,* trans. C. Enggass. University Park, Pa., 1966.

Barbier de Montault, C. *L'année liturgique à Rome.* Rome, 1862.

Barolsky, Paul. *Daniele da Volterra.* New York, 1979.

Bellarmino, Roberto. *Opera Omnia.* 12 vols. Paris, 1870–74.

———. *The Art of Dying Well (1620),* trans. J. Dalton. London, 1847.

———. *Dell'arte di ben morire,* trans. M. Cervini. Florence, 1620.

Bellori, G. P. *Le vite de'pittori, scultori e architetti moderni.* Rome, 1672.

Bernini, Domenico. *Vita del Cavalier Gio, Lorenzo Bernino.* Rome, 1713.

Bernstock, Judith. "Bernini's Memorials to Ippolito Merenda and Alessandro Valtrine." *Art Bulletin* 63, no. 2 (June 1981), 210–32.

Bertini, C. *La storia delle famiglie romane di Teodoro Amayden,* I. Rome, 1979.

Bjurström, Per, "Baroque Theater and the Jesuits." In *Baroque Art: The Jesuit Contribution.* New York, 1972, 99–110.

Blunt, Anthony. "Gianlorenzo Bernini: Illusionism and Mysticism." *Art History* 1, no. 1 (March 1978), 67–89.

Boncompagni, U. *Roma nel Rinascimento,* III and IV. Albano Laziale, 1929.

Brauer, H., and R. Wittkower. *Die Zeichnungen des Gianlorenzo Bernini.* Berlin, 1931.

Braun, Joseph. *Der Christliche Altar.* Hamburg, 1924.
Briesemeister, Dietrich. *Bilder des Todes.* W. Uhl, 1970.
Brinktrine, Johannes. *Die feierliche Papstmesse und die Zeremonien bei Selig Heiligsprechungen.* Rome, 1950.
Brummer, H. *The Statue Court in the Vatican Belvedere.* Stockholm, 1970.
Buchowiecki, Walther. *Handbuch der Kirchen Roms,* 3 vols. Vienna, 1974.
Callari, Luigi. *Palazzi di Roma.* Rome, 1944.
Carocci, G. *Lo stato della chiesa nella seconda metà del secolo XVI.* Milan, 1961.
Carol, J. B. "Our Lady's Part in the Redemption according to Seventeenth-Century Writers." *Franciscan Studies* 3 (March 1943), 3–20.
———. "Our Lady's Part in the Redemption according to Seventeenth-Century Writers." *Franciscan Studies* 3 (June 1943), 143–58.
Carreras, Emilia. "S. Francesco a Ripa." *Alma Roma* 20, nos. 1–2 (1979) 40–42.
Cavalli, Francesco. *Cose maravigliose città di Roma.* Rome, 1636.
Cecchelli, Carlo. *S. Francesco a Ripa,* II. Rome, 1924.
Celio, Gaspare. *Memoria fatta dal Sig. Gaspare Celio dell'habito di Christo, delli nomi dell'artefici delle pitture, che sono in alcune chiese, facciate e palazzi di Roma* (1638). Milan, 1967.
Chantelou, Paul Fréart de. *Diary of the Cavaliere Bernini's Visit to France,* trans. M. Corbett. Princeton, 1985.
Chastel, André. "Le Baroque et la mort." in *Atti del III Congresso internazionale di studi umanistici: Retorico e Barocco.* Rome, 1955.
Ciaconius, A. *Vitae et res gestae Pontificum Romanorum et S. R. E. Cardinalium,* II. Rome, 1677.
Congregatione Sacrorum Rituum. Romana Canonizationis Beatae Ludovicae Albertoniae Tertij Ordinis Sanct Francisci. Rome, 1671.
Contarino, Luigi. *L'antiquità di Roma.* Venice, 1575.
Costanzo, M. *Il gran teatro del mondo.* Milan, 1964.
Davies, G. *Renascence: The Sculptured Tombs of the Fifteenth Century in Rome.* London, 1910.
De Amadoris, Antonio. *I funere Clementis X. P.O.M. Oratio ad Eminentissimos S.R.E. Cardinales Habita in Basilica Vaticana Calend. Augusti.* Rome, 1676.
De Bildt, R. *Christine de Suède et le conclave de Clement X (1669–70).* Paris, 1906.
De Rossi, Giovanni Jacopo. *Disegni di vari altari e cappelle nelle chiese di Roma.* Rome, 1713.
Degni, P., and L. Porzio. "Il Convento di S. Francesco a Ripa in Roma." *Bollettino del centro di studi per la storia dell'architettura,* no. 27, 1980.
———. *Recupero di un monumento e del suo significato urbano: Tre interventi di restauro.* Rome, 1981, 45–48.
Delumeau, Jean. *Catholicism between Luther and Voltaire: A New View of the Counter-Reformation.* London, 1977.
Díaz Vara Calderón, G. *Grandezas y maravillas de la Incyta y Santa Ciudad de Roma.* Madrid, 1672.
Dionysius the Areopagite. *The Works of Dionysius the Areopagite,* trans. J. Parker. London, 1899.
Didier, Jean-Charles. *Death and the Christian,* trans. P. J. Hepburne-Scott. New York, 1961.
D'Onofrio, Cesare. *Roma nel seicento.* Florence, 1969.
D'Onofrio, Mario. *S. Andrea delle Fratte.* CXVI: *Le chiese di Roma,* 1971.
Enggass, Robert. *The Paintings of Baciccio.* University Park, Pa., 1964.
Erra, C. *Storia dell'imagine e chiesa di Santa Maria in Portico di Campitelli.* Rome, 1750.
Escobar, Mario. *Le dimore romane dei santi.* Bologna, 1964.
Esposita, Anna. "S. Francesca Bussa dei Ponziani: Società cittadina e religiosità laicale femminile a Roma nel secolo XV," unpublished manuscript.
Fagiolo dell'Arco, M. *Bernini.* Rome, 1967.
———. *La Roma dei Longhi,* exhibition catalogue. Rome, 1982.
Fasolo, F. *Le chiese di Roma nel '700,* I: *Trastevere.* Rome, 1949.
Fenlon, Dermot. *Heresy and Obedience in Tridentine Italy: Cardinal Pole and the Counter-Reformation.* London, 1972.
Ferrari, Giulio. *La tomba nell'arte italiana dal periodo preromano all'odierno.* Milan, 1917.
Florisoone, M. "Sur quelques récents problèmes de la peinture des XVII et XVIII siècles." *Revue des Arts,* no. 4 (1954), 249–56.
Forcella, V. *Iscrizioni delle chiese e d'altri edifici di Roma dal sècolo XI fino ai giorni nostri,* 14 vols. Rome, 1869–84.
Francis de Sales. *Introduction to the Devout Life,* trans. M. Day. Westminster, Md., 1956.
———. *The Love of God, A Treatise,* trans. V. Kerns. Westminster, Md., 1962.
———. *Trattato dell'Amor di Dio.* Rome, 1658.
Franzini, F. *Roma antica. . . .* Rome, 1668.
Fraschetti, S. *Il Bernini: La sua vita, la sua opera, il suo tempo.* Milan, 1900.
Frutaz, A. P. "Il culto delle reliquie e loro uso nella consacrazione degli altari." *Notitiae* 9 and 10 (1965), 309–15.
Gardner, Julian. "Arnolfo di Cambio and Roman Tomb Design." *Burlington Magazine* 115 (1973), 420–39.
Ghiberti, L. *I Commentari (1452–55).* II. Berlin, 1912.
Giachi, G. *S. Andrea al Quirinale.* In *Le chiese di Roma illustrata,* no. 107. Rome.
Gigli, G. *Diario Romano (1608–70).* Rome, 1958.

Gizzi, G. B. *Le due statue d'Alvernia: Discorso panegirico dedicato al card. A.* Rome, 1670.
Gnoli, D. *La Roma di Leo X.* Milan, 1938.
Golzio, V. "Note su Ottaviano Mascherino architetto in Roma." *Dedalo* 1 (1929–30), 164–94.
———. *Documenti artistici sul seicento nell'archivio Chigi.* Rome, 1939.
———. *Il seicento e il settecento.* Turin, 1950.
Golzio, V., and G. Zander. *Le chiese di Roma dall'XI al XVI sècolo.* Bologna, 1963.
Gonzaga, F. *De origine seraphicae religionis franciscanae, I.* pt. 2. Rome, 1587.
González-Palacios, A. "Bernini as a Furniture Designer." *Burlington Magazine* 112, no. 812 (November 1970), 719–22.
Gould, Cecil. *Bernini in France.* London, 1981.
Guarnieri, R. In *Dizionario degli Istituti di Perfezione,* VI. 1980, 1722–49, s.v. "Pinzochere."
Guerin, Paul. *Les Petits Bollandists: Vies des Saints de l'Ancien et du Nouveau Testament,* 17 vols. Paris, 1888.
Guibert, J. de. *La Spiritualité de la Compagnie de Jésus.* Rome, 1953.
Guida storico-artistica della chiese S. Francesco a Ripa. Rome.
Gumbinger, C. "The Primacy of Charity in Franciscan Theology." *Franciscan Studies* 24 (September 1943), 209–40.
Hamburgh, Harvey. "The Problem of *Lo Spasimo* of the Virgin in Cinquecento Paintings of the Descent." *The Sixteenth Century Journal* 12, no. 4 (Winter 1981), 45–75.
Harris, Anne. *Andrea Sacchi.* Oxford, 1977.
Haskell, Francis. *Patrons and Painters.* New York, 1971.
Haskell, Francis, and N. Penny. *Taste and the Antique.* New Haven, 1981.
Hibbard, Howard. *Bernini.* New York, 1965.
———. *Caravaggio.* New York, 1983.
Hinks, Roger. *Death of the Virgin.* London, 1953.
Honorato, M. *Historia di Santa Martina Vergine e Martina Romana.* Rome, 1635.
Hugo, Hermann. *Pia Desideria* (1624). Menston, 1971.
Huxley, Aldous. *Themes and Variations.* New York, 1950.
Ignacio de Loyola. *The Spiritual Exercises of St. Ignatius* (1548), trans. L. Puhl. Westminster, Md., 1951.
Imparato, F. "Documenti relativi al Bernini e a suoi contemporanei." *Archivio storico dell'arte,* III, 1890, 142ff.
Jacob, Henriette. *Idealism and Realism: A Study of Sepulchral Symbolism.* Leiden, 1954.
Jameson, A. *Legends of the Madonna.* Boston, 1895.
Johns, Christopher. "Some Observations on Collaboration and Patronage in the Altieri Chapel." *Storia dell'Arte* 50 (January–April 1984), 43–47.
Juan de la Cruz. *The Complete Works of Saint John of the Cross,* trans. P. Silverio de Santa Teresa, 4 vols. Westminster, 1945.
———. *Opere spirituali,* trans. Fr. Alessandro di S. Francesco. Rome, 1634.
Jungmann, Joseph. *The Mass of the Roman Rite,* trans. F. Brunner. New York, 1959.
Kaftal, G. *Iconography of the Saints in Central Italian Schools of Painting.* Florence, 1965.
Kauffmann, Hans. *Giovanni Lorenzo Bernini.* Berlin, 1970.
Kenseth, Joy. "Bernini's Borghese Sculptures: Another View." *Art Bulletin* 63, no. 2 (June 1981), 191–209.
King, Archdale. *Liturgy of the Roman Church.* London, 1957.
Kleinschmidt, Beda. *Die Heilige Anna.* Düsseldorf, 1930.
Kosareva, Nina. "A Terracotta Study by Gianlorenzo Bernini for the Statue of the Blessed Ludovica Albertoni." *Apollo* 100 (1974), 480–85.
Künstle, Karl. *Ikonographie der Christlichen Kunst,* 2 vols. Freiburg im Breisgau, 1928.
Lalemant, R. *Les Saints désirs de la mort ou recueil de quelques pensées des Pères de l'Eglise.* Brussels, 1713.
Lanciani, Rodolfo. *The Golden Days of the Renaissance in Rome.* Boston, 1906.
Landwehr, John. *Etchings of Romeyn de Hooghe.* Amsterdam, 1970.
Lavagnino, Emilio, et al. *Altari barocchi in Roma.* Rome, 1959.
Lavin, Irving. "The Bozzetti of Gianlorenzo Bernini." Ph.D. dissertation, Harvard University, 1955.
———. "Bozzetti and Modelli: Notes on Sculptural Procedure from the Early Renaissance through Bernini." In *Stil und Überlieferung in der Kunst des Abendlandes: Akten Des 21. internationalen Kongresses für Kunstgeschichte in Bonn 1964,* III. Berlin, 1967, 93–104.
———. "Bernini's Death." *Art Bulletin* 54 (1972), 159–86.
———. "Afterthoughts on 'Bernini's Death.' " *Art Bulletin* 55 (1973), 729–36.
———. "Calculated Spontaneity: Bernini and the Terracotta Sketch." *Apollo* 107 (1978), 398–405.
———. *Bernini and the Unity of the Visual Arts.* New York, 1980.
Lavin, Irving, et al. *Drawings by Gianlorenzo Bernini from the Museum der Bildenden Künste Leipzig, German Democratic Republic,* exhibition catalogue. Princeton, 1981.
Lavin, Marilyn. "The Joy of the Bridegroom's Friend: Smiling Faces in Fra Filippo, Raphael, and Leonardo." In *Art the Ape of Nature: Studies in Honor of H. W. Janson.* New York, 1981, 193–210.
Levi D'Ancona, M. *The Garden of the Renaissance: Botan-*

ical Symbolism in Italian Painting. Florence, 1977.

Liutprando, R. *Mirabilia Urbis Romae.* Rome, 1618.

Magnum Bullarium Romanum, I. Venice, 1671.

Mâle, Emile. *L'Art religieux après le Council de Trent.* Paris, 1951.

Mancini, G. *Considerazioni sulla pittura,* mss. of c. 1617–21.

Manni, Giovanni Battista. *Ritratta della gloria del paradiso.* Venice, 1670.

———. *La prigione eterna.* Venice, 1673.

Marchese, F. *Unica speranza del peccatore che consiste nel Sangue del N. S. Giesù Cristo.* Rome, 1670.

———. *Vite de' cinque Santi cioè S. Gaetano Tieneo, S. Francesco Borgia, S. Filippo Benitii, S. Ludovico Bertrando, S. Rosa di S. Maria, Canonizati dalla Santità di Nostro Signore Papa Clemente X.* Rome, 1671.

Marchiori, C. *La leggenda di S. Alessio nella tradizione popolare italiana.* Genoa, 1975.

Mariani, V. "Bozzetti Berniniani." *Bollettino d'Arte* 9 (1929–30), 59–65.

Marracci, L. *Memorie di S. Maria in Portico ora in Campitelli.* Rome, 1871.

Martimort, Aime, ed. *L'Eglise en Prière: Introduction à la liturge.* Paris, 1961.

Martinelli, Valentino. *Bernini.* Verona, 1953.

———. "Novità berniniane: Le sculpture per gli Altieri." *Commentari* 10 (1959), 204–27.

Martirologio Romano, publicato per ordere del Sommo pontefice Gregorio XIII riveduto per autorità di Urbano VIII & Clemente X. Vatican, 1931.

Matzulevitsch, G. "Tre bozzetti di G. L. Bernini all'Ermitage." *Bollettino d'Arte* 48 (1963), 67–74.

Mazzara, B. *Leggendario francescano,* I. Venice, 1689.

Menichella, Anna. *San Francesco a Ripa.* Rome, 1981.

Millin, A. *Antiquités nationales ou recueil de monumens,* I. Paris, 1790.

Miloni, F. *Per l'esaltazione della S. tà di N. S. Clement X panegirico . . . dedicato al . . . card. A.* Rome, 1670.

Mola, G. B. *Breve racconto delle miglioni opere dell'architettura, scultura et pittura fatte in Roma et alcune fuori de Roma.* Rome, 1663.

Montenovesi, O. "Pietro da Cortona e Santa Martina." *Roma* 10 (1932), 171–80.

Noehles, Karl. "Gio. Battista Mola e la sua Guida romano del 1663." *Arte lombarda* 2 (1966), 192–96.

———. *La chiesa dei SS Luca e Martina nell'opera di Pietro da Cortona.* Rome, 1970.

Nussdorfer, Laurie. "City Politics in Baroque Rome, 1623–44." Ph.D. dissertation, Princeton University, 1985.

O'Connor, Mary Catherine. *The Art of Dying Well: The Development of the Ars Moriendi.* New York, 1942.

Olphe-Galliard, M. "L'Abandon à la providence divine et la tradition Salesienne." *Revue d'ascetique et de mystique* 149 (January 1962), 324–53.

Orsenigo, C., et al. *San Carlo Borromeo nel terzo centenario della canonizzazione,* nos. 1–26, 1908–10, 3–632.

Palladio, Andrea. *Descrizione delle chiese.* Rome, 1554.

Panciroli, Ottavio. *I tesori nascosti nell'alma città di Roma.* Rome, 1625.

Panofsky, Erwin. "Imago Pietatis." In *Festschrift für Max J. Friedlander zum 60. Geburtstage.* Leipzig, 1927, 261–308.

———. *Tomb Sculpture.* New York, 1964.

———. "Mors Vitae Testimonium: The Positive Aspect of Death in Renaissance and Baroque Iconography." In *Studien zur toskanischen Kunst: Festschrift für Ludwig Heydenreich zum 23 März 1963,* ed. W. Lotz. Munich, 1964, 221–36.

Parks, Randolph. "On Caravaggio's 'Dormition of the Virgin' and Its Setting." *Burlington Magazine* 127, no. 988 (July 1985), 438–48.

Partner, Peter. *Renaissance Rome, 1550–1559.* Los Angeles, 1976.

Passeri, Giovanni Battista. *Vite de pittori, scultori, ed architetti che hanno lavorate in Roma morti dal 1641 al 1673.* Rome, 1772.

Pastor, Ludwig von. *The History of the Popes,* XXX. Saint Louis, 1940.

Pauolo, Giovanni. *Vita della B. Ludovica Albertoni . . .* Rome, 1672.

Pecchiai, Pio. *Il Campidoglio nel cinquecento.* Rome, 1950.

———. *Il Gesù di Roma.* Rome, 1952.

Perlove, Shelley. "Bernini's Androclus and the Lion: A Papal Emblem of Alexandrine Rome." *Zeitschrift für Kunstgeschichte* 45 (1982), 287–96.

———. "Gianlorenzo Bernini's *Blessed Lodovica Albertoni* and Baroque Devotion." Ph.D. dissertation, University of Michigan, 1984.

Pesci, B. *San Francesco a Ripa,* XLIX: *Le chiese di Roma illustrati.* Rome, 1959.

Peterson, Robert T. *The Art of Ecstasy: Teresa, Bernini and Crashaw.* New York, 1970.

Piazza, G. *Opere pie di Roma.* Rome, 1679.

Pohle, Joseph, and Arthur Preuss. *The Sacraments,* III. London, 1956.

Pollak, Oskar. *Die Kunsttätigkeit unter Urban VIII,* I. Vienna, 1928.

Pope-Hennessy, John. *Italian High Renaissance and Baroque Sculpture,* 3 vols. Greenwich, Conn., 1963.

Poschmann, Bernhard, *Penance and the Anointing of the Sick,* trans. F. Courtney. New York, 1964.

Posse, H. *Der römische Maler Andrea Sacchi.* Leipzig, 1925.

Praz, Mario. *Studies in Seventeenth-Century Imagery.* Rome, 1964.

Quarles, Francis. *Emblems Divine and Moral,* I. London, 1942, 196.

Rahner, Karl. *On the Theology of Death,* trans. C. Henkey. New York, 1961.

Réau, Louis. *L'Iconographie de l'art chrétien,* 3 vols. Paris, 1958.

Robert, C. *Die Antiken Sarkophag Reliefs,* III. Berlin, 1904.

Rome, Archivio Segreto Vaticano. *S. Visitatio Apost,* II. Miscellanea Arm. VII, 112, fols. 84–89.

Rome, Archivio Segreto Vaticano. *Diversorum Clemen. X,* Lib. I (1669–70). Sec. Brev. 1581, fol. 250.

Rome, Archivio Segreto Vaticano. *Diversorum Clemen. X,* Lib. IV (1672–73). Sec. Brev. 1584, fols. 51–54.

Rome, Archivio Segreto Vaticano. *Diversorum Clemen. X,* Lib. V (1674–75). Sec. Brev. 1585, fols. 337–45.

Rome, Archivio di S. Francesco a Ripa. Ludovico da Modena. *Cronaco della Riforma dal 1519 al 1722. Fondazione e Riforma del convento di S. Francesco a Ripa,* busta 12.

Rome, Archivio di S. Francesco a Ripa. *Elenco SS. Reliquie,* busta 261, undated.

Rome, Archivio di S. Francesco a Ripa. F. M. Nicolini da Collamato. *Vita de Servi di Dio. Francescani dal 1630–1685,* busta 16.

Rome, Archivio di Stato. Alexius de Paregrinis. *Archivio dei Notari Capitoline,* busta 1257, fols., 199–200.

Rome, Archivio di Stato. Pacificus de Pacificus. *Archivio dei Notari Capitoline,* busta 1181, carte 674v, 733r.

Rome, Archivio di Stato. *Stato dell'Eredità della ch. me. dell Card. Paluzzi,* June 1698, busta 1.

Rome, Roma calcografia. *L'immagine di San Francesco nella controriforma.* exhibition catalogue, 1982–83.

Rosci, M. *I quadroni di San Carlo del Duomo di Milano.* Milan, 1965.

Rosenberg, Pierre. *La "Mort de Germanicus" de Poussin.* Paris, 1973.

Rossi, E. "Palazzo Altieri." *Roma* 18 (1940), 57.

———. "Palazzo Altieri." *Roma* 19 (1941), 29–30.

Rudolf, R. *Ars Moriendi.* Cologne, 1957.

Rushforth, G. "Funeral Lights in Roman Sepulchral Monuments," *Journal of Roman Studies* 5, pt. 2 (1915): 149–64.

Santini, Bernardino. *I voli d'amore panegirico per la b. Ludovica Albertoni Paluzzi Altieri del Terz Ordine di S. Francesco alla presenza dell'Em. mo e Rev. mo Prencipe Paluzzo Cardinal Altieri.* Bologna, 1673.

Schiavo, A. *La donna nelle sculture del Bernini.* Milan, 1942.

———. *Palazzo Altieri.* Rome, 1963.

Schillebeeckx, E. *The Eucharist,* trans. N. Smith. London, 1968.

Sommer, Frank. "The Iconography of Action: Bernini's *Ludovica Albertoni.*" *Art Quarterly* 36 (1970), 30–38.

Spila, B. *Memorie,* I. Rome, 1892.

Stella, A. In *Dizionario biografico degli italiani,* II, 1960. 561–64, s.v. "Altieri (Paluzzo degli Albertoni), Paluzzo."

Supplement to *Burlington Magazine* 123 (1981), 63.

Tapié, Alain. *L'Allégorie dans la peinture: La répresentation de la charité au XVII siècle,* exhibition catalogue. Caen, 1986.

Tenenti, Alberto. *Il senso della morte e l'amore della vita nel rinascimento.* Turin, 1957.

Theresa of Jesus. *Complete Works of St. Theresa,* trans. A. Peers, 3 vols. London, 1957.

———. *Opere spirituali della S.M. Teresa di Giesù,* trans. Fr. Filippo di S. Giacomo, 2 vols. Rome, 1641.

Thomas à Kempis. *The Imitation of Christ,* trans. E. Waugh and M. Oakley. New York, 1959.

Thurston, Herbert. *The Physical Phenomena of Mysticism.* London, 1952.

Titi, F. *Studio di pittura, scoltura et architettura.* Rome, 1674.

———. *Ammaestramento utile e curioso di pittura, scoltura et architettura . . .* Rome, 1686.

———. *Descrizione delle pitture, sculture e architetture esposte al pubblico in Roma.* Rome, 1763.

Totti, Pompilio. *Ritratto di Roma moderna.* Rome, 1638.

Vauchez, André. *La sainteté en Occident aux dernières siècles du moyen âge d'après les procès de canonisation et les documents hagiographiques.* Rouen, 1975.

Vichi, Umberto. "La capella di S. Antonio nella Basilica di Aracoeli in Roma." *Il Santo* 9 (1969), 283–88.

Visconti, P. *Città e famiglie nobili e celebri dello stato pontifico,* III. Rome, 1847.

Voragine, Jacobus de. *The Golden Legend,* trans. G. Ryan. New York, 1969.

Vovelle, Michel. *Mourir autrefois: Attitudes collectives devant la mort aux XVIIe et XVIIIe siècles.* Mesnil-sur-l'Estrée, 1974.

Wadding, Luke. *Annales Minorum seu Trium Ordinum a S. Francesco institutorum* (continued by P. Aniceto Chiappini), XXVI, XXXII 1623–27, Florence, 1933.

Weibel, W. "The Representation of Ecstasy." In *Bernini in Perspective.* Englewood Cliffs, N.J., 1976.

Weil, Mark. "The Devotion of the Forty Hours and Roman Baroque Illusions." *Journal of the Warburg and Courtauld Institutes* 37 (1974), 218–48.

Wittkower, Rudolf. *Bernini.* New York, 1955.

Wright, Georgia. "Caravaggio's Entombment Considered *in situ.*" *Art Bulletin* 60 (1978), 35–42.

Index

Note: S.F.R. = San Francisco a Ripa

Illustrations

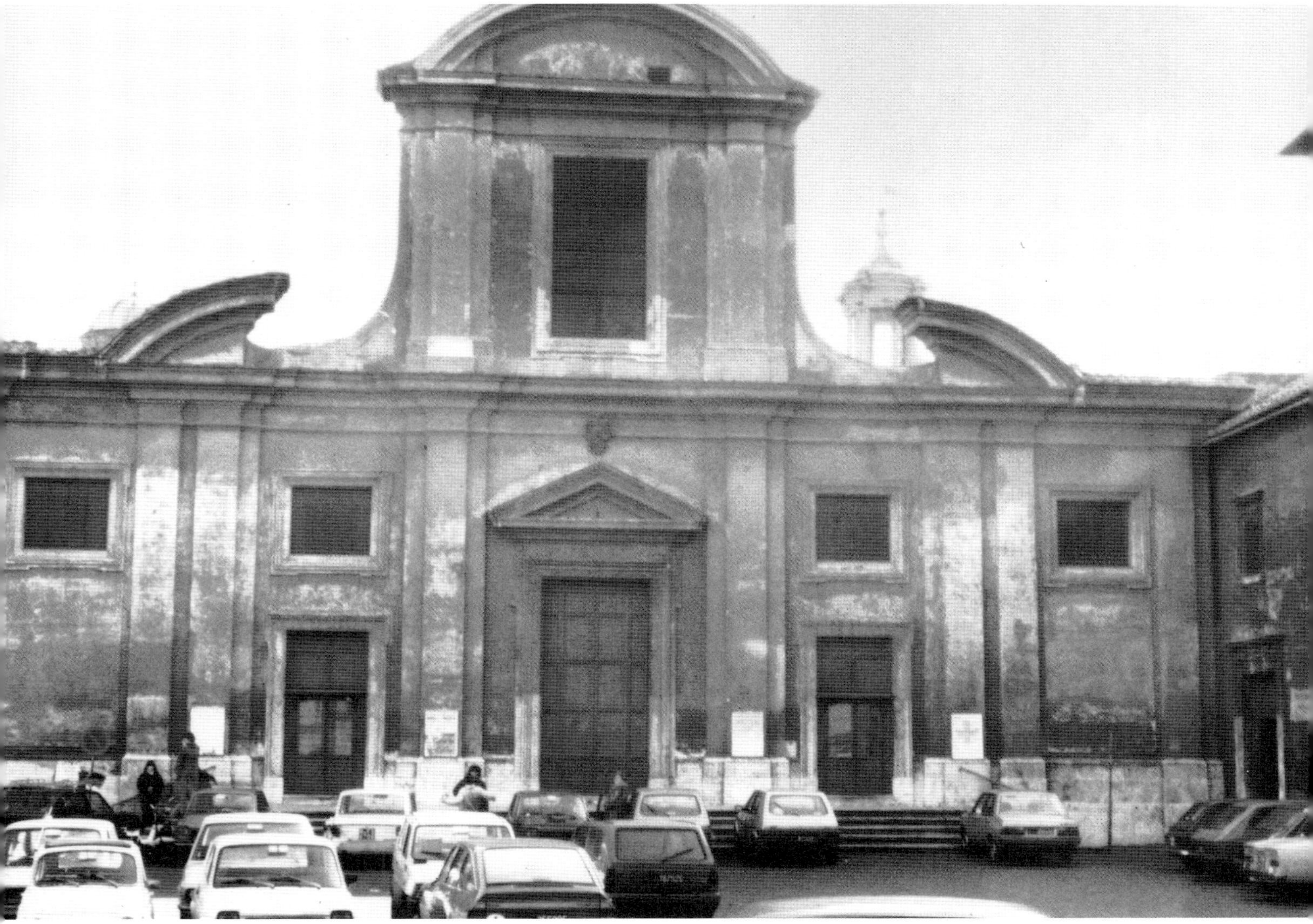

PLATE 1. Matthia de' Rossi, facade, c. 1681–82, San Francesco a Ripa

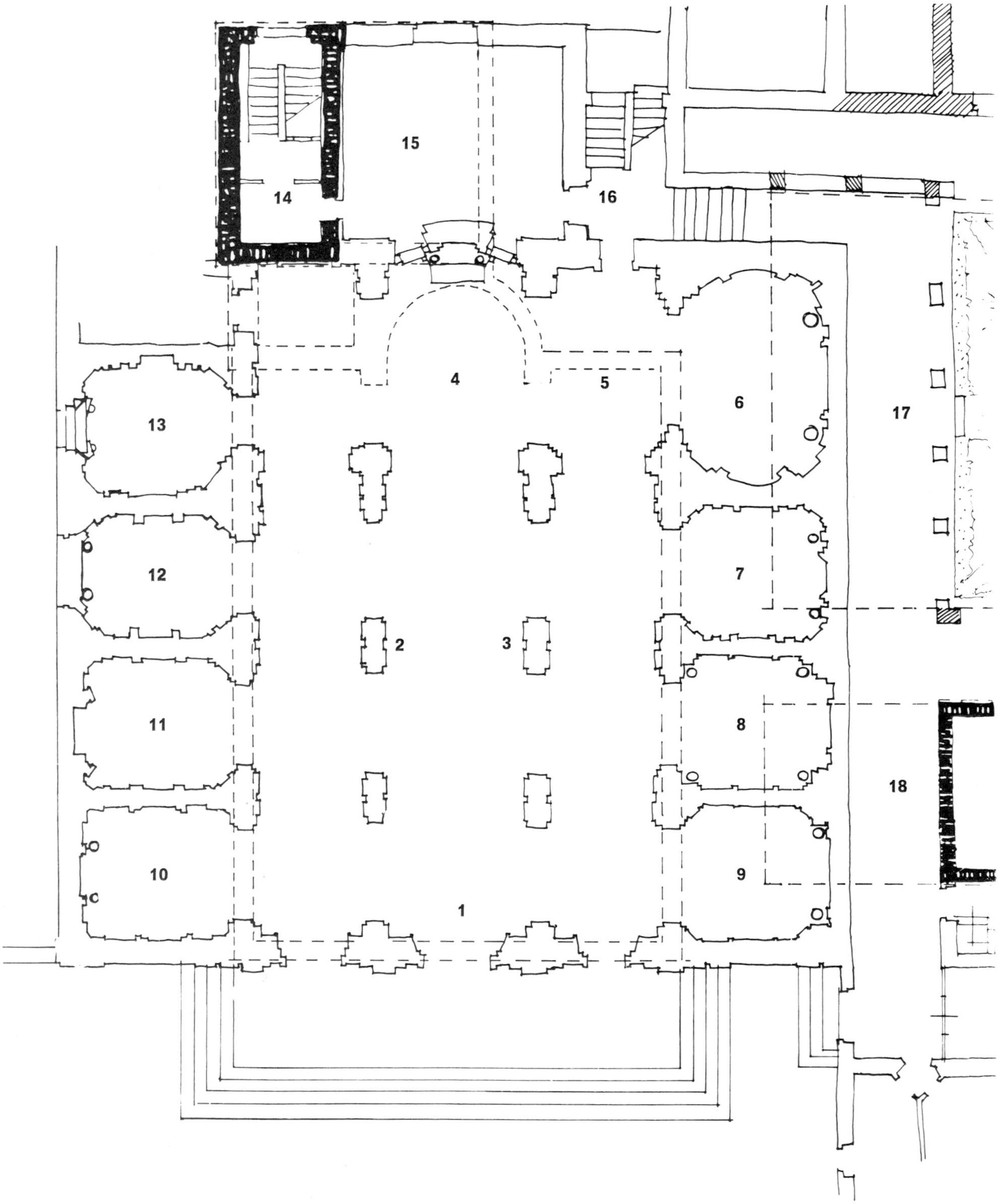

NAVATA CENTRALE

1. Ingresso
2. Monumento Ven. Francesco da Chiusa
3. Monumento Bartolomeo da Salutio
4. Altare maggiore

NAVATA DESTRA

5. Altare S. Giacinto Morescotti
6. Capp. S. Pietro d'Alcantara
7. Capp. S. Giuseppe
8. Capp. S. Giovanni da Capestrano
9. Capp. SS. Crocefisso

NAVATA SINISTRA

10. Capp. Immacolata
11. Mon. Annunziata
12. Mon. S. Carlo
13. Mon. B. Ludovico

14. Sacrestia - Cella S. Francesco
15. Coro e ingresso
16. Chiostro
17. Chiostro
18.

PLATE 2. Plan of the church, San Francesco a Ripa

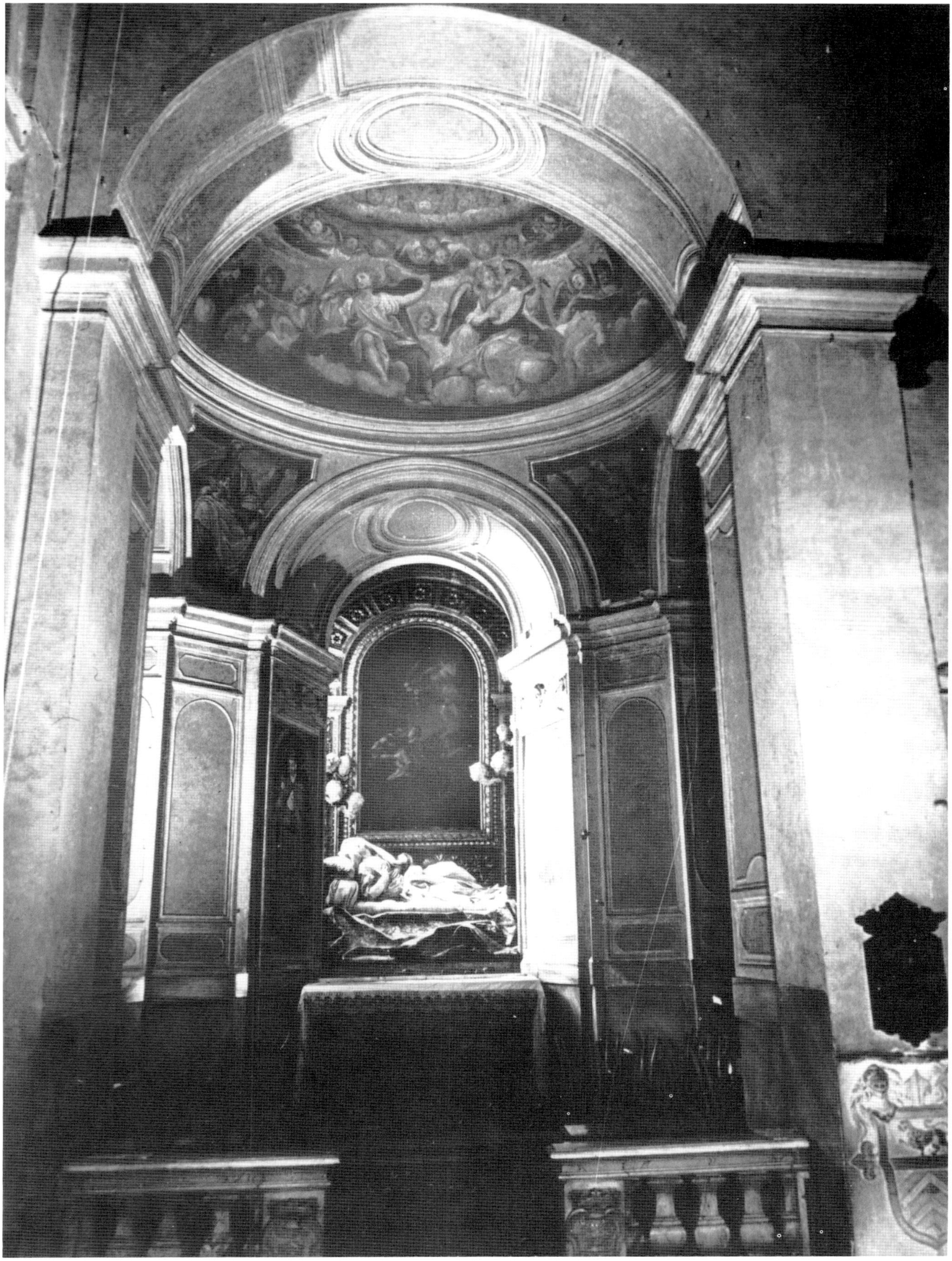

PLATE 3. Altieri Chapel, San Francesco a Ripa

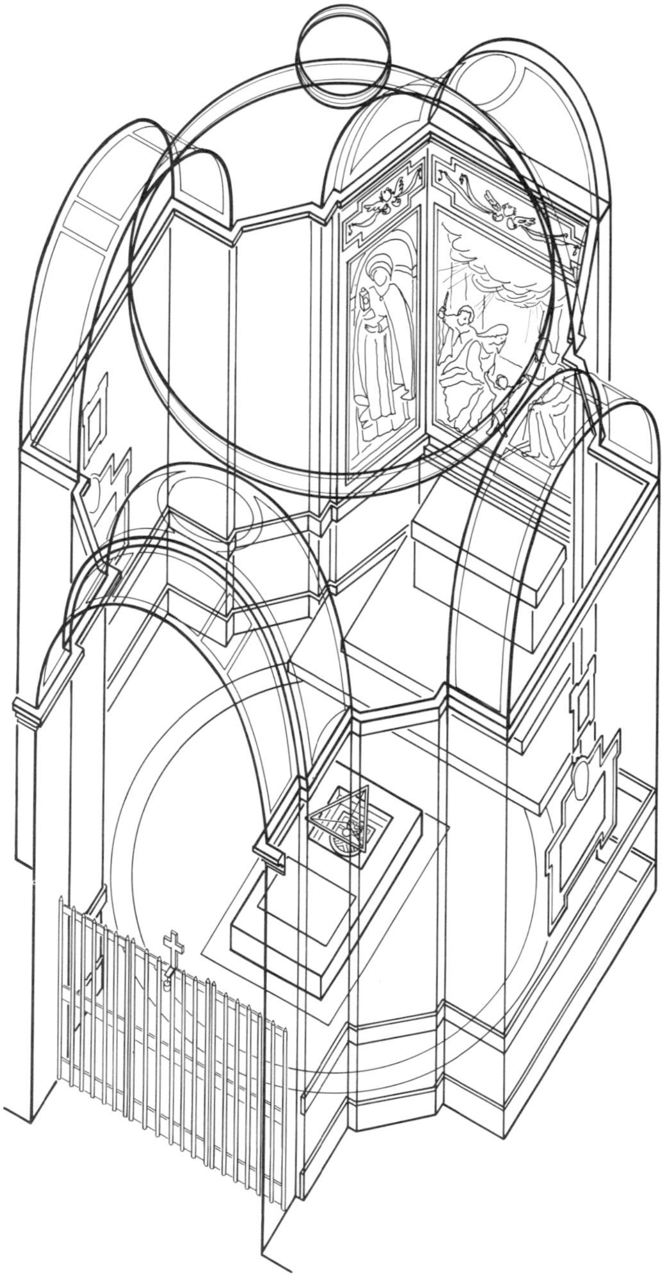

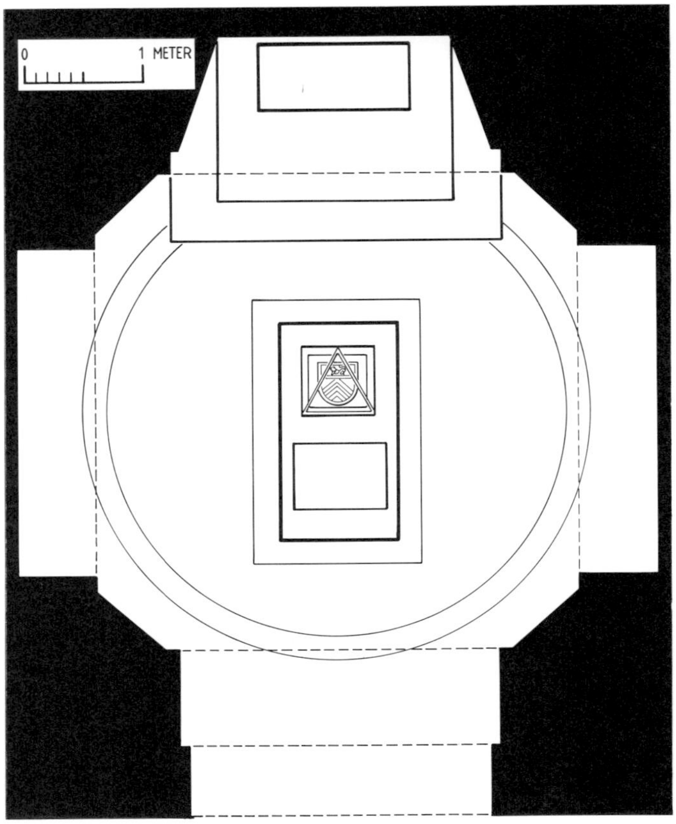

PLATE 5. Reconstruction drawing of the plan of the Altieri Chapel as it looked prior to Bernini's intervention

PLATE 4. Reconstruction elevation drawing of the Altieri Chapel as it looked prior to Bernini's intervention

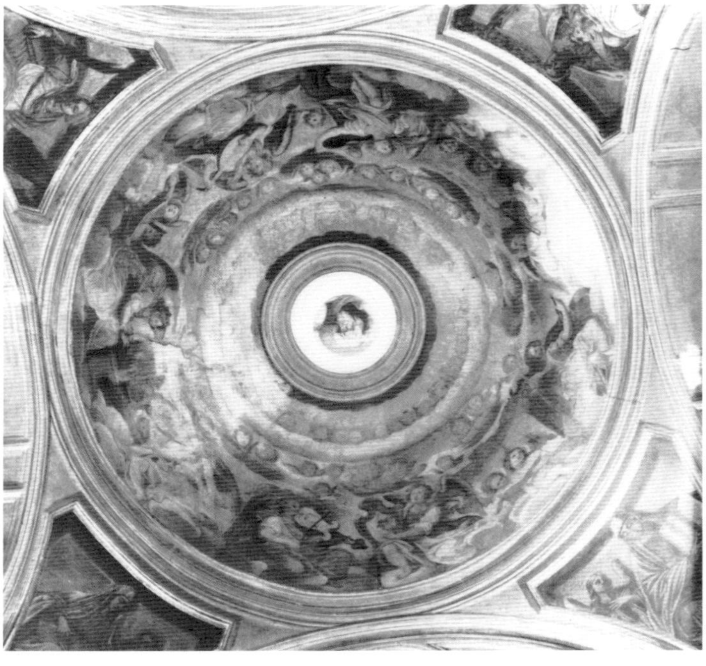

PLATE 6. Gaspare Celio, *Musical Angels with God the Father,* fresco of the dome and lantern, c. 1622, Altieri Chapel, San Francesco a Ripa

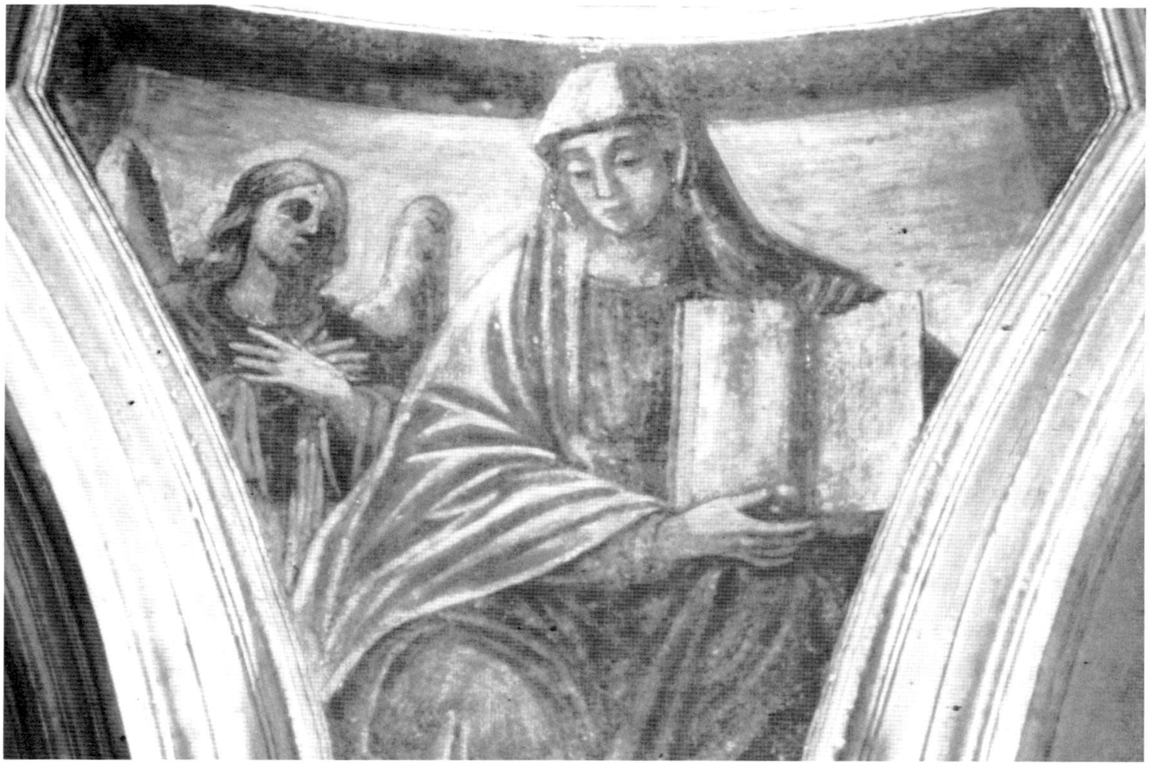

PLATE 7. Assistant of Gaspare Celio, *Santa Francesca Romana,* fresco of the pendentive, c. 1622, Altieri Chapel, San Francesco a Ripa

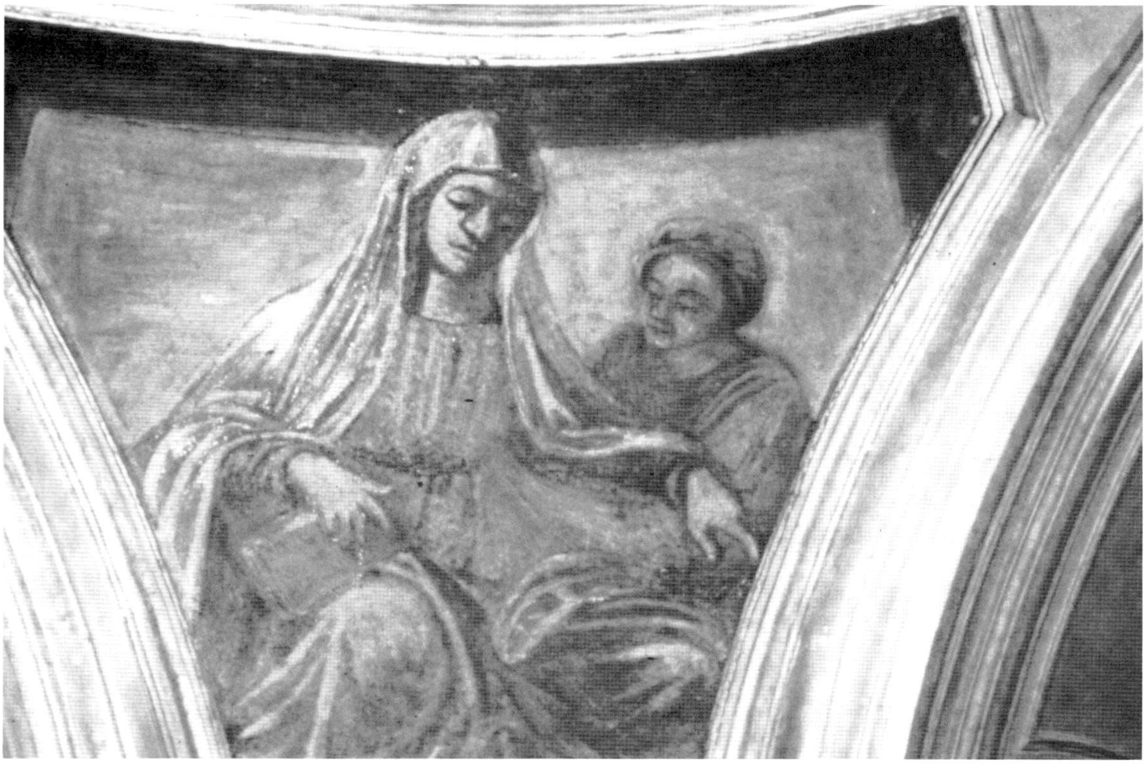

PLATE 8. Assistant of Gaspare Celio, *Blessed Ludovica,* fresco of the pendentive, c. 1622, Altieri Chapel, San Francesco a Ripa

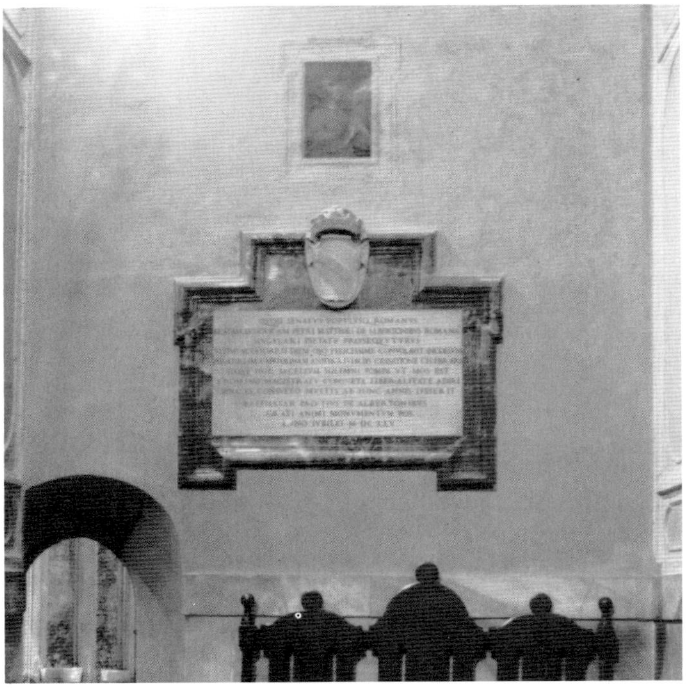

PLATE 9. Left lateral wall with inscription plaque and fresco of Saint Carlo Borromeo, Altieri Chapel, San Francesco a Ripa

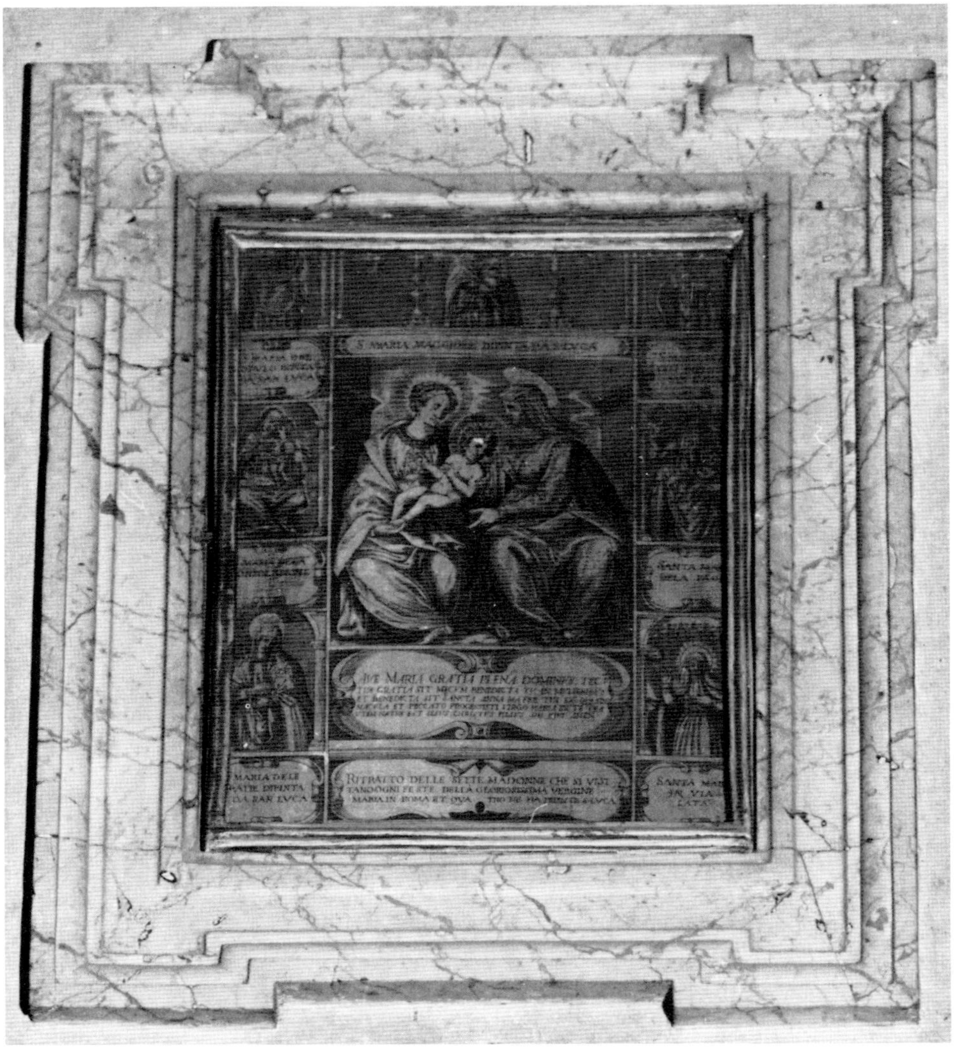

PLATE 10. *Holy Family and Saint Anne,* print, Altieri Chapel, San Francesco a Ripa

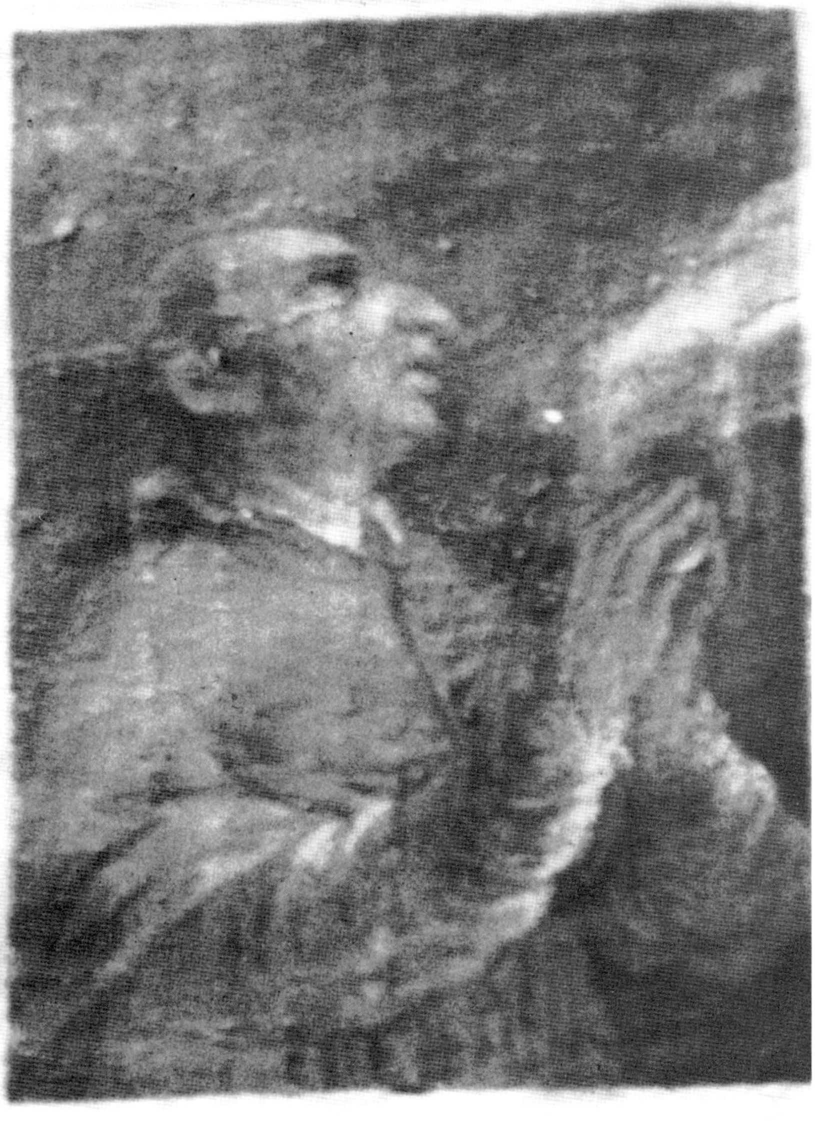

PLATE 11. Assistant of Gaspare Celio, *Saint Carlo Borromeo,* fresco, c. 1622, Altieri chapel, San Francesco a Ripa

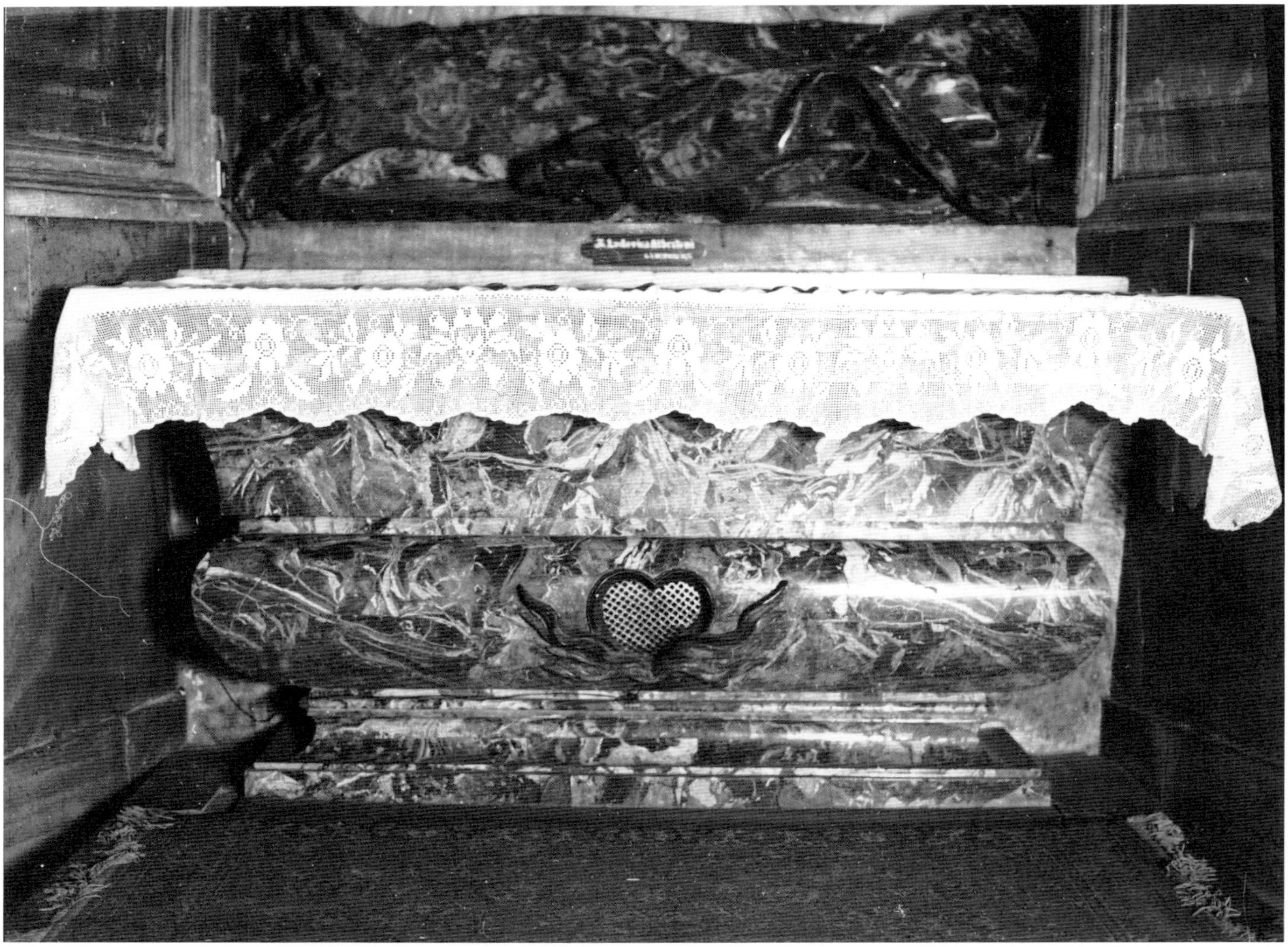

PLATE 12. Altar of the Altieri Chapel, San Francesco a Ripa

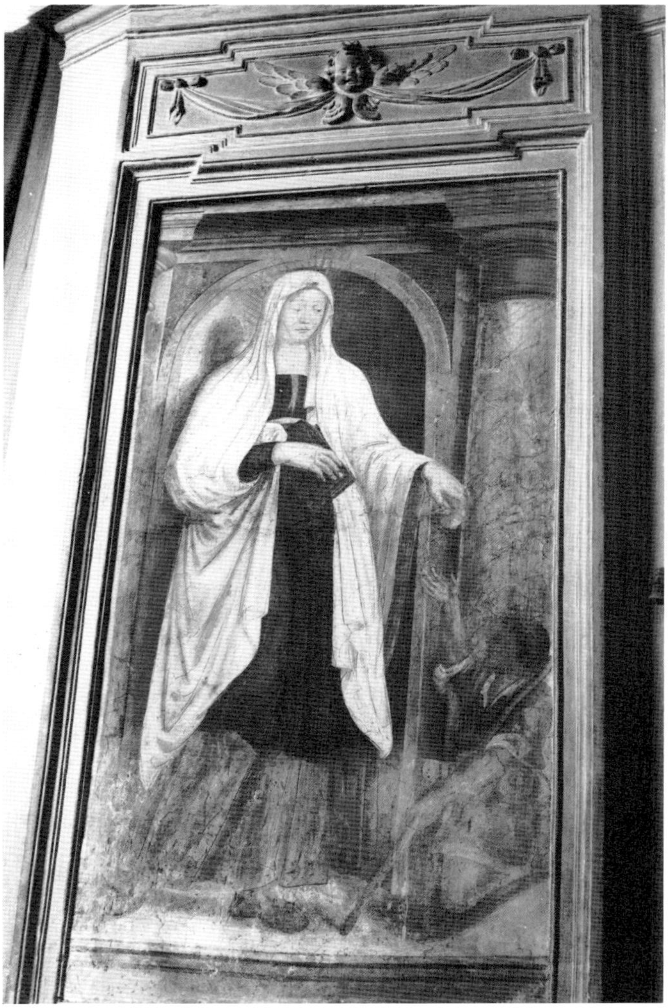

PLATE 13. *Ludovica Giving Bread to a Poor Pilgrim,* fresco on the epistle side of the altar, Altieri Chapel, San Francesco a Ripa

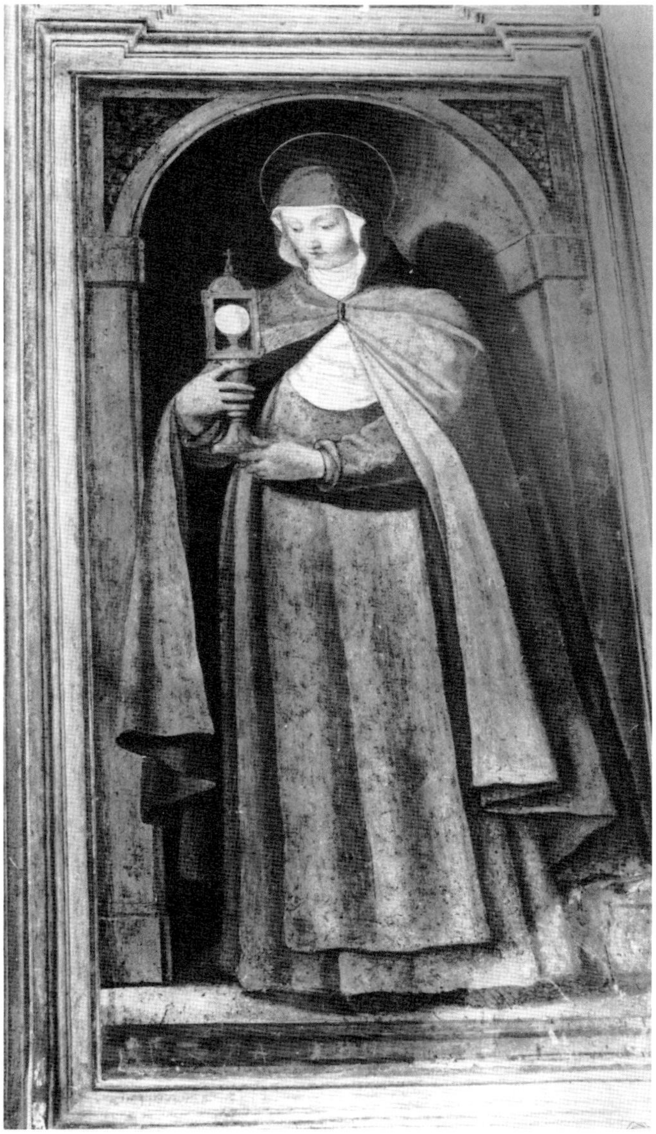

PLATE 14. *Saint Clare Holding a Monstrance,* fresco on the evangelical side of the altar, Altieri Chapel San Francesco a Ripa

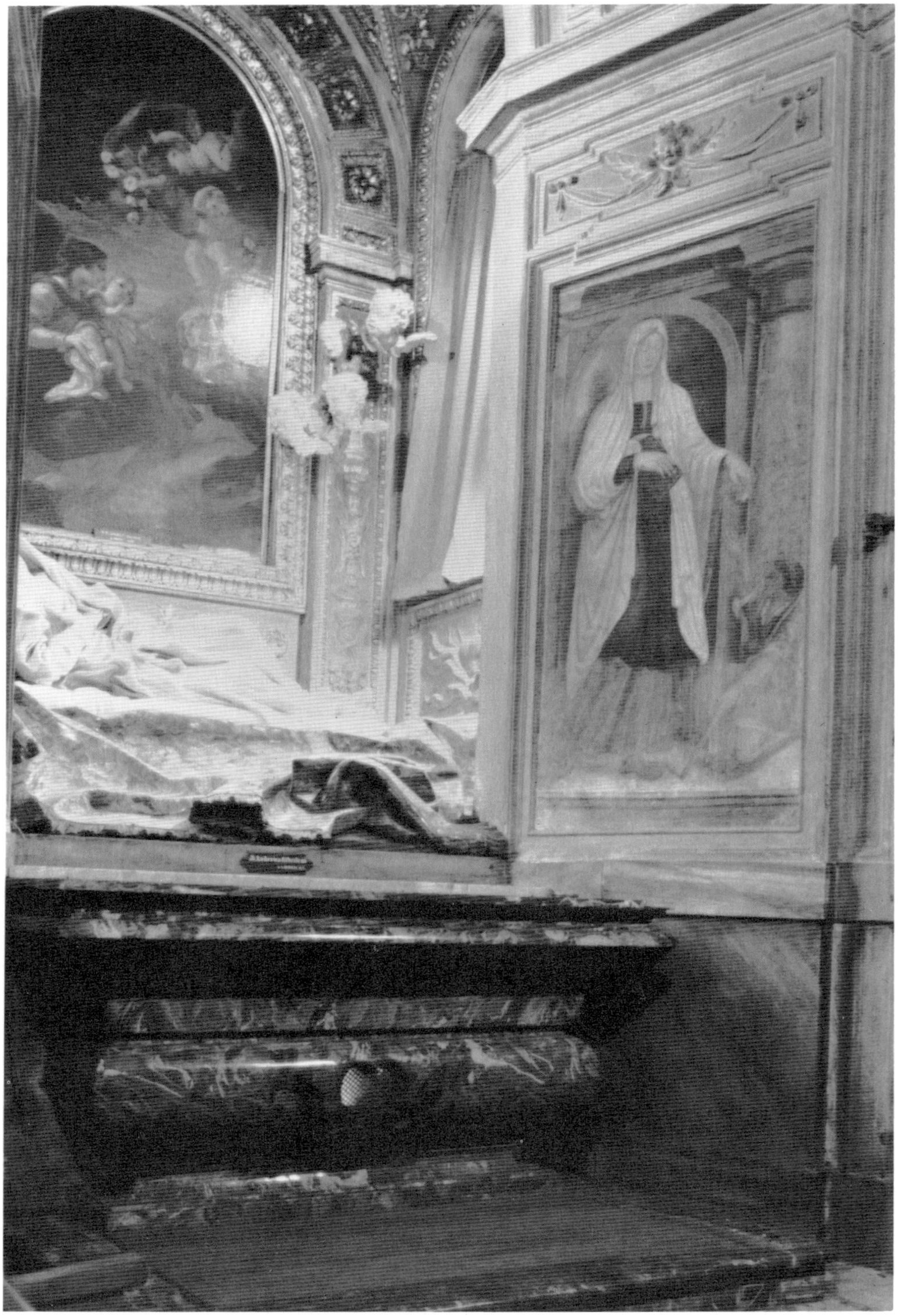

Plate 15. Recess, Altieri Chapel, San Francesco a Ripa

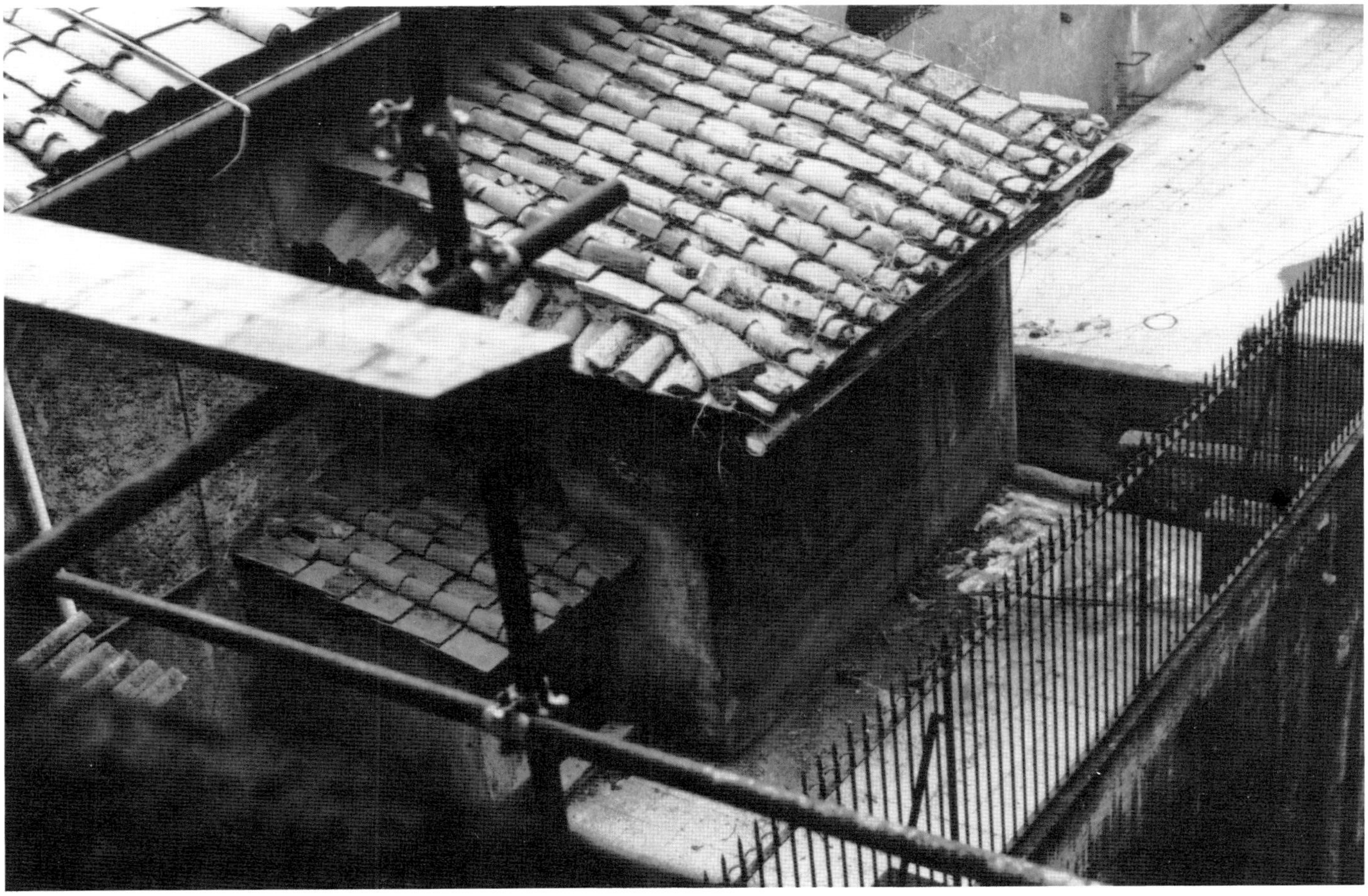

PLATE 16. Recess, Altieri Chapel, San Francesco a Ripa

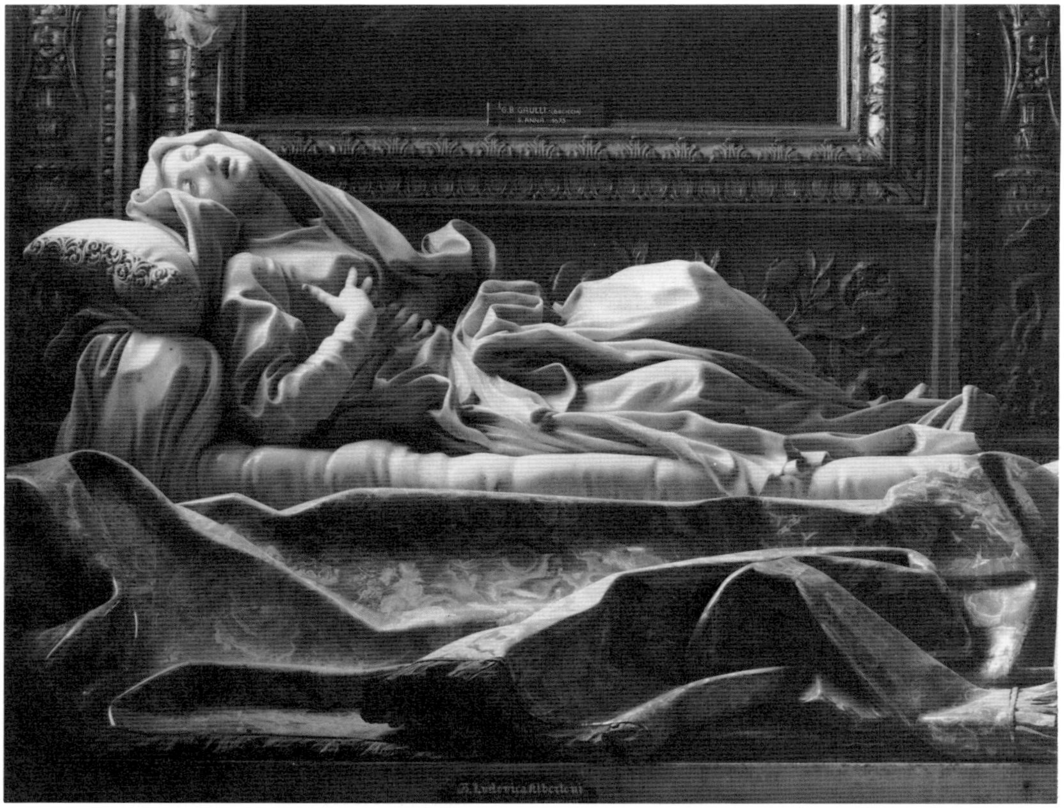

PLATE 17. Gianlorenzo Bernini, *Blessed Ludovica Albertoni,* 1672–74, Altieri Chapel, San Francesco a Ripa

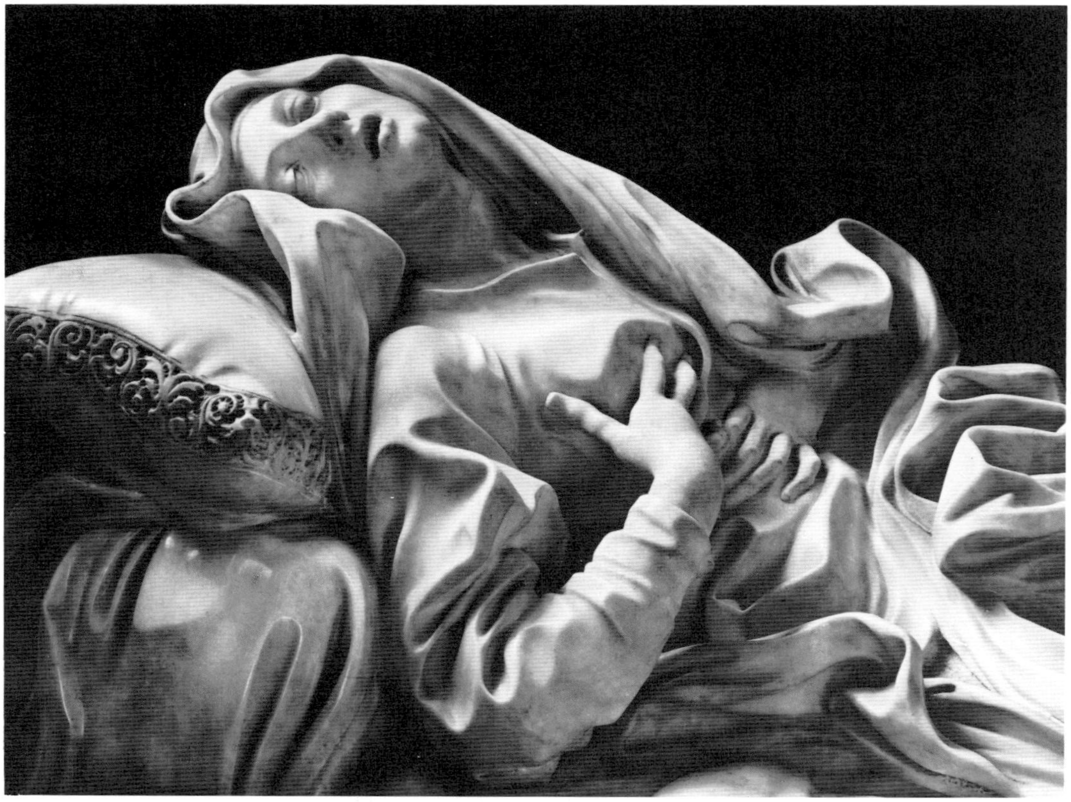

PLATE 18. Gianlorenzo Bernini, *Blessed Ludovica Albertoni* (detail of upper torso, 1672–74), Altieri Chapel, San Francesco a Ripa

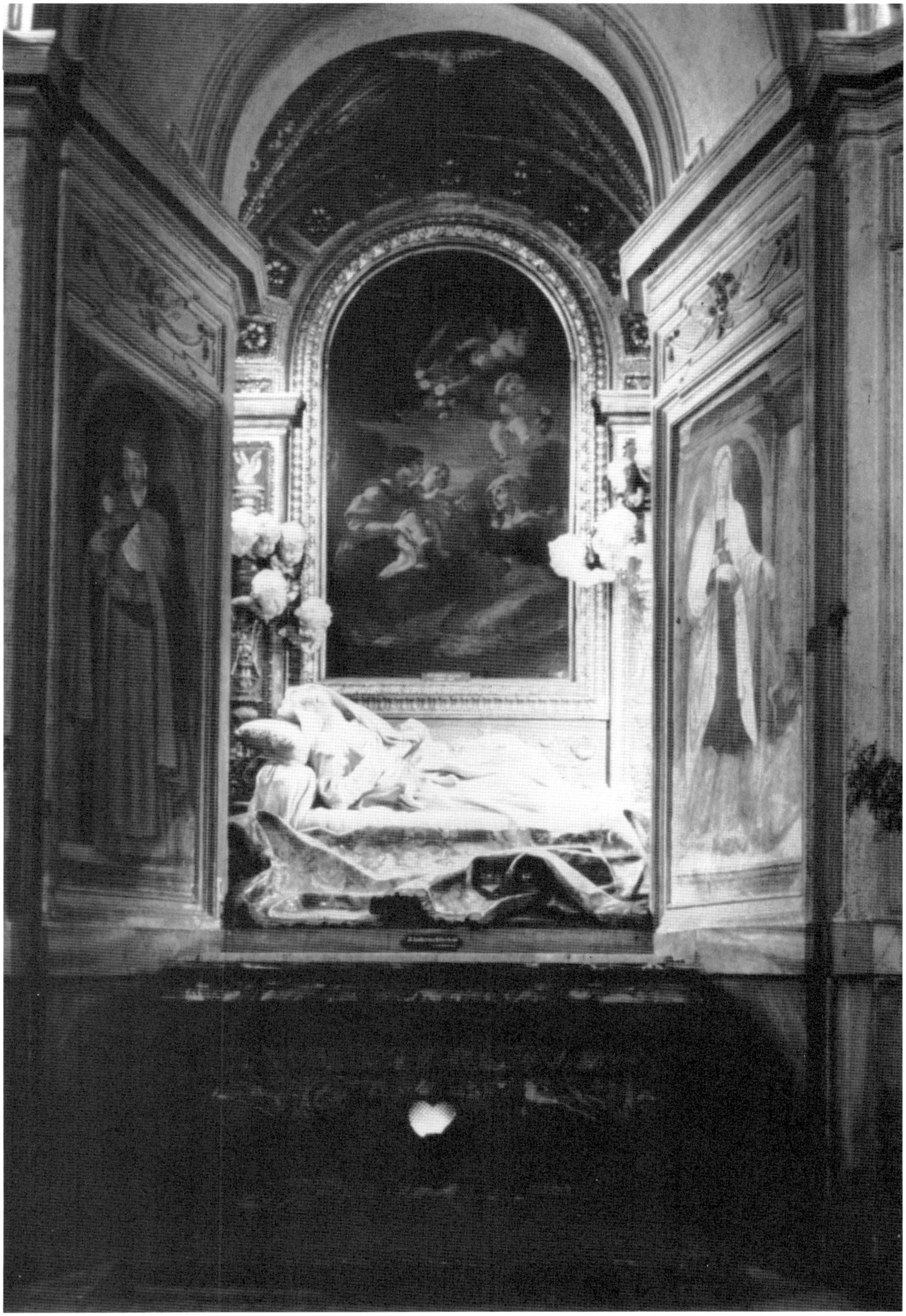

PLATE 19. Recess, Altieri Chapel, San Francesco a Ripa

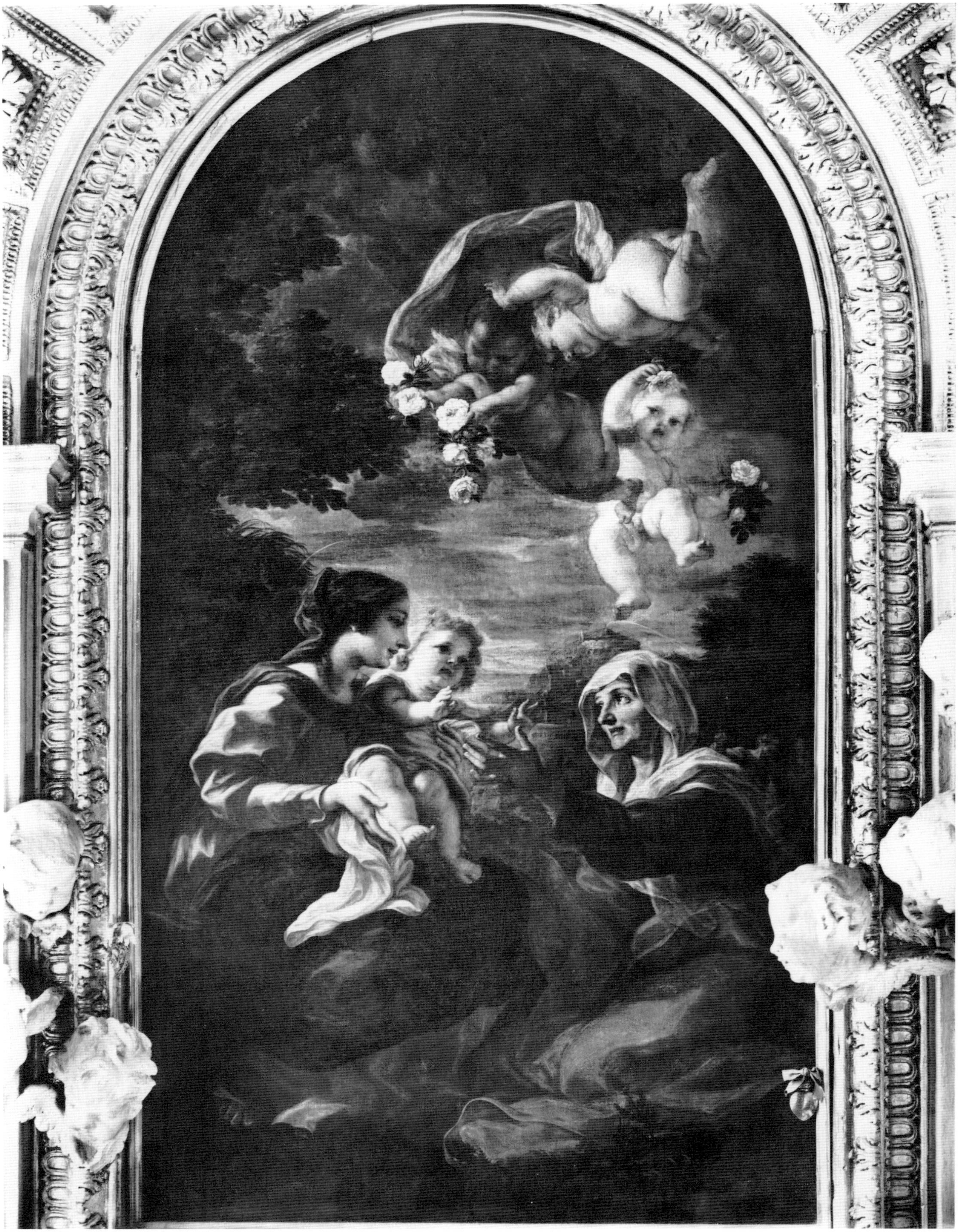

OPPOSITE:
PLATE 20. Giovanni Battista Gaulli, called "Baciccio," *Virgin and Child with Saint Anne,* oil on canvas, c. 1674, Altieri Chapel, San Francesco a Ripa

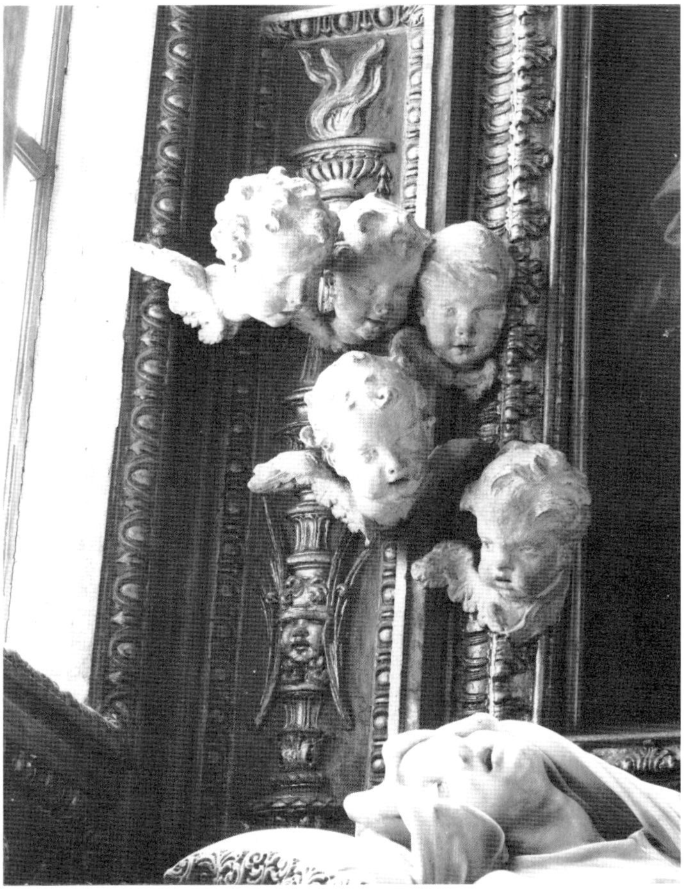

PLATE 21. Frame of the altarpiece (left side), Altieri Chapel, San Francesco a Ripa

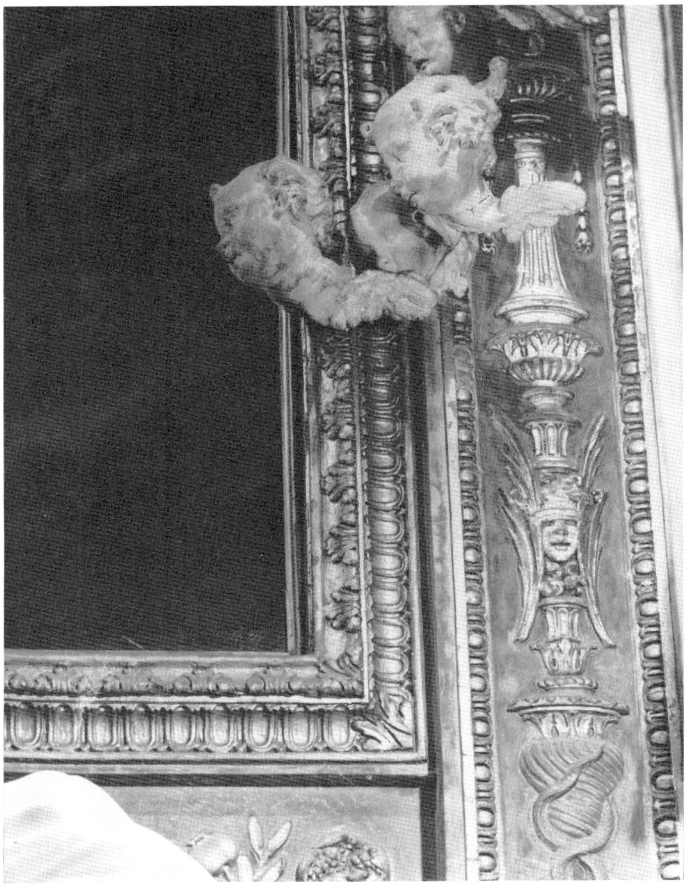

PLATE 22. Frame of the altarpiece (right side), Altieri Chapel, San Francesco a Ripa

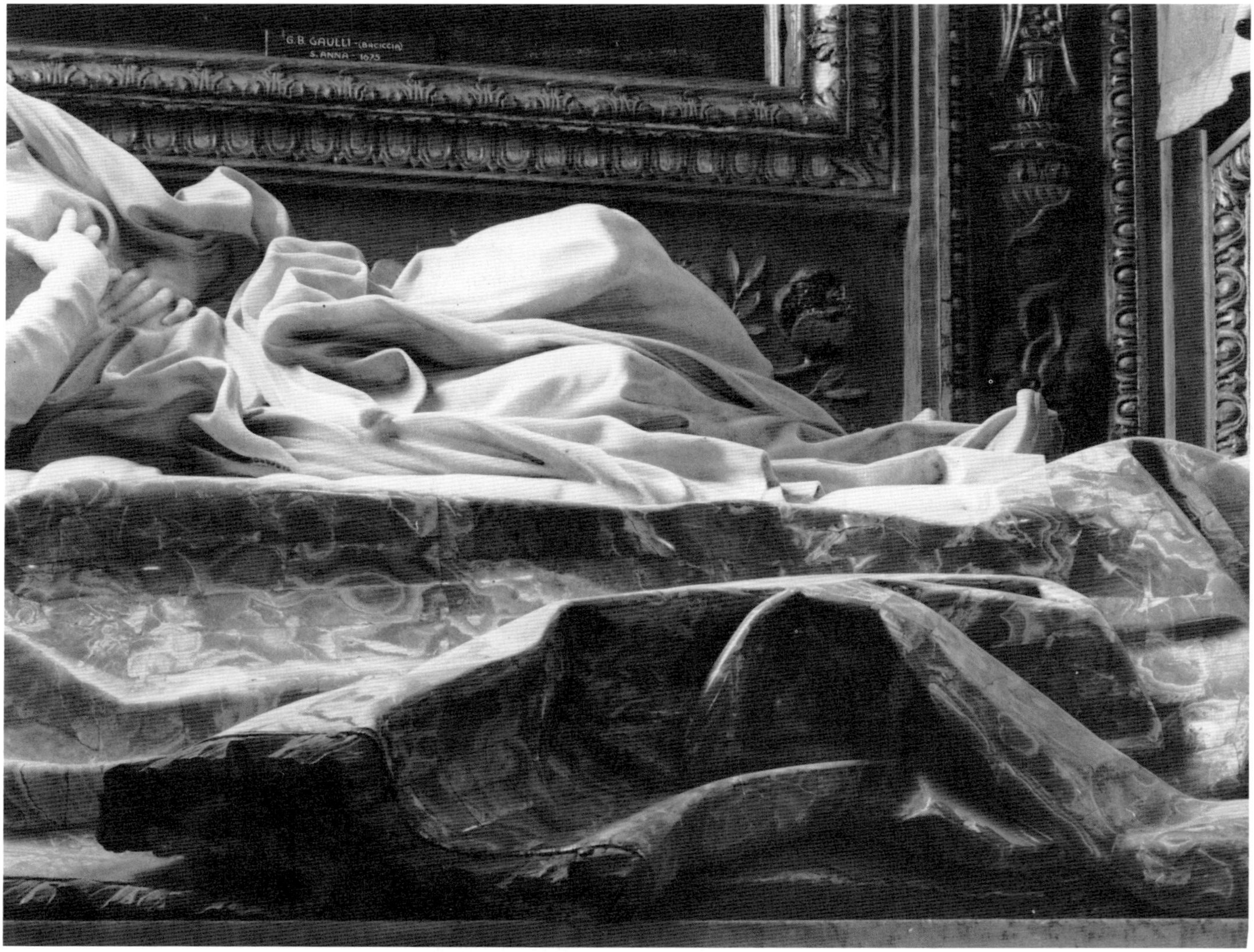

PLATE 23. Frame of the altarpiece and panel decorated with pomegranates, Altieri Chapel, San Francesco a Ripa

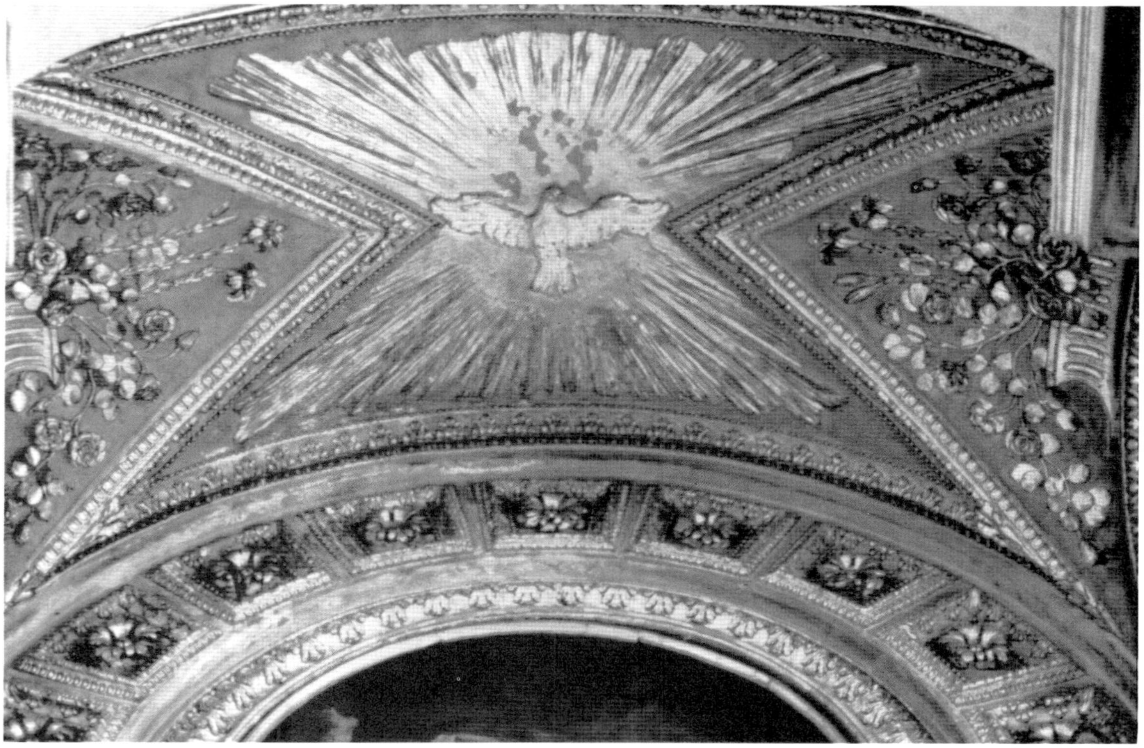

PLATE 24. Vault of the recess with dove of the Holy Spirit, Altieri Chapel, San Francesco a Ripa

PLATE 25. Flaming heart, panel beneath the right window, Altieri Chapel, San Francesco a Ripa

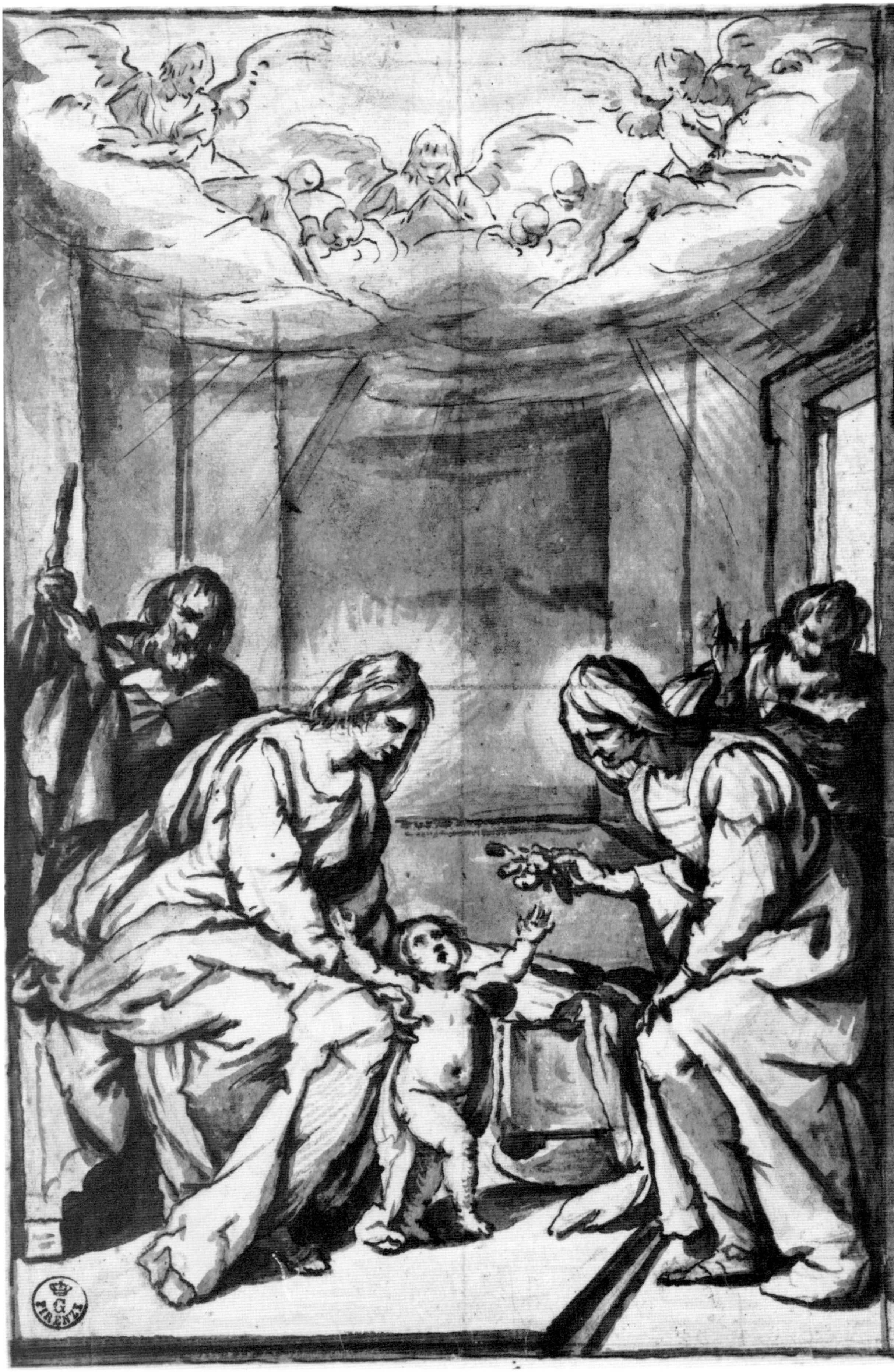
G
FIRENZE

OPPOSITE:
PLATE 26. Gaspare Celio, *Madonna and Child with Saint Anne, Joseph, and Joachim,* pen-and-ink wash drawing, c. 1628

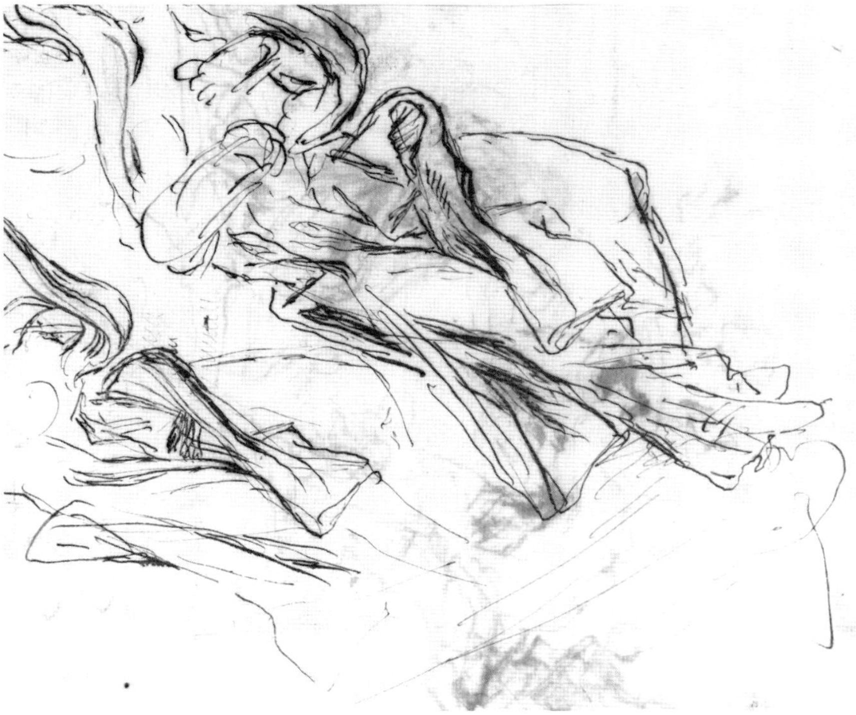

PLATE 27. Gianlorenzo Bernini, study for the *Ludovica Albertoni,* pen and ink, c. 1672

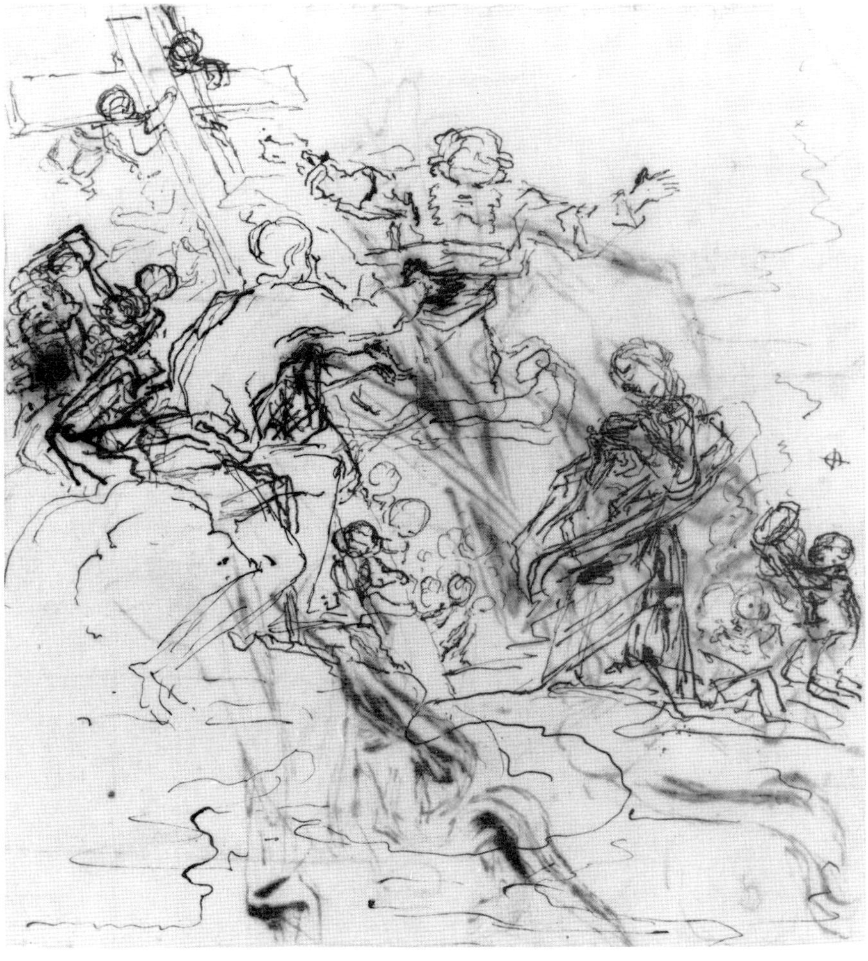

PLATE 28. Gianlorenzo Bernini, *Intercession of Christ and the Virgin,* study for the dome fresco of the Gesù, pen and ink

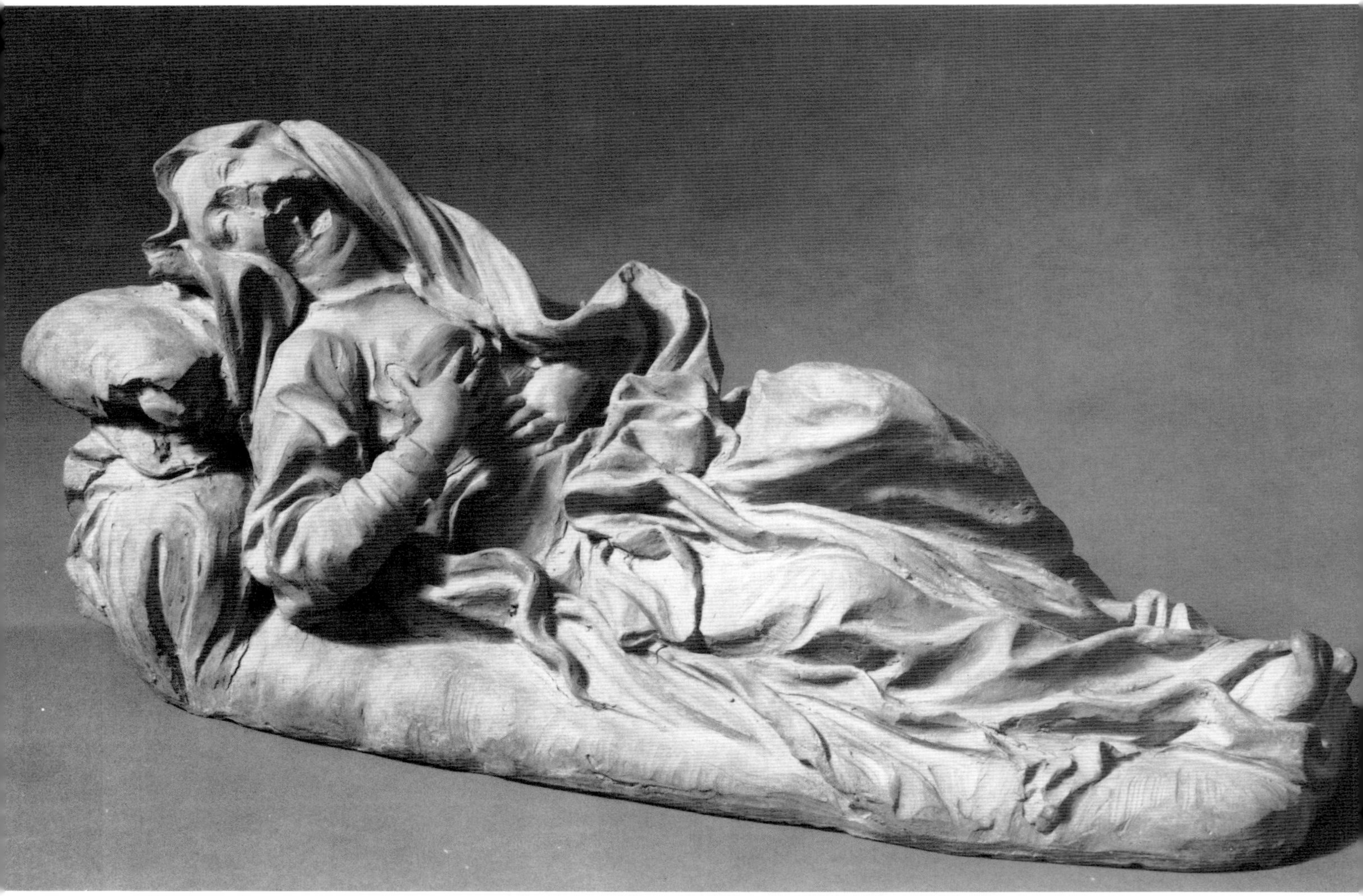

PLATE 29. *Bozzetto* of the *Ludovica,* terra-cotta

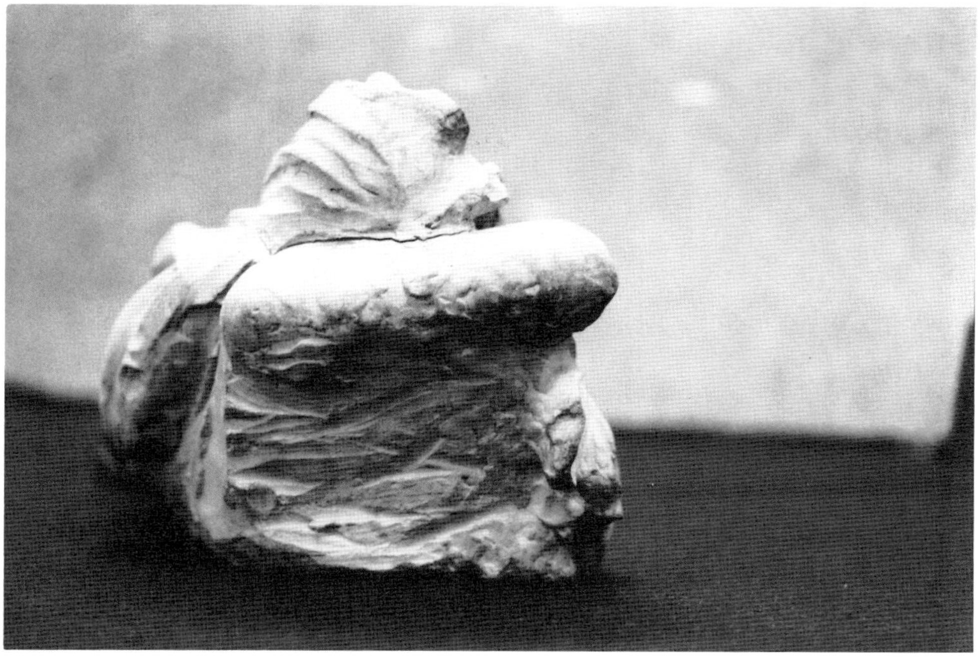

Plate 30. End view of the pillow and bolster, *bozzetto* of the *Ludovica,* terra-cotta

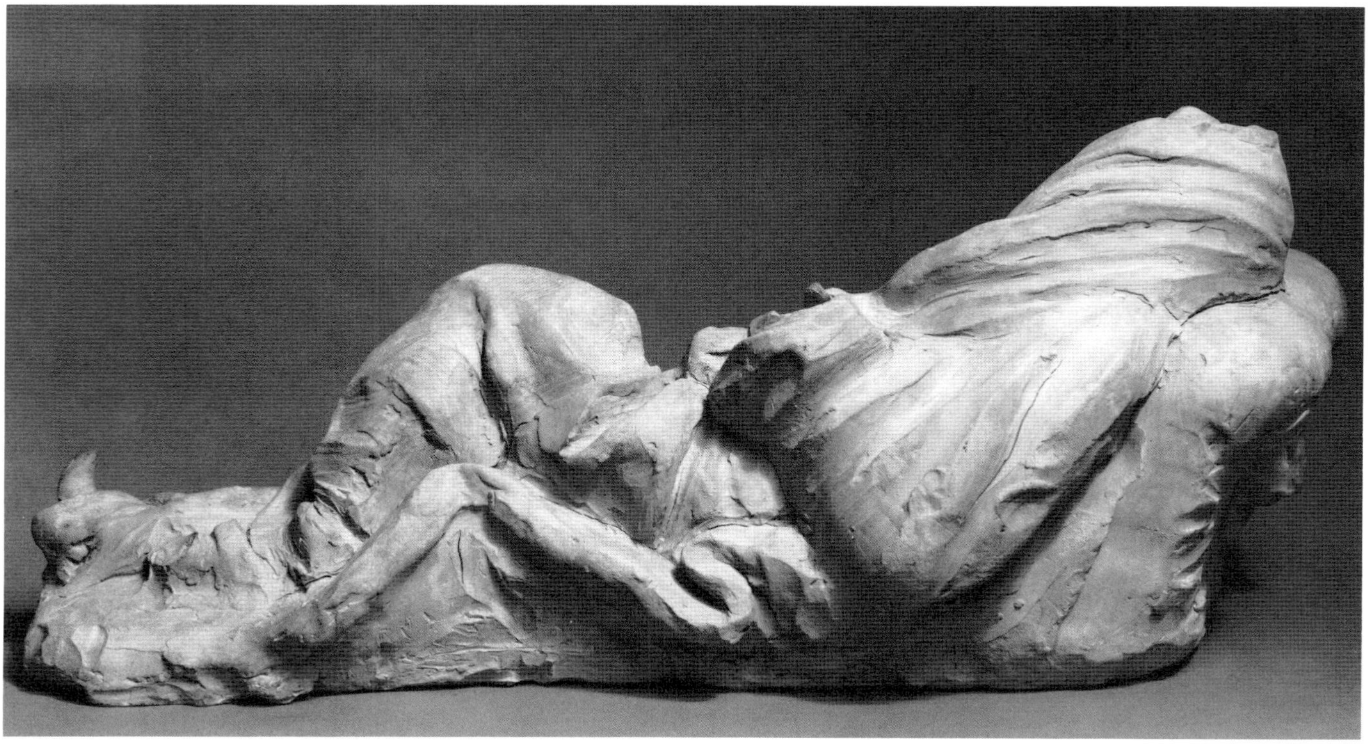

Plate 31. Back view of the statuette, *bozzetto* of the *Ludovica,* terra-cotta

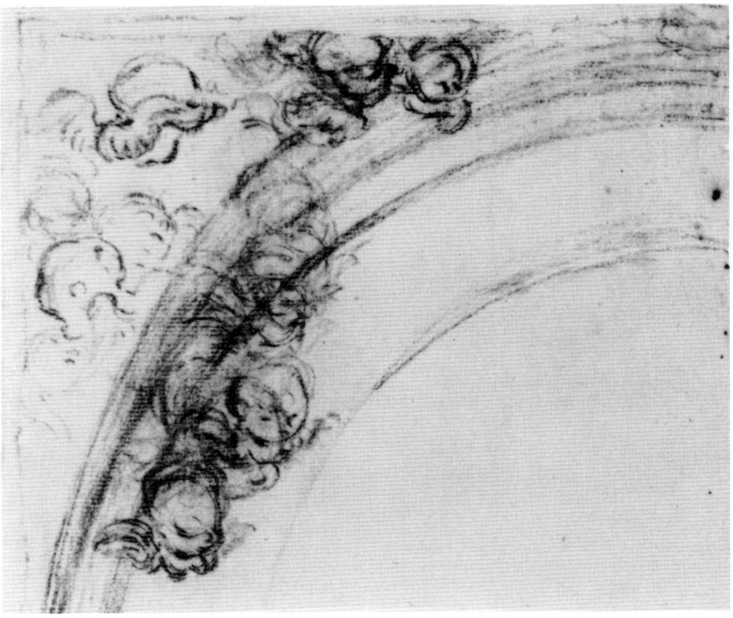

PLATE 32. Gianlorenzo Bernini, study for the recess of the Altieri Chapel, black chalk

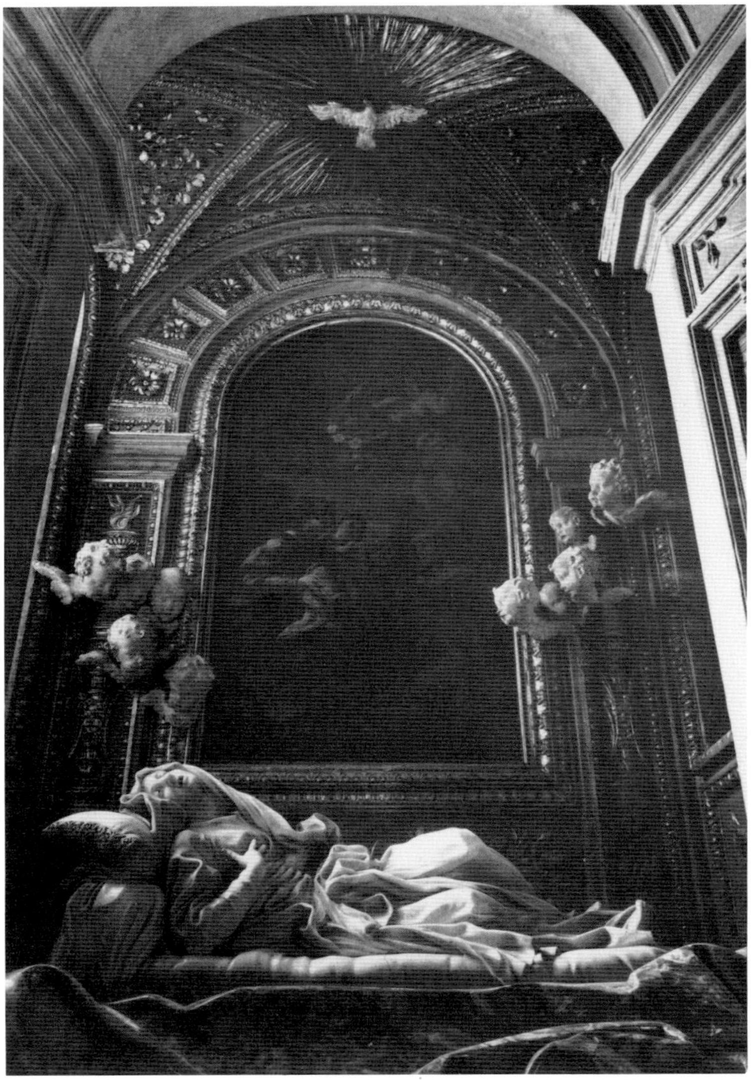

PLATE 33. Recess, Altieri Chapel, San Francesco a Ripa

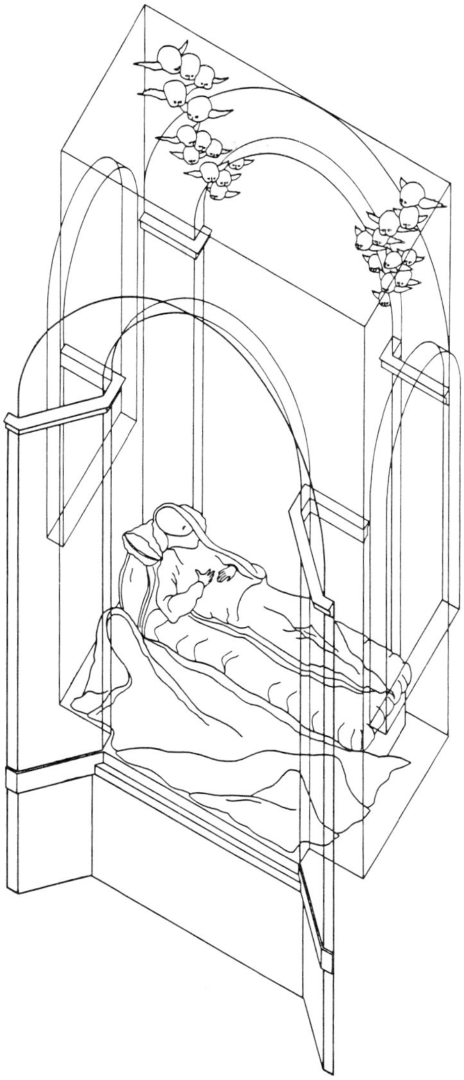

PLATE 34. Reconstruction based on Bernini's early ideas for the recess of the Altieri Chapel, pen and ink

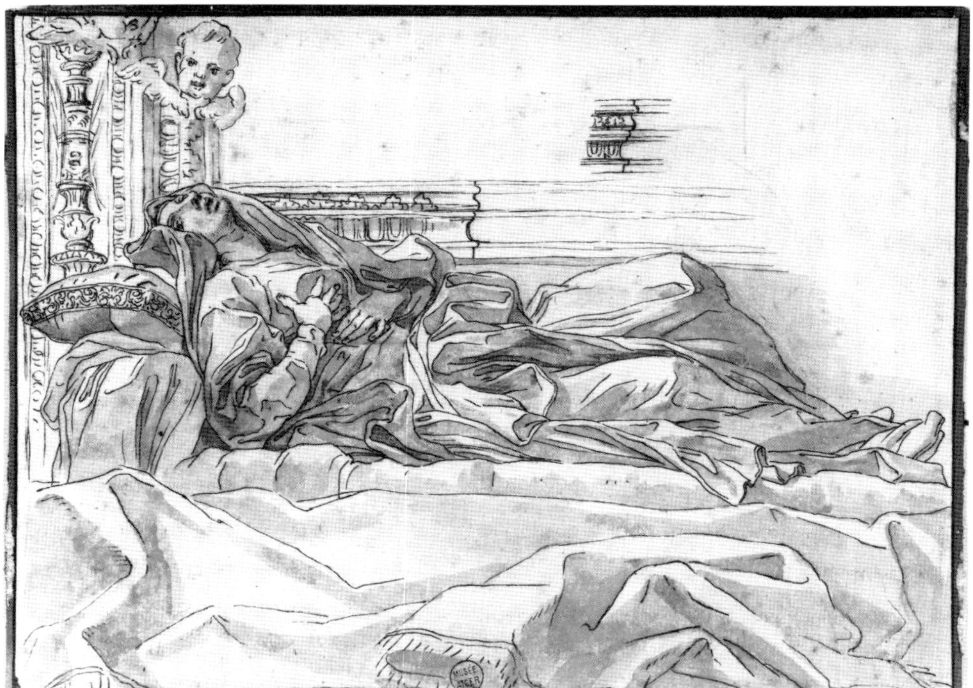

PLATE 35. Giovanni Battista Gaulli, called "Baciccio," drawing after the *Ludovica,* pen and ink, c. 1674

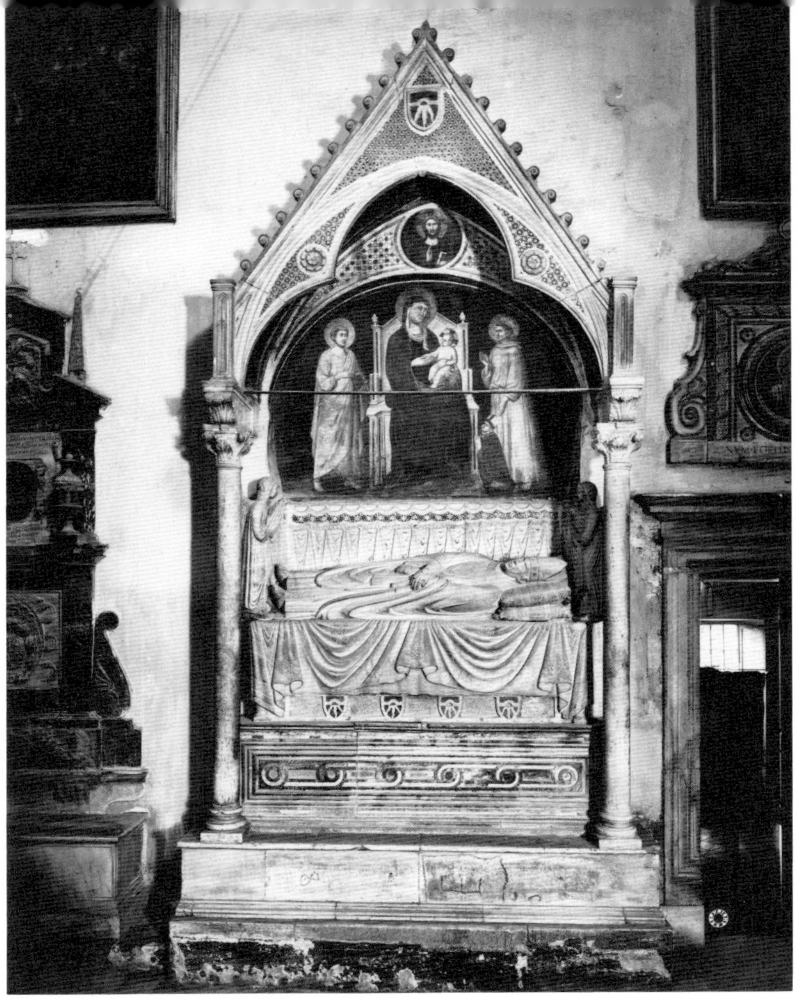

Plate 36. Tomb of Cardinal Matteo d'Acquasparta (d. 1302), Santa Maria in Aracoeli

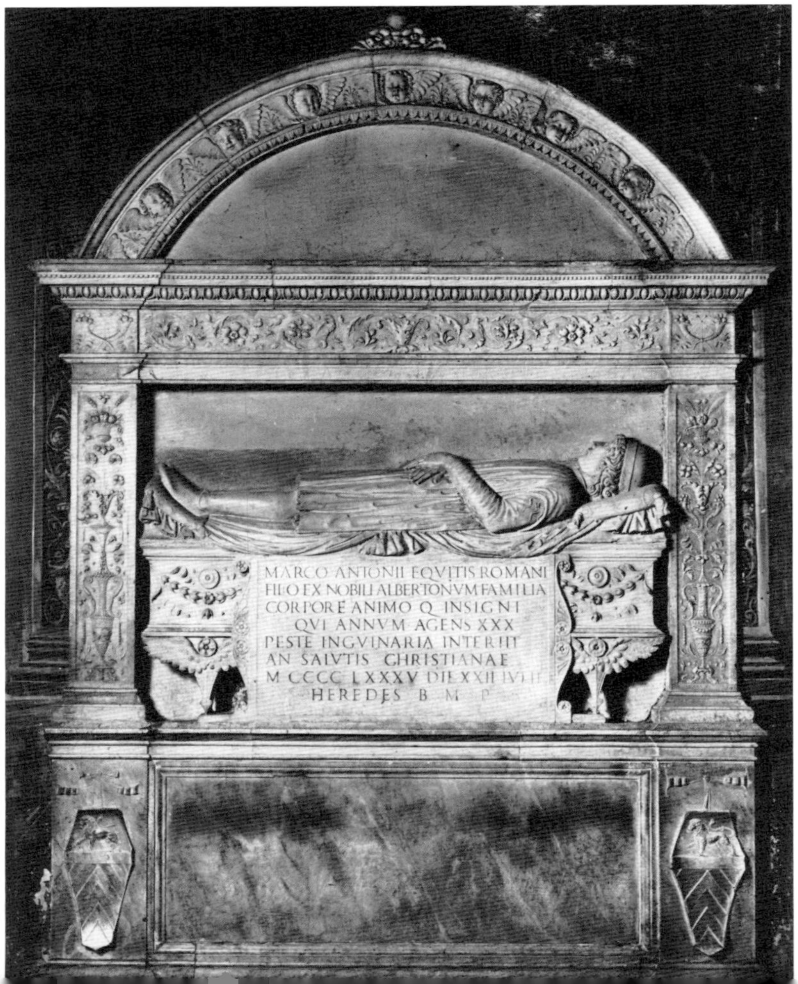

Plate 37. Tomb of Marco d'Antonio Albertoni (d. 1485), Santa Maria del Popolo

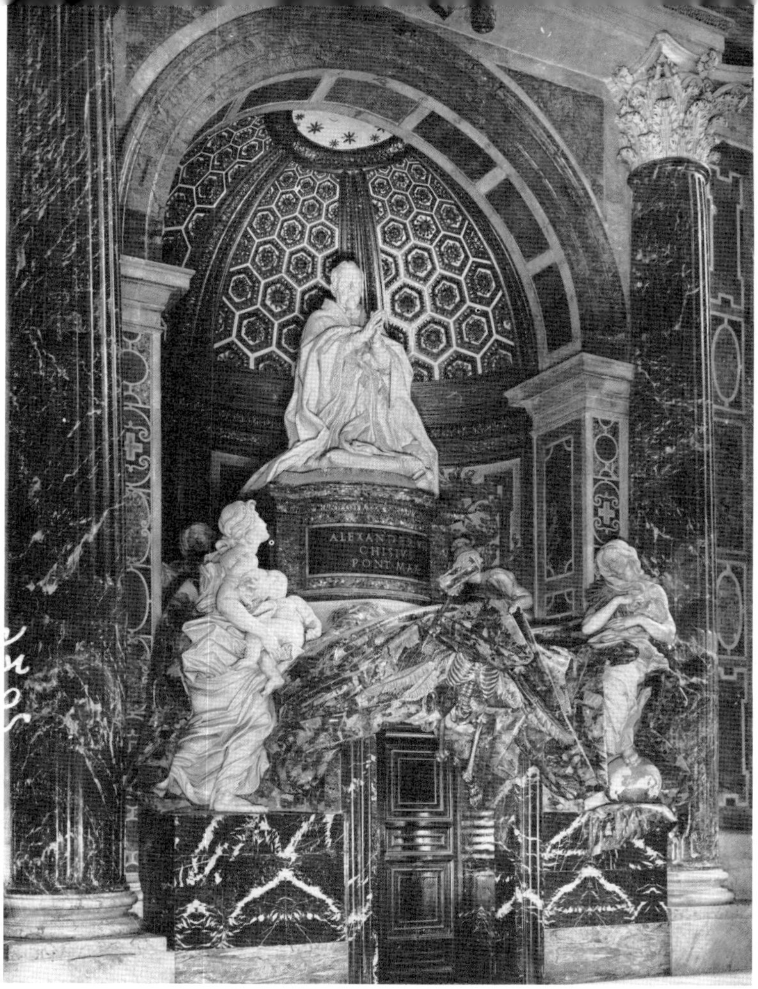

PLATE 38. Gianlorenzo Bernini, tomb of Alexander VII, 1672–78, Saint Peter's

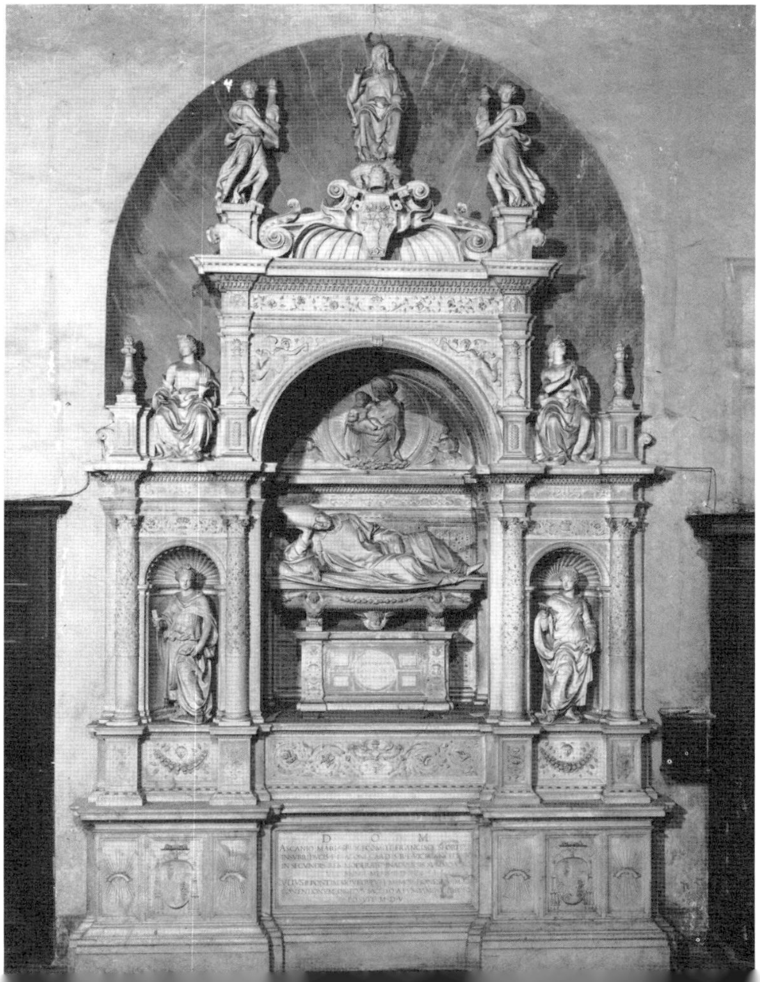

PLATE 39. Andrea Sansovino, tomb of Cardinal Ascanio Sforza (d. 1505), Santa Maria del Popolo

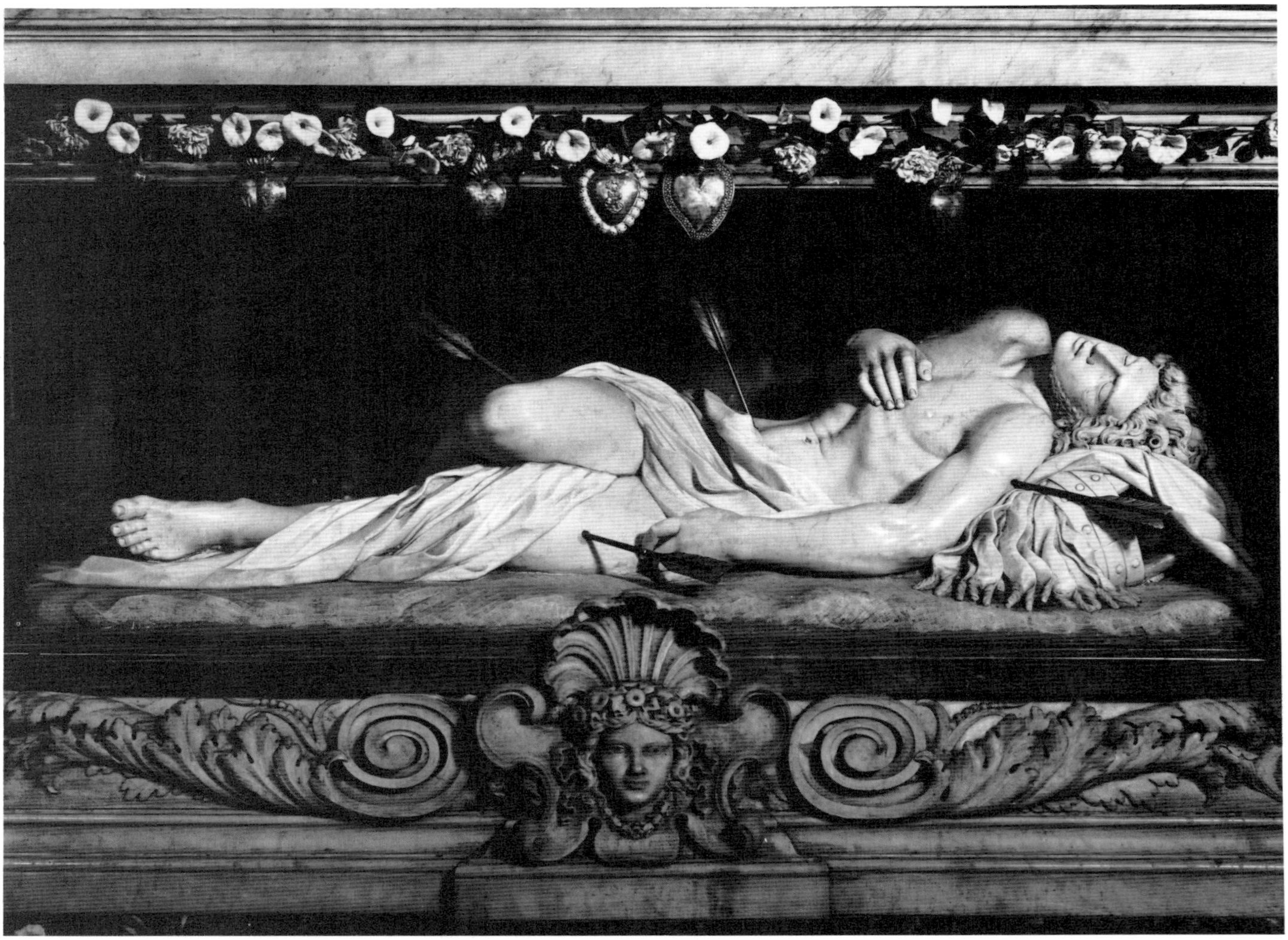

PLATE 40. G. Giorgetti, *Saint Sebastian*, c. 1672, San Sebastiano

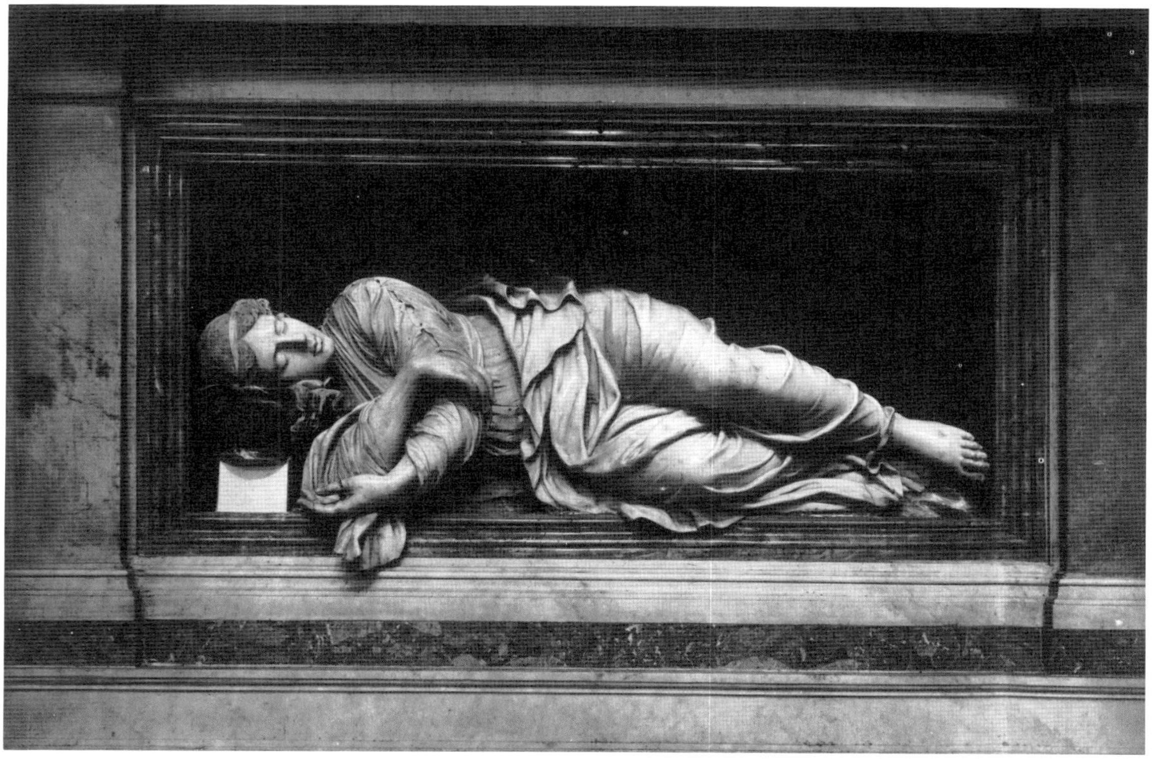

PLATE 41. Niccolò Menghini, *Saint Martina,* 1635, SS. Martina e Luca

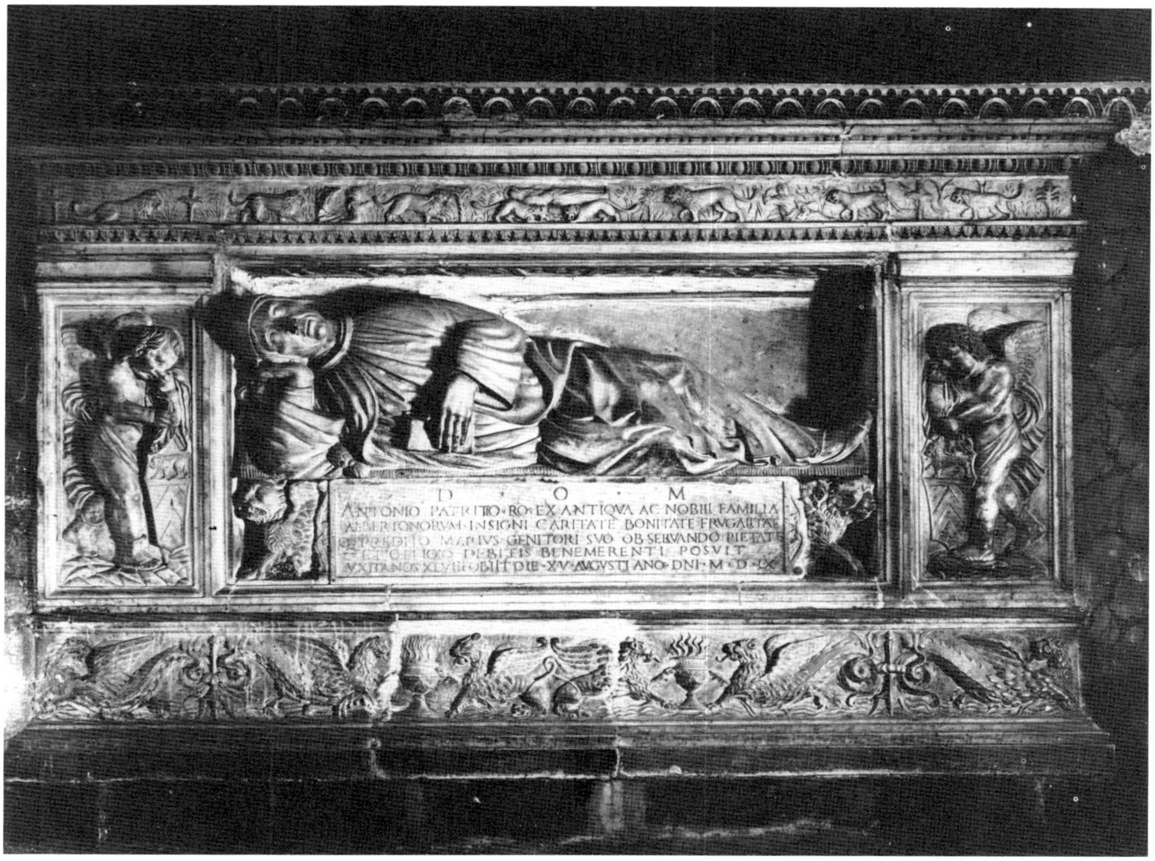

PLATE 42. Tomb of Antonio Albertoni (d. 1509), Chapel of San Antonio, Santa Maria in Aracoeli

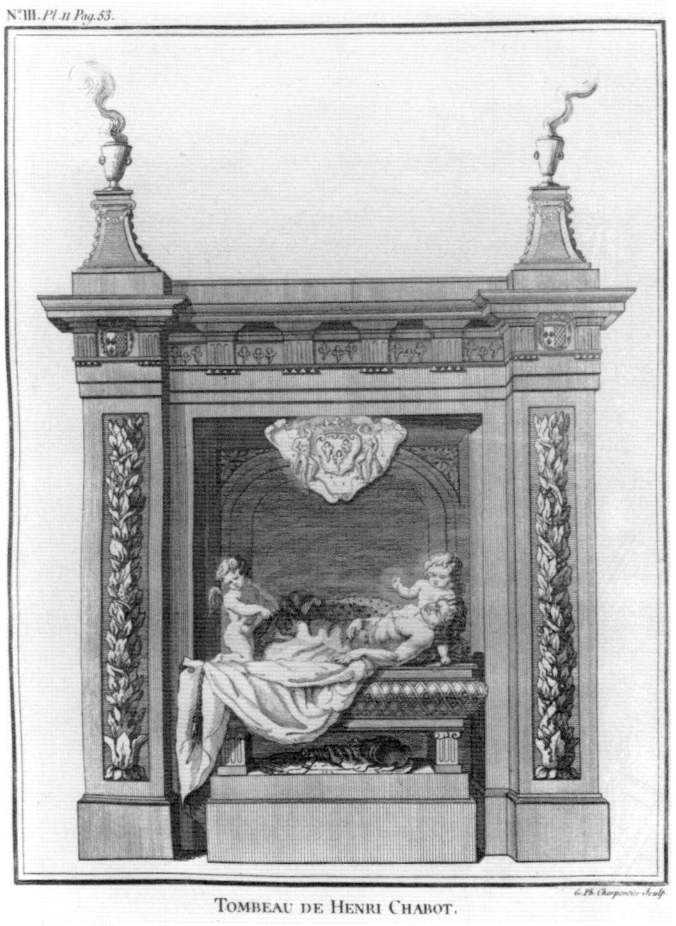

PLATE 43. Engraving of François Anguier's tomb of Henri Chabot, Orléans Chapel, Church of the Celestines, Paris

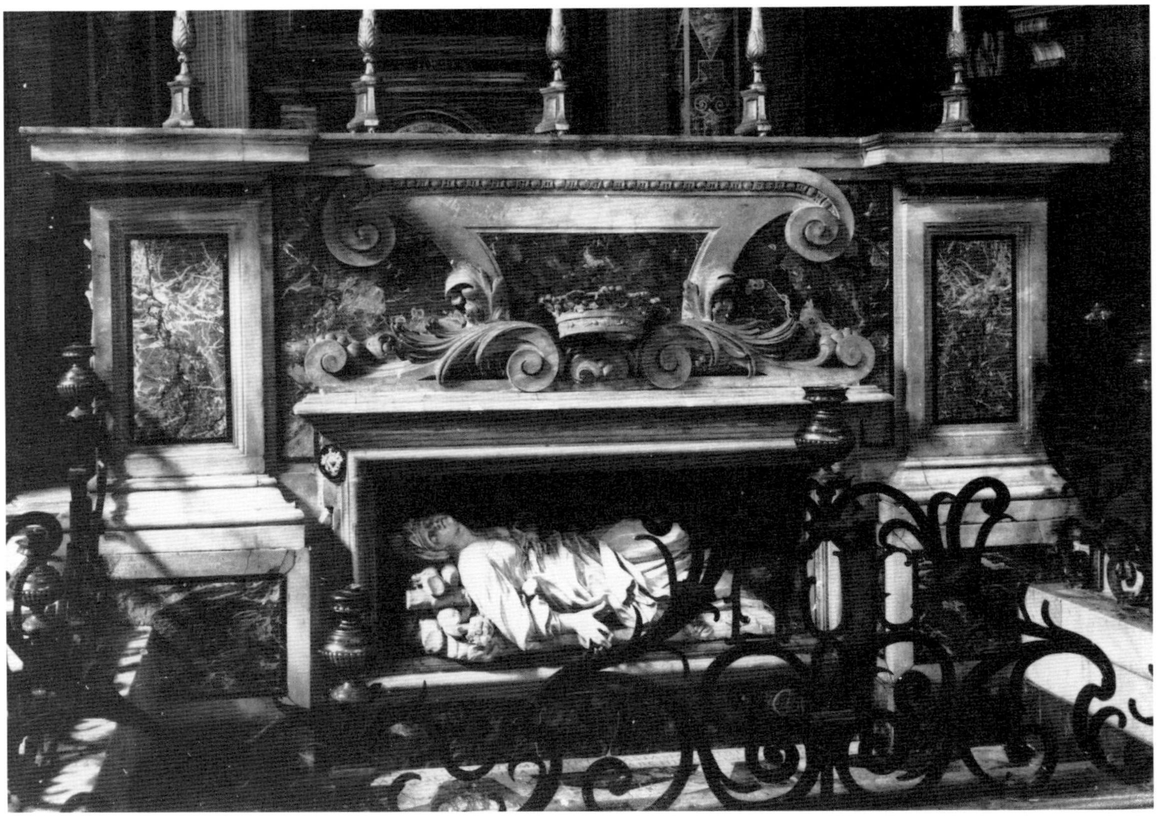

PLATE 44. Francesco Aprile, *Saint Anastasia*, 1685, Sant' Anastasia

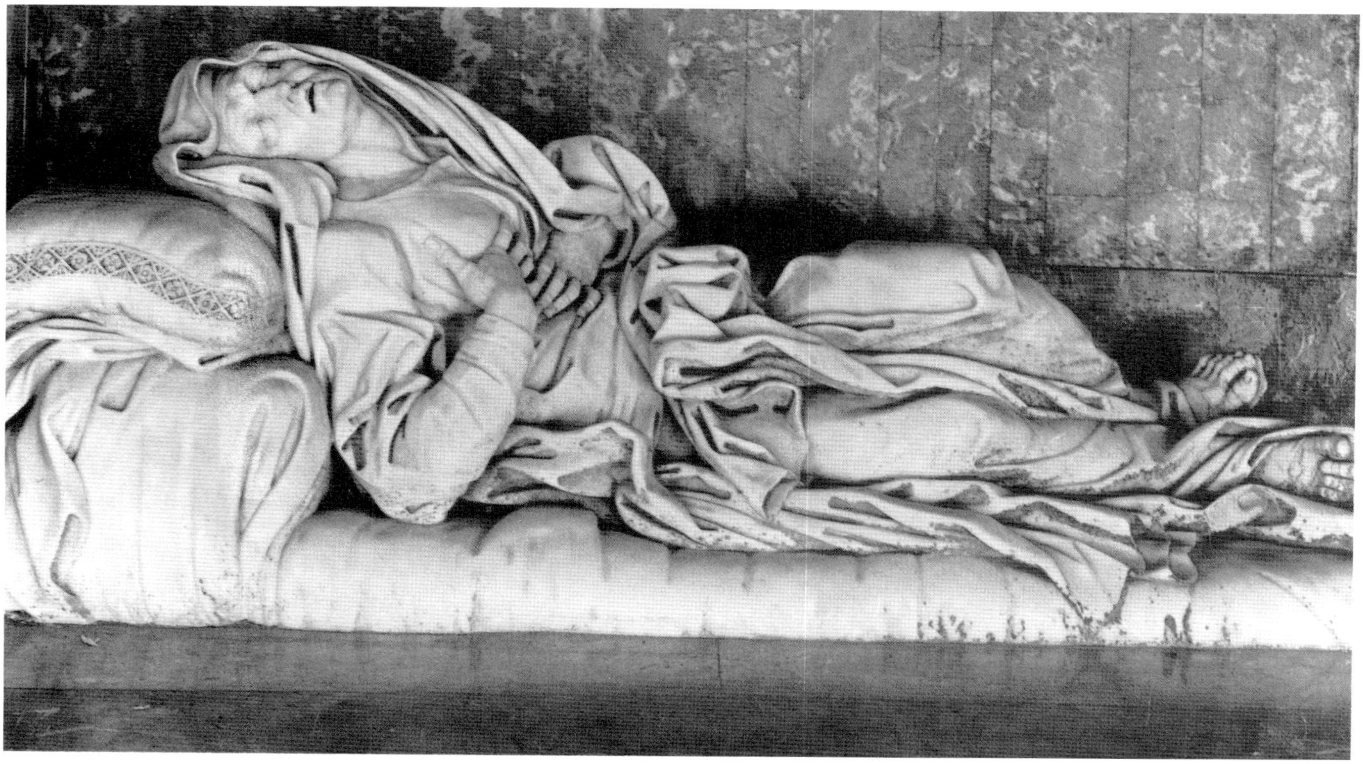

PLATE 45. Attributed to Giovanni Battista Maini, *Saint Anne*, Sant' Andrea delle Fratte

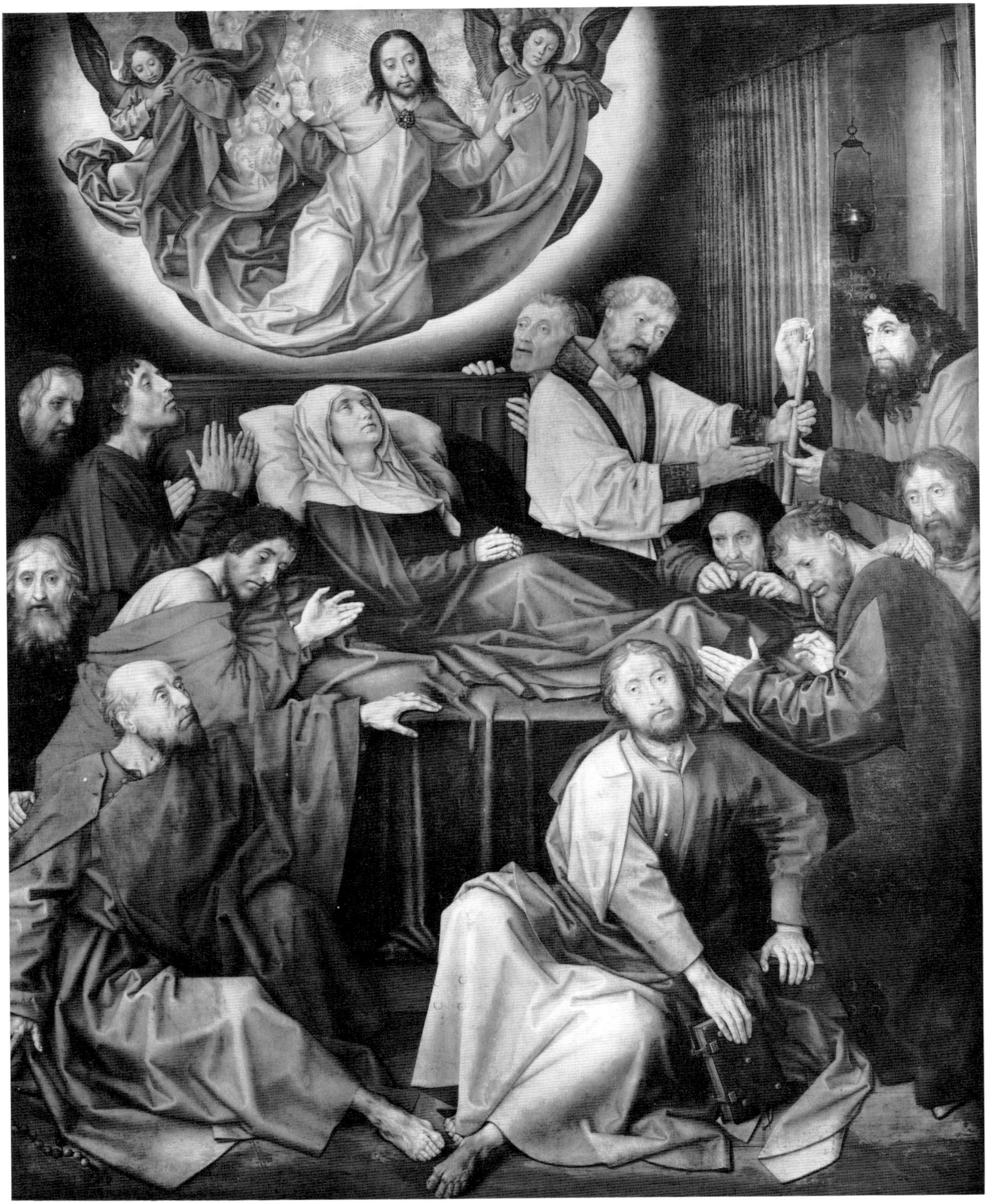

PLATE 46. Hugo van der Goes, *Death of the Virgin,* c. 1481

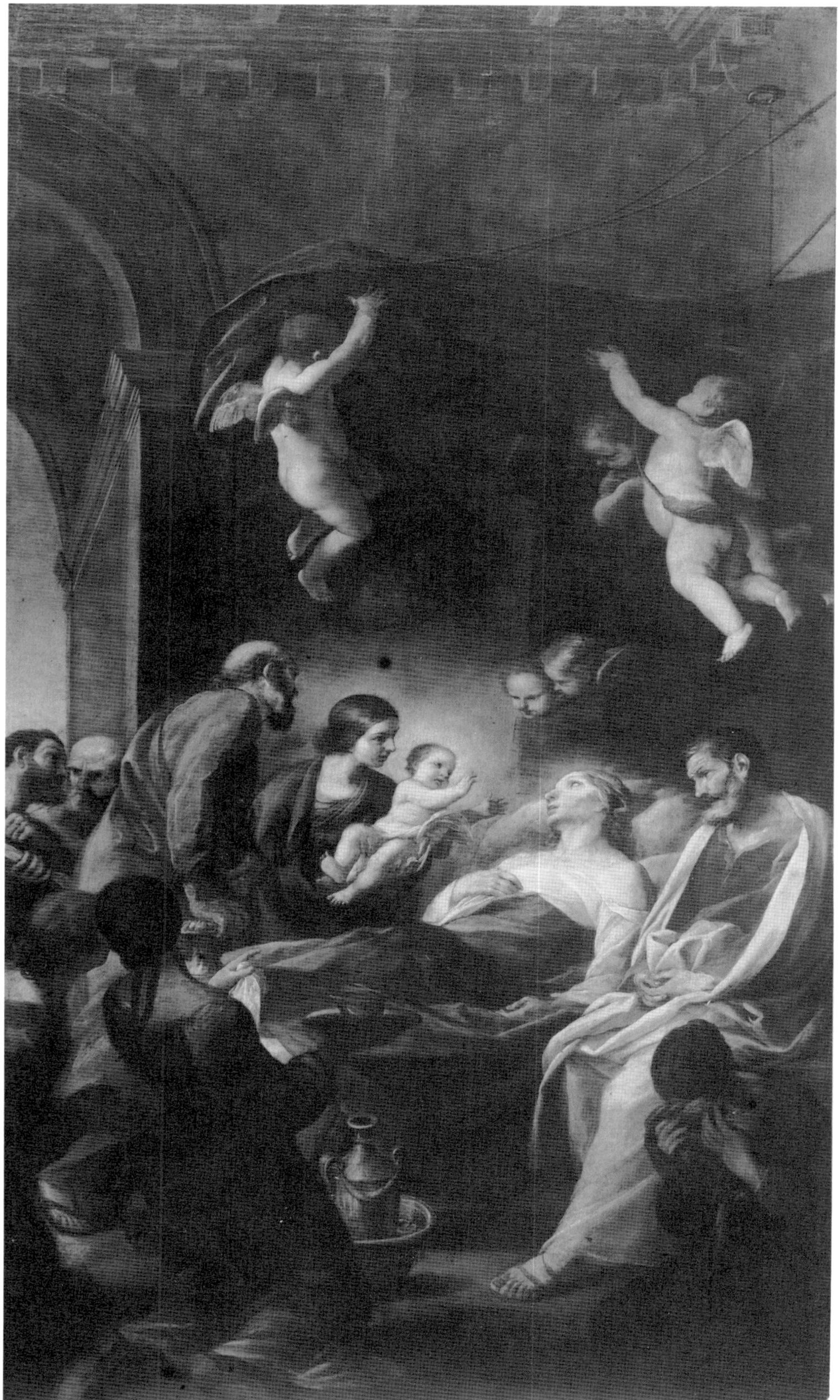

PLATE 47. Andrea Sacchi, *Death of Saint Anne,* 1649, San Carlo ai Catinari

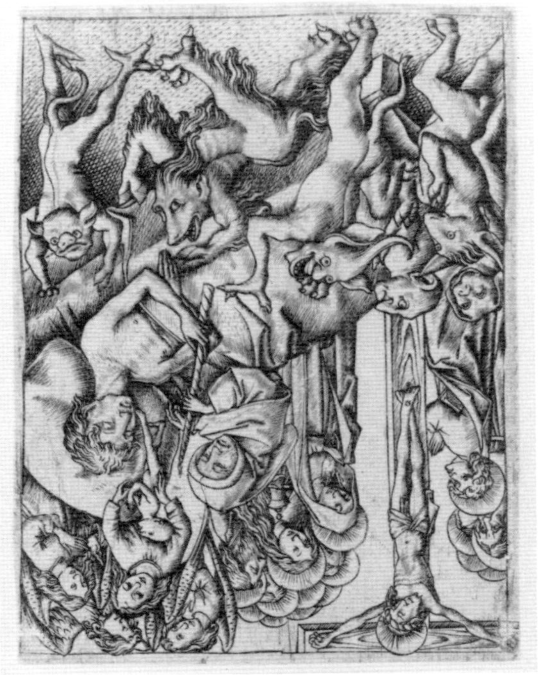

Plate 48. Master E.S., *The Final Triumph over all Temptations at the Hour of Death,* from the *Ars Moriendi,* print

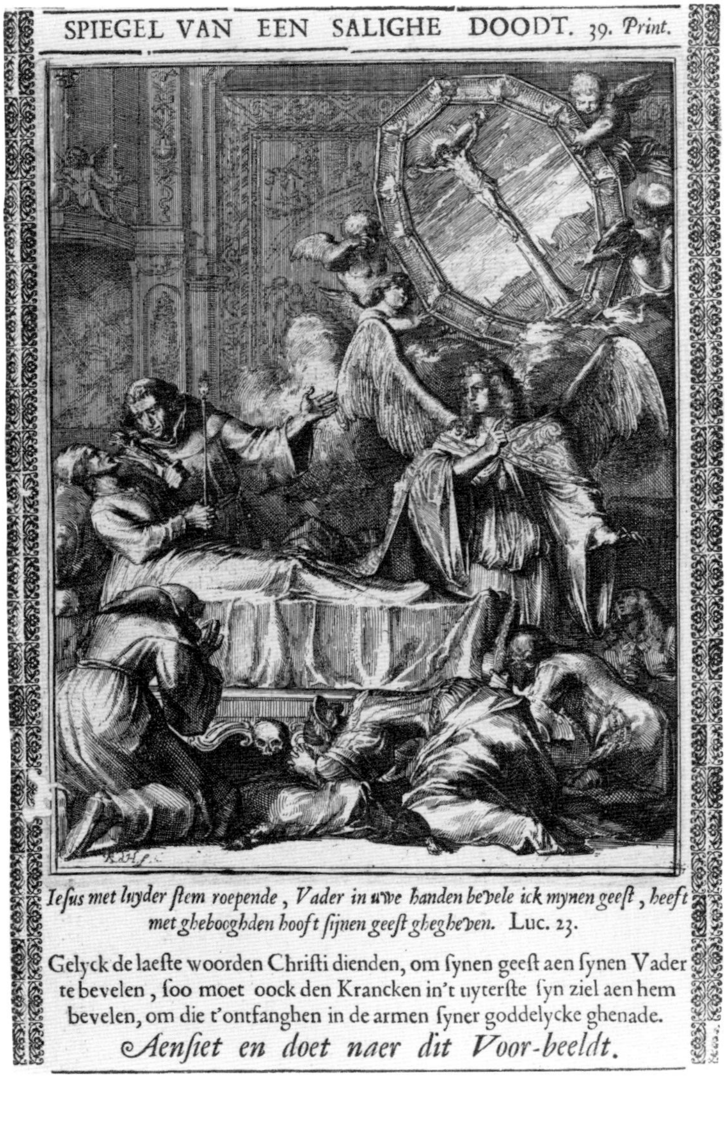

Plate 49. Romeyn de Hooghe, *Death of Moriens,* engraving from David de la Virra, *Spiegel van een salighe Doodt,* Antwerp, 1673

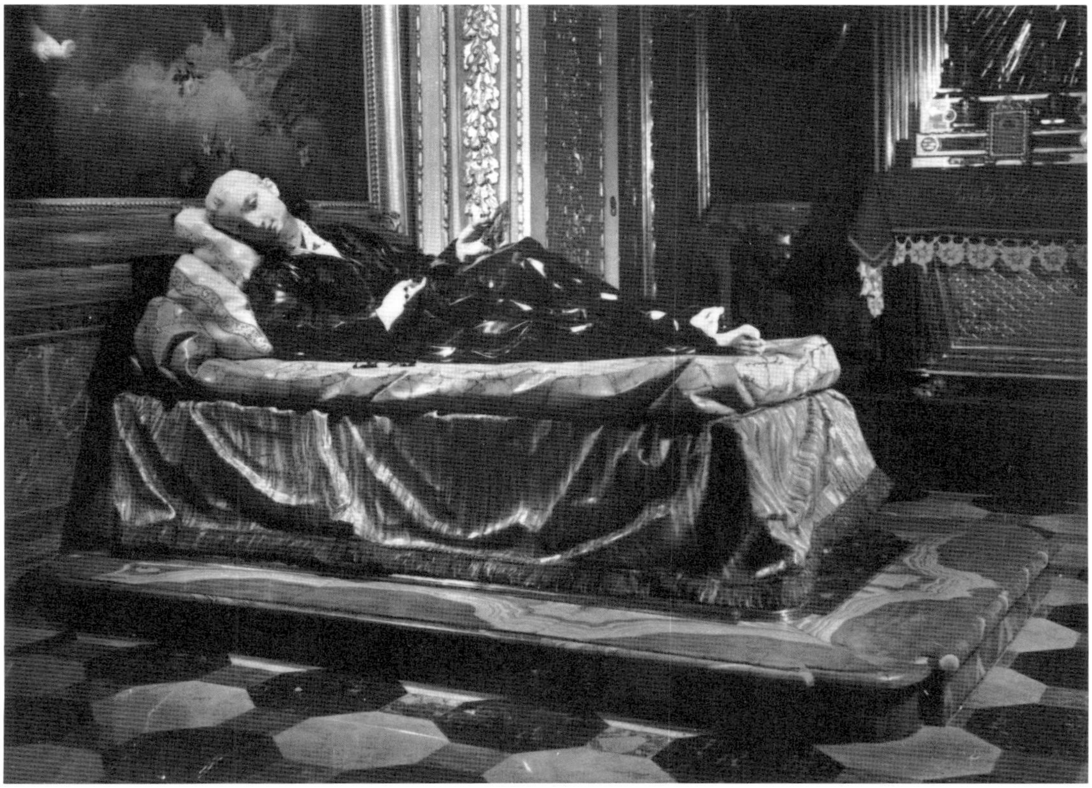

PLATE 50. Pierre Legros, *Blessed Stanislas Kostka,* c. 1703, Sant' Andrea al Quirinale

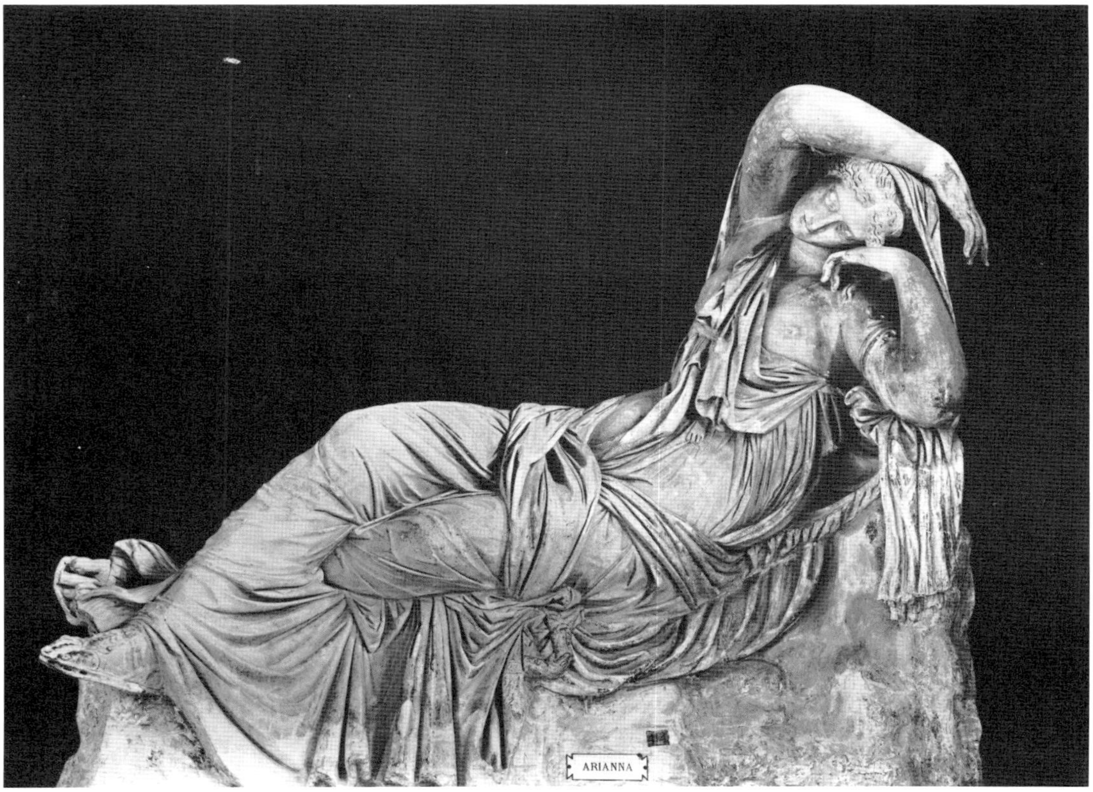

PLATE 51. *Sleeping Ariadne* (*Dying Cleopatra*), late Hadrianic or early Antonine copy of a Hellenistic work, Vatican

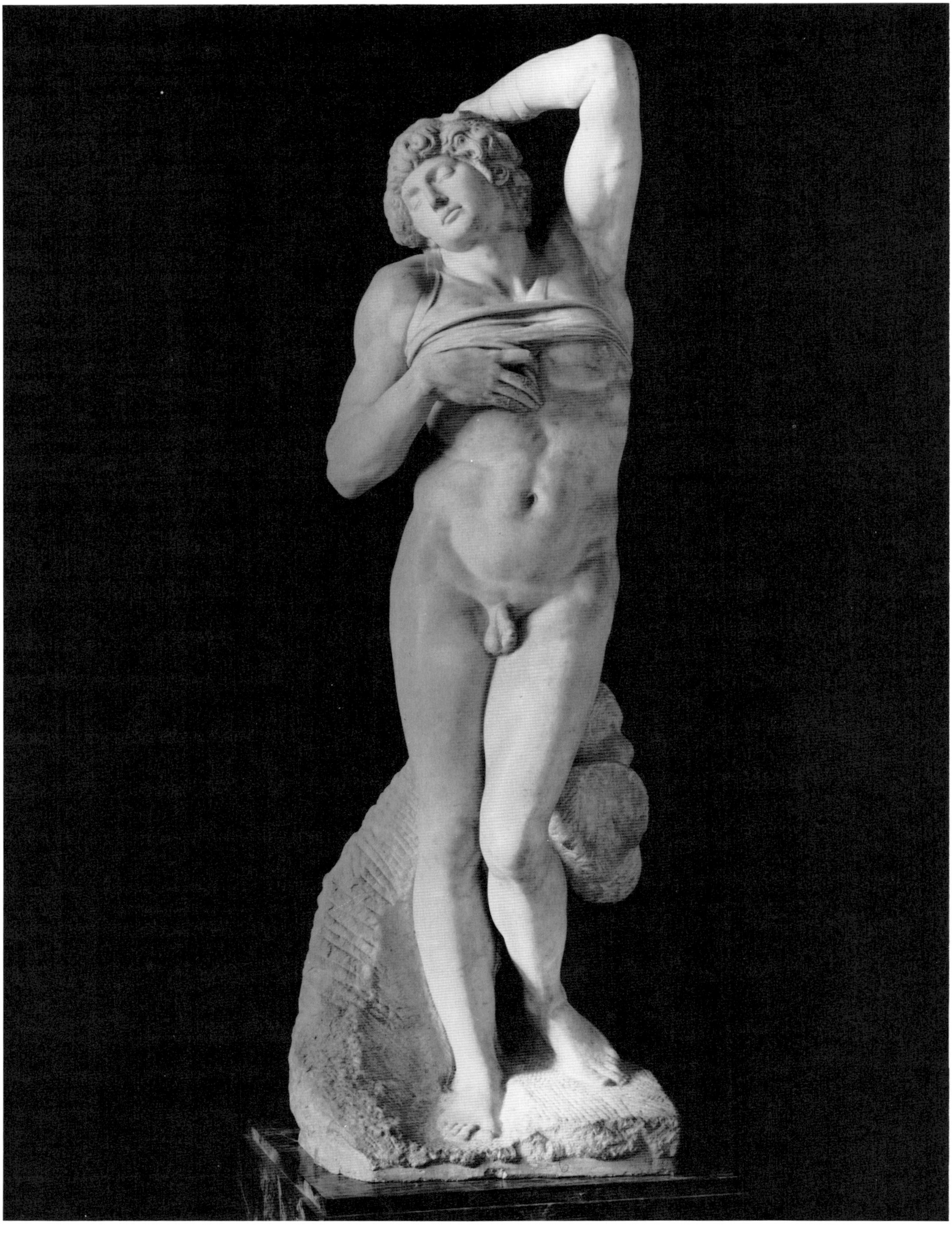

PLATE 52. Michelangelo, *Dying Slave,* before 1513

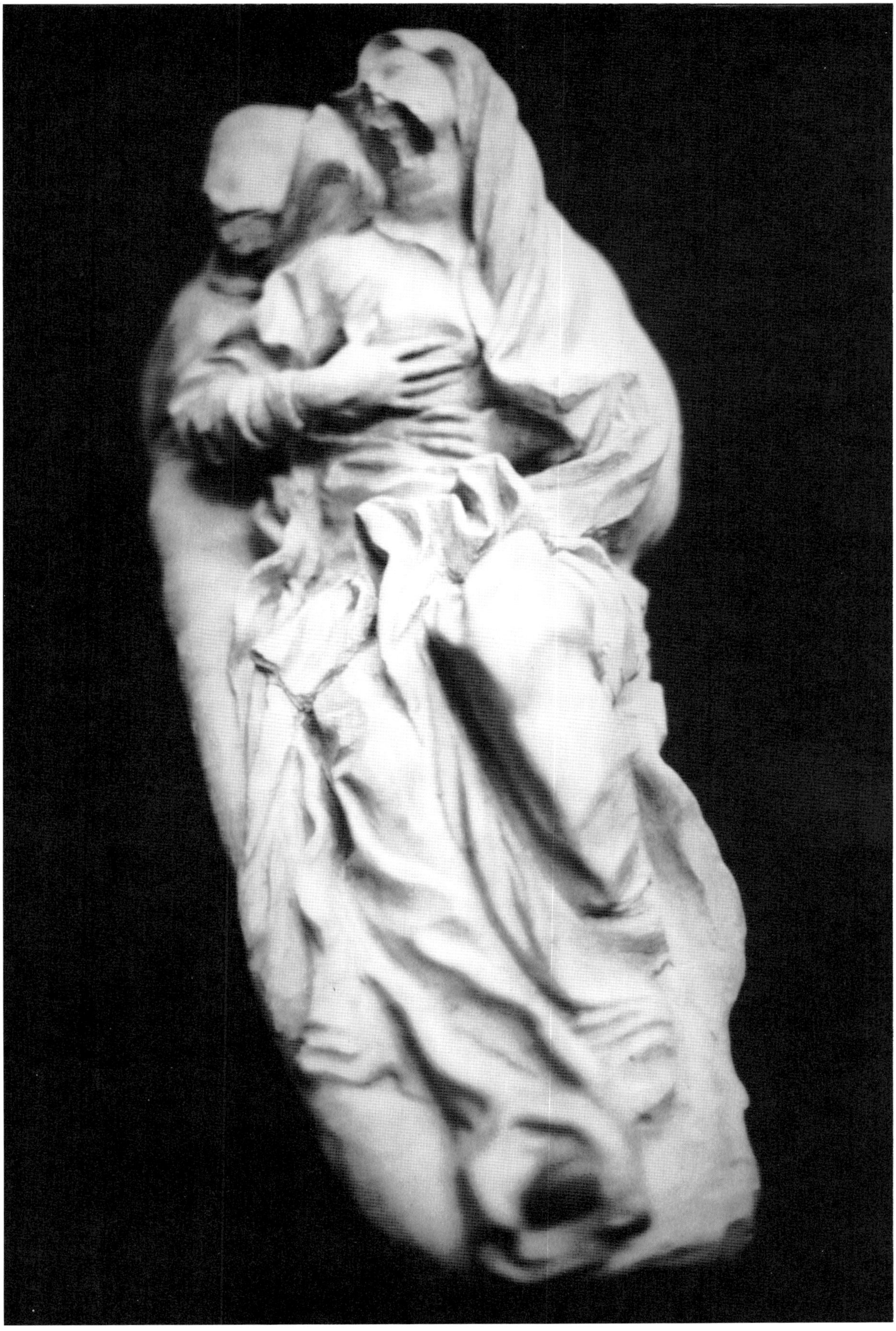

PLATE 53. Top view, *bozzetto* of the *Ludovica,* terra-cotta

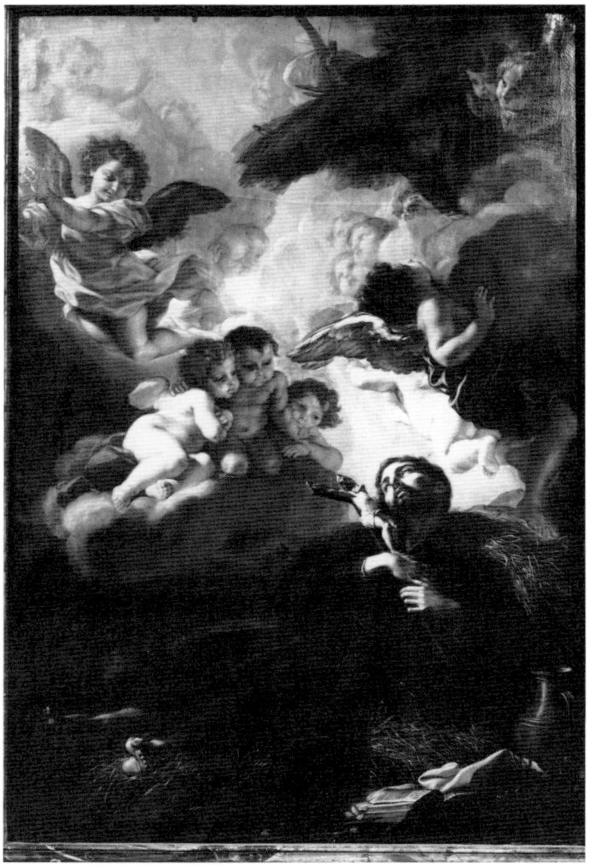

PLATE 54. Baciccio, *Death of Saint Francis Xavier,* 1676, Sant' Andrea al Quirinale

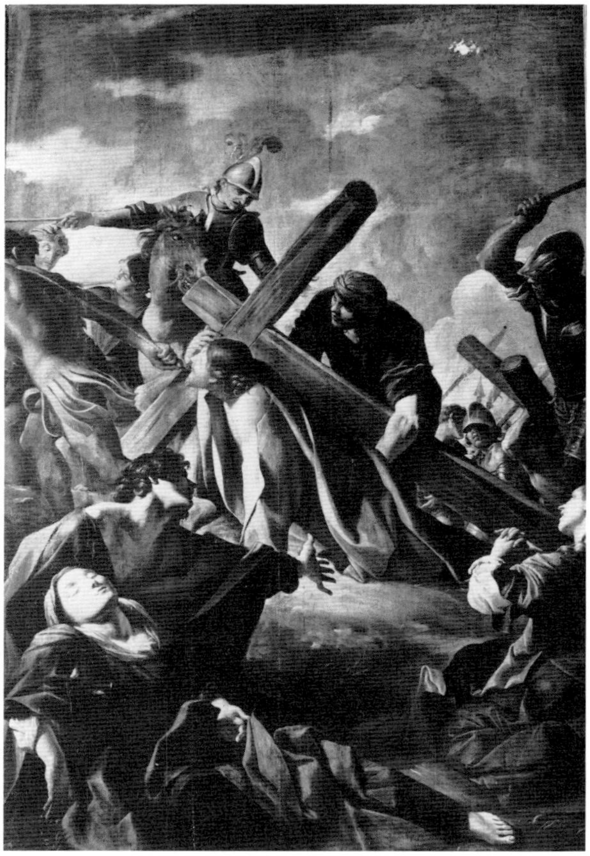

PLATE 55. Giovanni Lanfranco, *Road to Calvary,* San Giovanni dei Fiorentino

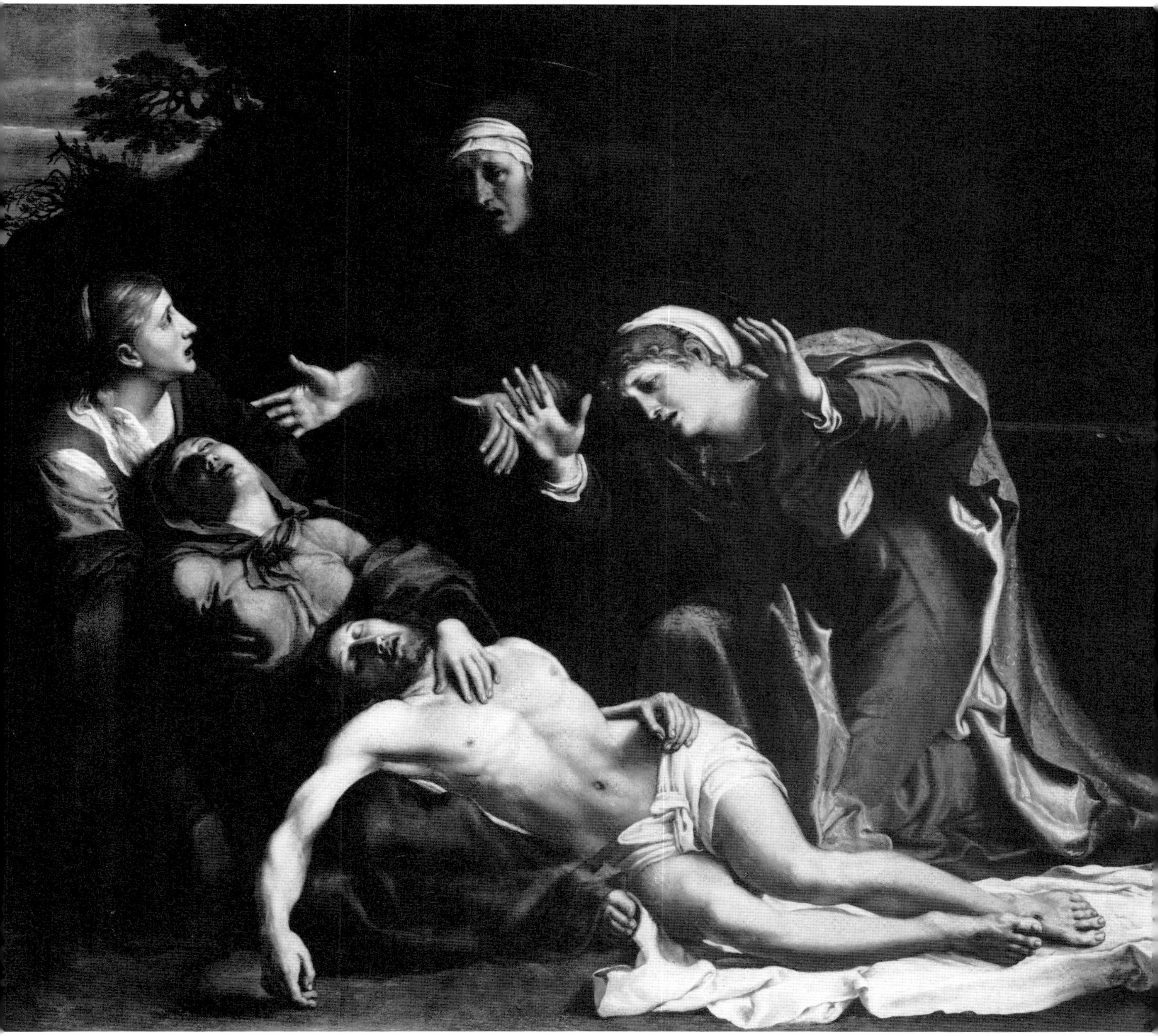

Plate 56. Annibale Carracci, *Pietà with the Three Maries*, c. 1606

OPPOSITE:
PLATE 59. Michelangelo, *Pietà,* 1498, Saint Peter's

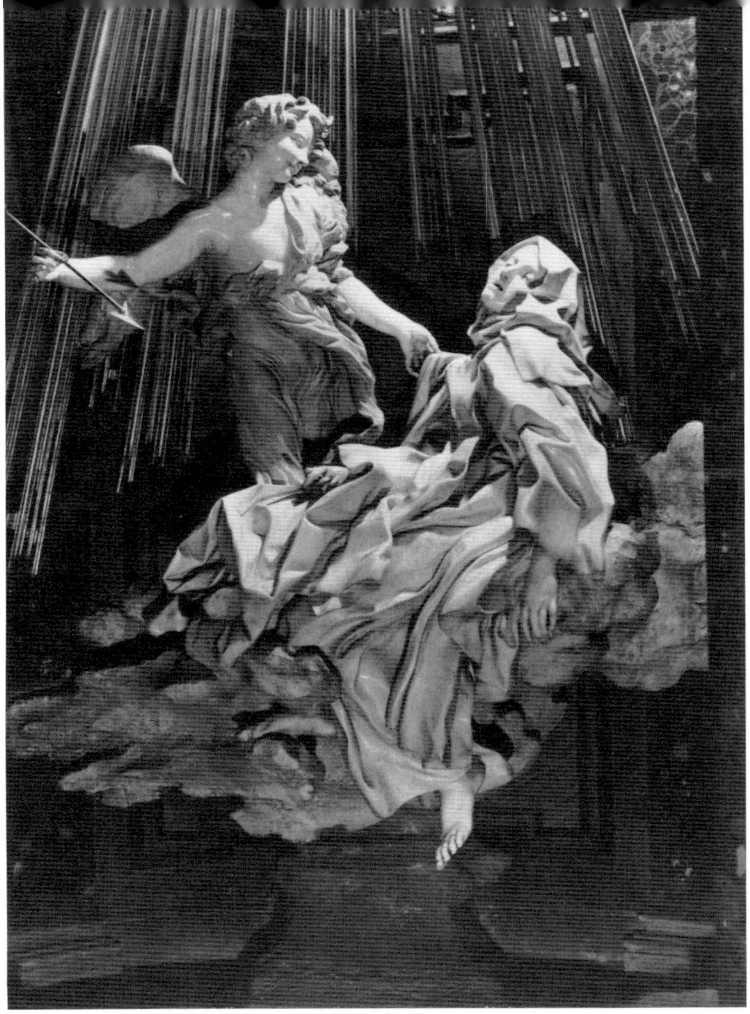

PLATE 57. Gianlorenzo Bernini, *Saint Theresa,* c. 1647, Cornaro Chapel, Santa Maria della Vittoria

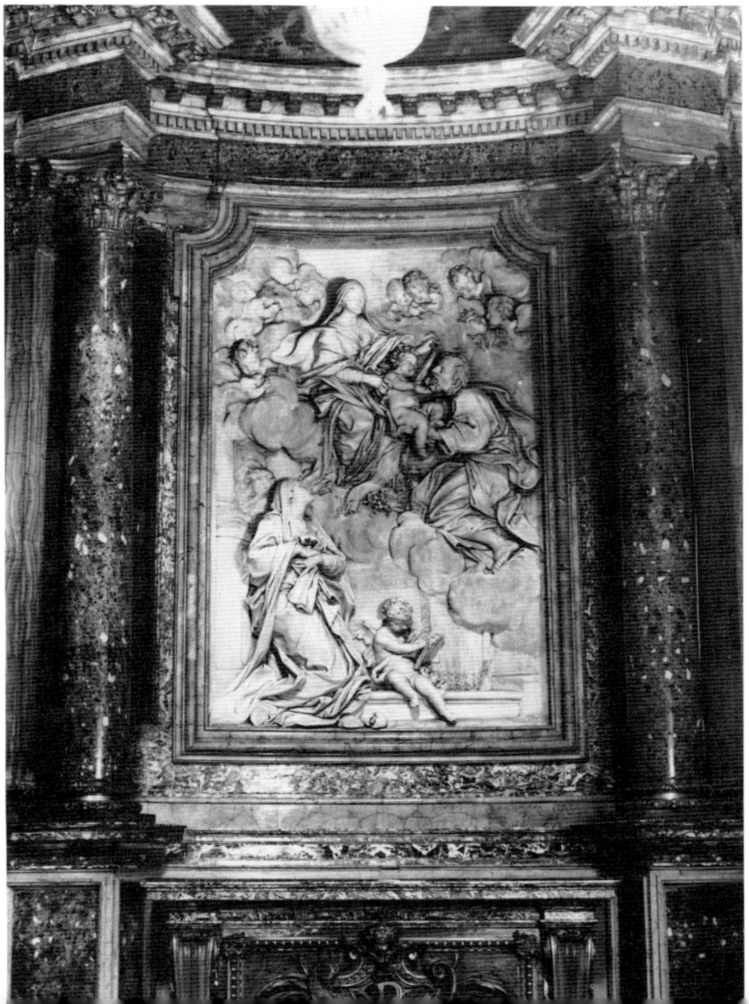

PLATE 58. Lorenzo Ottoni, *Madonna and Child with Saint Joseph and Ludovica Albertoni,* c. 1706, Chapel of Saint Joseph and the Blessed Ludovica Albertoni, Santa Maria in Campitelli

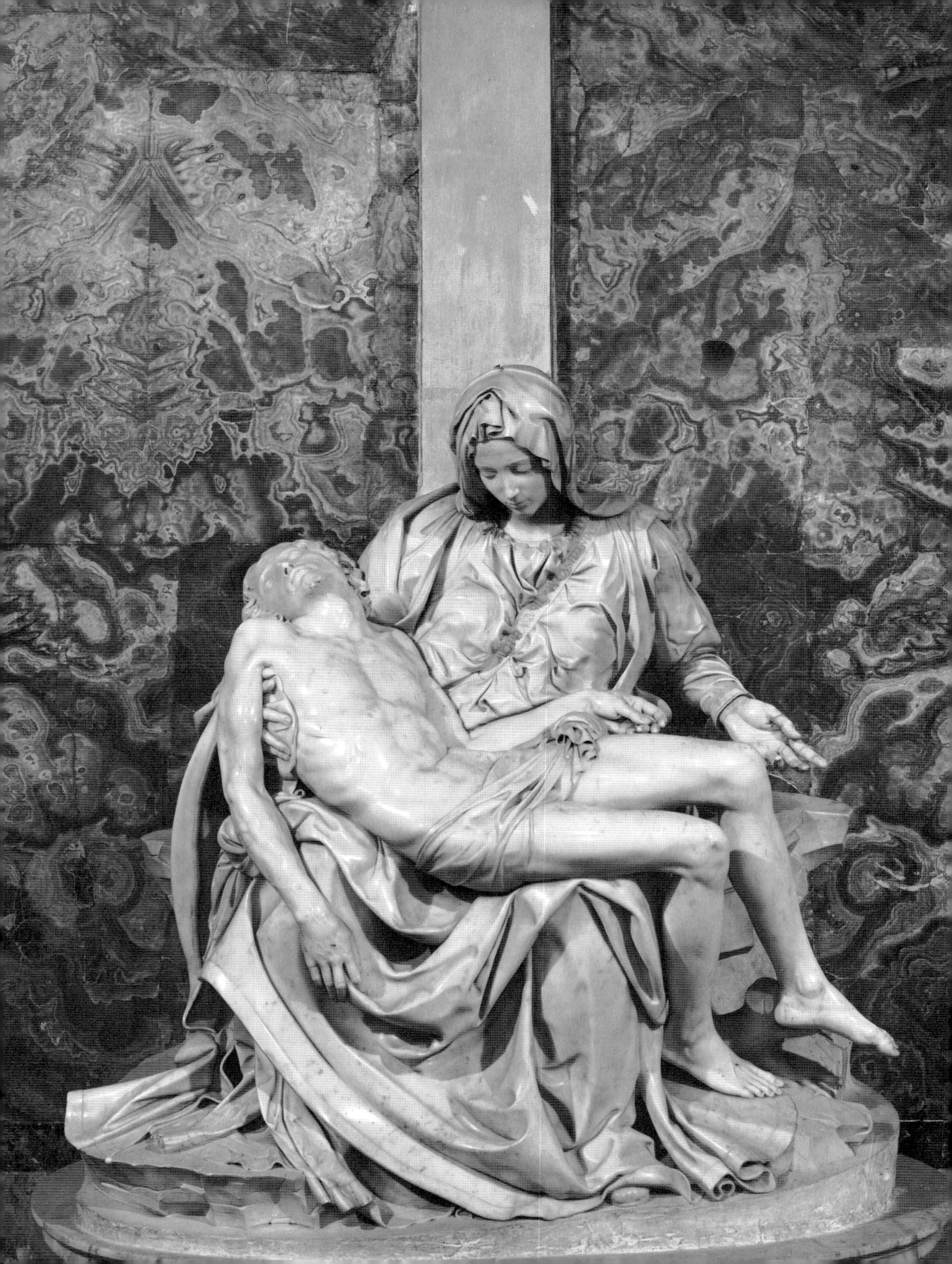

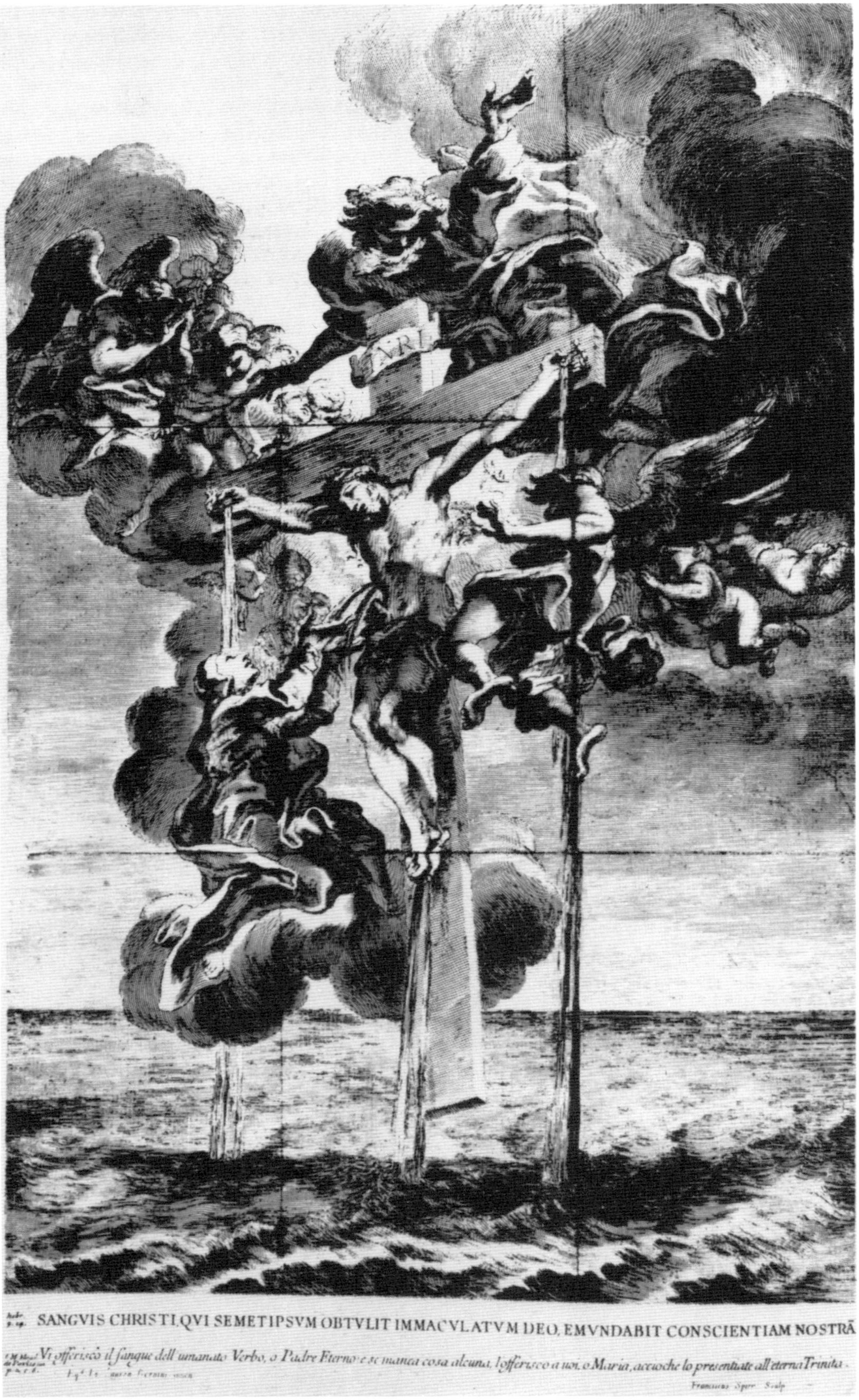

Plate 60. Gianlorenzo Bernini, *Sangue di Cristo,* 1670, engraved by F. Spierre, frontispiece of F. Marchese's *Unica speranza del peccatore,* Rome, 1670